METROPOLITAN AREAS,
METROPOLITAN GOVERNMENTS

METROPOLITAN AREAS, METROPOLITAN GOVERNMENTS

A READER

Second Edition

Edited by

Gary Helfand

New York Institute of Technology

KENDALL/HUNT PUBLISHING COMPANY
Dubuque, Iowa

$7.95

Contents

Acknowledgments

Thanks are hereby given to the Advisory Commission on Intergovernmental Relations and the Committee for Economic Development for permitting the reprint of their hard-to-find and most excellent case studies on metropolitan government.

Introduction

The subject of metropolitan areas and metropolitan governments is currently undergoing intensive study by professionals from a multitude of disciplines, including psychologists, economists, political scientists, planners, lawyers, and the so-called management analysts. In 1970, the extent of metropolitanization in this country was revealed by the Census Bureau's observation that the number of metropolitan areas that could be clearly outlined on a United States map had increased to about two hundred and forty. These areas (designated as Standard Metropolitan Statistical Areas or SMSA's) then contained about seventy percent of the U.S. population, but, incredibly, only took up about ten percent of the total land area of the nation. In other words, seventy percent of the people lived on ten percent of the land, and this portion of the land was considered to be "metropolitan."

In the works to follow, the reader will be exposed to the various trends and types of experimentation that have been attempted by political and civic leaders and public administrators to restructure or reform governmental machinery in metropolitan areas. In some of these cases, the reforms have worked and have caused tremendous gains to be made in the sense of having greatly improved the quality of services offered by government for the price being paid by the taxpayer. In other instances, however, the assessment is, at best, mixed. The reader should therefore attempt to critically evaluate the successes and failures apparent in each case study, and relate these to the type of changes that were made in governmental institutions and the political process.

It is the hope of the editor that this selection of metropolitan case studies fills a gap in the literature of domestic politics. While such distinguished groups as the Advisory Commission on Intergovernmental Relations and the Committee for Economic Development have, in the past, made attempts to publish these metropolitan case studies, the average reader has not found them readily available. In order to correct this problem, the current reader has been assembled.

Introduction

Joan Aron's article seeks to make some sense out of the hodgepodge of state and local government organizations that presently exist in the New York metropolitan region, and the relative responsibilities and effectiveness of each.

In reading the piece, one begins to experience an increasing sense of uneasiness and finally utter exasperation with the multitude of confusing and often mutually exclusive Boards, Agencies, Authorities, Compacts, Commissions, Corporations, Districts, Councils, and Associations that have been created in an attempt to provide a higher level of services—often within the context of a regional focus—for the New York/New Jersey/Connecticut metropolitan region.

When reading some of the later selections dealing with different forms of metropolitan **consolidation,** one should bear in mind the fragmented mess that currently exists in the New York SMSA.

THE NEW YORK INTERSTATE METROPOLIS*

Joan Aron
Assistant Professor of Public Administration
New York University

HISTORICAL NARRATIVE

The Regional Setting

The New York metropolitan region is the largest, most populous, most diverse, and most complex metropolitan area in America. Nineteen million people live within its 7,900 square miles: 12.0 million in New York, 5.4 million in New Jersey, and 1.6 million in Connecticut. About 8.4 million people are employed here. No other metropolitan area in the country is remotely comparable in size to this "tenth of the nation."

The most commonly accepted definition of the metropolitan region is that used by the Tri-State Regional Planning Commission, the official planning agency of the metropolitan area. It includes twelve counties in New York State (including the five counties of New York City), nine counties in northern and central New Jersey, and six planning regions in southwestern Connecticut. (See map for the jurisdiction of the Tri-State Regional Planning Commission.)

The governmental structure of the region is noteworthy for its complexity. In addition to the three states and 27 counties and planning districts, the region includes about 1,500 units of local and special-purpose government. The Federal government also plays an important role in regional governance. Since local jurisdictions exhibit great variety in size, structure, formal powers, and political arrangements, a large number of autonomous decision-making centers attempt to cope with the problems commonly associated with urban growth: polluted air and water, deteriorating transit facilities, housing shortages, and racial and economic segregation.

From: *Regional Governance—Promise and Performance: Substate Regionalism and the Federal System,* Vol. II—Case Studies, May, 1973, p. 200.

*I am indebted to Hugh O'Neill, staff member of the New York City Commission on State-City Relations, for his help in the research and writing of the historical narrative and performance sections.

As the Nation's largest metropolis in terms of population, economic wealth, education, and cultural resources, New York City occupies the dominant position among the region's local governments. It contains nearly eight million people and four million jobs within its 320 square miles. Large and medium-sized cities that would dominate other parts of the country—Newark, Jersey City, Bridgeport, New Haven, Yonkers—lie in the shadow of their giant neighbor. Each of them has an urban life independent of New York City, but each is also inextricably involved in the life of the region.

As in most metropolitan areas of the nation, the older cities of the region have ceased to grow in population. During the 1960s, the region's population grew from 17 to 19 million, with the entire increase taking place in the suburban counties. Economic growth is also an increasingly suburban phenomenon. In the last decade, the suburban counties gained three times as many new jobs as New York City. At the same time, the older central cities contain increasingly large concentrations of low-income, unskilled black and Puerto Rican families. By 1970, New York City alone had approximately 1,845,000 non-whites, or about two-thirds of the region's non-whites. This demographic change has been accompanied by severe social and economic dislocations which intensify the split between city and suburb and sharpen the need for regional accommodations.

Despite its great diversity and complexity, the New York region forms, in many ways, a single interdependent community. A limited degree of "regional consciousness" has been helping to shape policy and policy-making institutions in the region for half a century. The development of this awareness is traced in the following section.

The Development of Regionalism

Emerging Regionalism, Private and Public. A "regional consciousness" first emerged in the New York area during the first two decades of this century. While the greater New York City government created in 1898 was in many respects a true metropolitan government, absorbing two giant cities, outlying suburbs, and rural farms and villages, it soon became clear to planning advocates that the city did not encompass the network of social and economic interactions that comprised the metropolitan community.

Thus, Charles D. Norton, chairman of New York City's Advisory Commission on the City Plan, wrote in 1915:

> No plan of New York will command recognition unless it includes the area in which all New Yorkers earn their livelihood and make their home.
> From City Hall a circle must be swung which will include the Atlantic Highlands and Princeton; the lovely Jersey hills back of Morristown and

Tuxedo; the incomparable Hudson as far as Newburgh; the Westchester lakes and ridges, to Bridgeport and beyond; and all of Long Island.[1]

Norton campaigned tirelessly for the formulation of a New York regional plan, persuading the Russell Sage Foundation in 1921 to finance a tri-state planning project. The work was begun the following year with the creation of the Committee on the Regional Plan. The committee conducted extensive physical and economic surveys of the metropolitan area, and formulated a variety of proposals for regional development. Between 1929 and 1939, it published ten survey volumes and its *Regional Plan of New York and its Environs.*

The Regional Plan Association (RPA), a private civic association, was formed in 1929 to promote the adoption of proposals included in the *Regional Plan*. During the 1930s, RPA helped governments in the region plan and execute a variety of Federally aided public works projects originally proposed in the plan.[2]

TRI-STATE REGION

Counties and Planning Regions

During this same period, the public sector also began to display an interest in regional approaches. In 1921, New York and New Jersey created the Port of New York Authority to plan and effectuate coordinated development of the immense complex of pier, terminal, and transit facilities on both sides of the Hudson River. By the early 1930s, the Port Authority had acquired or constructed a half dozen major river crossings. Tolls collected on these facilities enabled the authority to become self-supporting by the mid-1930s and to undertake a variety of development projects related to the port.

In 1936, New York and New Jersey established the interstate Sanitation Commission to control pollution in a new sanitation district embracing the tidal waters of the region. Connecticut joined the compact in 1941, extending the commission's jurisdiction along the eastern portion of Long Island Sound. In 1937, New York and New Jersey entered into another compact providing for the creation of the Palisades Interstate Park Commission. The compact formalized a long-standing cooperative agreement between the two States to preserve and maintain the Palisades Interstate Park. The commission now exercises jurisdiction over 52,000 acres of park lands and operates a large number of different types of recreational facilities.

In the 1940s, the States continued to rely on special-purpose agencies to operate within different geographic sectors of the metropolitan region. The Port Authority continued to expand, most notably through the leasing and operation of LaGuardia, New York International, Newark, and Teterboro Airports. The Triborough Bridge and Tunnel Authority was created in 1946 to consolidate a number of previous authorities which operated bridges and roadways within New York City. Like the Port Authority, the Triborough used toll revenues and the proceeds of bond issues to construct additional facilities. Between 1948 and 1952, the New York Thruway Authority and the New Jersey Turnpike and Highway Authorities were created to build major limited-access highways between cities and suburbs in the region. Coordination among the different transportation networks was enhanced by the regional presence of Robert Moses, who, by virtue of his many official positions, was able to relate transportation arteries with housing and recreational projects in the region.

The 1950s: Recognition of Regional Problems. During the 1950s and early 1960s, a new kind of regional awareness developed out of a regional transit crisis stemming from the decline of the commuter railroads. Increased operating costs coupled with reduced revenues led the railroads to neglect commuter services and to seek permission to raise fares and reduce services on their least profitable lines. Several railroads went into bankruptcy. Pressure was brought on the three States to keep the commuter trains running and to finance improvements in the quality of service.

In 1954, a coalition of groups interested in rail transportation persuaded

New Jersey and New York to create a bi-state Metropolitan Rapid Transit Commission to develop a plan for transit facilities in the metropolitan area. The commission proposed creation of a new bi-state agency, the Metropolitan Transit District, which would provide financial assistance to the commuter railroads and construct a new trans-Hudson rail link between New York City and New Jersey. Legislation embodying this proposal was enacted in New York but was killed in 1958 in the New Jersey legislature.[3]

The States subsequently embarked on unilateral short-term programs to meet the mounting transportation pressures in the New York region. Largely as a result of the interpersonal relationships that developed out of the periodic crises and because of the prodding of the Regional Plan Association and the Metropolitan Regional Council (an organization of local officials), the three Governors created a Tri-State Transportation Committee in 1961 to study and recommend measures to meet regional transportation problems.

Local recognition of regional problems also emerged in the mid-1950s. In June 1956, chief elected executives of local communities in the New York metropolitan area met at New York City Hall to discuss the possibility of joint action for problems transcending local boundary lines. Their efforts resulted in the creation of the Metropolitan Regional Council (MRC), a voluntary organization of 37 county and municipal governments in the tri-state area, chaired by New York City's Mayor Robert Wagner. MRC undertook studies in transportation, water and air pollution, water supply, recreation and land use, and law enforcement, and determined to secure legal recognition of its efforts. Because of strong resistance by suburban interests, the attempt to gain legal status was abandoned in 1963. Although most of the local officials who participated in MRC's activities were convinced of its value, they were unsuccessful in persuading their local legislative bodies to ratify an agreement pledging regular financial contribution to the council. MRC could not recover from its downward course. By the early 1960s it became clear that the council would not be an important force in formulating regional plans or developing regional programs.

During this same period, the Regional Plan Association undertook sponsorship of the New York Metropolitan Region Study, a massive survey of physical, economic, social, and political developments in the tri-state area. Ten volumes were published between 1959 and 1961 and sparked new interest in regional affairs.

The 1960s: State and Federal Regional Initiatives. During the 1960s, Federal and State programs turned toward the use of regional approaches as a means of solving major metropolitan problems. Largely as a response to provisions of the Federal Aid Highway Act of 1962, which required that all Federally aided highway projects in urban areas be based on a comprehensive transportation planning process, a compact was drawn up in 1963 to convert the informal Tri-State Transportation Committee into a tri-state commission. Because of objections by New Jersey legislators to a compact provision calling for operating as well as planning authority, the compact was amended to limit the agency to a planning role. In 1965, the legislatures of the three States agreed to create a Tri-State Transportation Commission to perform transportation planning in the New York metropolitan region and to "consider all land-use problems related to the development of proper transportation plans."

In the next few years, the States became more and more directly involved in the region's transportation operations. In 1965, New York created the Metropolitan Commuter Transportation Authority to rehabilitate and operate the Long Island Railroad and improve transportation services throughout the New York sector of the region. Connecticut created the Connecticut Transportation Authority to finance and supervise improvements on the New Haven Railroad. New Jersey created the region's first Department of Transportation and authorized it to make direct grants to New Jersey's commuter lines. Both New York and Connecticut also created State transportation departments.

The era of regional institution-building by the States culminated in the creation by New York and New Jersey of three agencies with broad regional authority. New York created the Metropolitan Transportation Authority in 1967 to extend and improve mass transit facilities within a 12-county area. The legislation was coupled with a $2.5 billion transportation bond issue, the largest of its kind in the Nation's history. New York established the Urban Development Corporation in the following year in an effort to overcome the many obstacles that had limited the effectiveness of conventional urban renewal and housing development programs. New Jersey created the Hackensack Meadowlands Development Commission in 1968 to plan and effectuate the development of a large tract of undeveloped land in Hudson and Bergen Counties into an urban complex. Like the Urban Development Corporation, it is empowered to act without regard to many local limitations.

Meanwhile, the Federal government had been encouraging the development of regional perspectives in State and local decision making. Between 1960 and 1965, Federal grants were made contingent upon areawide planning in many different functional fields: open space acquisition, highways, mass transit, and water and sewerage facilities. The Housing and Urban Development Act of 1965 made Federal planning assistance available to groups such as councils of government and stimulated the revival of the dormant Metropolitan Regional Council. The Demonstration Cities and Metropolitan Development Act of 1966 required that local applications for grants or loans in a large number of urban programs be submitted for review to an areawide agency. The Tri-State Transportation Commission gradually assumed responsibility for additional planning and review functions and it was designated as the official review body under OMB Circular A-95. Largely because of pressure from HUD, Tri-State's enabling legislation was amended in 1971 and its name was changed to the Tri-State Regional Planning Commission to reflect its expanded responsibilities.

Despite the existence in the New York region of two Federally supported regional bodies, only the Federal Departments of Transportation and Housing and Urban Development (in the case of Tri-State) and the Law Enforcement Assistance Administration (in the case of MRC) have utilized these agencies to implement metropolitan programs. Other Federal programs incorporating regional approaches, such as community action, comprehensive health planning, law enforcement planning, air quality control, and manpower area planning, have been assigned to different agencies within the States and localities.[4]

At present, then, the New York area contains a small number of regional advisory bodies and some powerful, single-purpose bodies. It is also affected by a large number of State and Federal programs with regional impact. All of these forces exert some pressure over regional growth and development. The relative influence of the major regional bodies will be discussed in the following section.

ANALYSIS OF MAJOR REGIONAL BODIES

Advisory Bodies

Metropolitan Regional Council and Interlocal Cooperation. MRC, the local COG, is the prime example of interlocal cooperation in the New York region. It was revived and incorporated on November 2, 1966, pursuant to the Membership Corporations Law of New York State, as an agency "through which elected chief executive officers of municipalities . . . may, by association, consultation, and study, aid each other in dealing with governmental and community problems that transcend the geographic borders of their individual communities and are of common interest."[5] The by-laws provide that any elected chief executive officer of a municipality in the metropolitan region may become a member simply by notifying the executive secretary of his desire to join and paying his annual dues. Since the term "municipality" is broadly defined as a "county, city, town or village," membership in MRC is available to some 600 local communities. Presently, only two-thirds of the region's population, or roughly 12 million people, including New York City, are represented by the 16 elected officials who are dues-paying members of the council. Many large and important communities, containing about six million residents, are not supporting members. Population disparities among MRC's members are enormous:

member communities range in size from Westport, Connecticut, with 21,000 people, to New York City, with nearly 8 million. According to the by-laws, each member community, regardless of size, has one vote.

The by-laws provide for a nine-man board of directors—four from New York, three from New Jersey, and two from Connecticut—to serve for one year. A chairman and vice-chairman may be elected from these nine members to serve as president and vice-president of the council respectively. The by-laws also call for membership on MRC committees and participation in MRC activities by representatives from the three States and interstate agencies but do not confer on such representatives the right to vote.

MRC has had financial problems since its inception. Once it developed into a legal entity, it became eligible for 701 planning assistance funds and it has received Federal planning grants of from $100,000 to $150,000 per year since 1968. Annual membership dues based on a population formula were used to provide matching funds to Federal grants. Dues payments range from a high of $40,000 for a community with over 4 million in population (i.e., New York City) to a low of $5,000 for a community with a population of less than 50,000. In 1970, HUD recognized the Tri-State Transportation Commission as the sole applicant for comprehensive planning assistance funds in the New York metropolitan region and MRC now receives Federal funds through a subcontractual arrangement with Tri-State.

Since 1967, MRC has functioned with a small staff (ranging from five to eight professionals) and an annual budget of less than $200,000. It has supported a small number of programs, including narcotics prevention services, a waterfront cleanup project, a volunteer service and urban corps-work study project, and a public information and educational program—undertaken jointly with RPA. MRC's sponsorship with RPA of public meetings throughout the region to promote discussion of RPA's 2nd Regional Plan has provided its major exposure to the general public. Other than this, its public contacts have been limited to specialized public and private groups.

The council's most important current projects include the coordination of law enforcement programs in narcotics control and the construction and operation of a closed circuit television network linking counties and major cities of the tri-state region. When it is operational, the TV system will be used to coordinate law enforcement activities, to televise conferences and meetings of public officials, and to train municipal employees. The council has recently received two grants to support these activities: $115,000 from the Law Enforcement Assistance Administration to form a regional narcotics task force, and $102,000 from the National Science Foundation to conduct a study of communicating patterns and practices among the region's local officials.

Because of MRC's limited program concerns, its narrow membership base, and its relative anonymity, it plays a small role in bringing local governments together to develop solutions to major regional problems. It feels constrained by its membership of diverse, highly specialized, local communities, and by its voluntary character, to consider only "safe" issues which lend themselves to consensus-building activities and to shun regional issues which might tend to provoke conflict among its members. It has thus carved out a niche for itself as a service agency for local governments—rather than as a spokesman for local interests in formulating regional policy decisions.

Aside from MRC, there is little organized effort to effectuate collective action on the part of the region's local governments. Intergovernmental agreements at the local level have been limited both in geographic scope and in programs that have been covered. Robert Wood, a well-known observer of local governmental behavior, pointed out more than ten years ago that cooperative arrangements require "highly complex and cumbersome procedures . . . protracted negotiations, and . . . a political and administrative finesse which (the region's) local units do not ordinarily possess."[6] Cooperative patterns appear to have changed little in the intervening time.

The most notable instances of interlocal cooperation center on the joint planning undertaken by some of the region's local governments. In 1965, for example, Nassau and Suffolk Counties in New York joined in creating the Nassau-Suffolk Regional Planning Board to analyze changing patterns of regional growth and development on Long Island. Both counties contribute equal amounts to the board's total planning budget of approximately $200,000. The board issued a major regional plan in 1970. It presently serves as the review body for local applications for Federal grants and furnishes technical assistance to local municipalities.

The six regional planning agencies in the Connecticut sector of the New York metropolitan region furnish another example of interlocal effort to deal with regional problems. These agencies are organized on an official basis following an affirmative vote of at least 60 percent of the municipalities in a defined planning region. They receive financial assistance from the State and Federal governments and from member municipalities.

Despite these few examples, the region's local governments exhibit little sense of regional consciousness. The dominant local government, New York City, has not actively related its own planning efforts to regional planning activities or defined regional issues of importance to itself; nor has it assumed leadership in formulating and sustaining a regional strategy. The city's master plan, a massive series of documents issued in 1969 after many years of preparation by the City Planning Commission and outside consultants, neither discusses regional issues nor considers suburban resources that would be useful to the city.[7] The region's other communities are equally parochial; they frequently refrain from joint action even when they seek a common end. When local communities are located within different States, regional bonds are virtually non-existent.

In the absence of regional policy generated by the region's local governments, a greater impetus has been given to direct intervention in regional affairs by the States. The State programs raise the possibility of positive collaboration between State and local interests, but, thus far, local participation in State-sponsored programs has been limited.

Tri-State Regional Planning Commission and Comprehensive Planning. The Tri-State Regional Planning Commission is basically State-oriented and State-controlled. Since its creation, it has consisted of 18 members, five representatives from each of the party States and three non-voting members from Federal agencies. The States are represented mainly by the commissioners of departments of State government and include, in all cases, representatives of transportation and planning agencies. Before the compact was amended in May 1971, local interests and citizens were represented on the policy-making board by the chairman of the New York City Planning Commission from New York State, two private citizens from New Jersey, and the chief executive officer of a Connecticut municipality, all appointed by the respective governors. Under the new compact, membership from New York and Connecticut remains unchanged; New Jersey members now include two State commissioners and three public members appointed by the Governor, two of whom are to be local officials from the New Jersey sector of the region. In the new compact, then, State commissioners still outnumber local interest by a ratio of 2-1, and the governors retain veto power over plans affecting their respective State sectors.

By virtue of its parity of members from each of the three party States, Tri-State's representation is skewed in terms of population. The New York portion of the Region has more than twice the population of the New Jersey portion, and New Jersey, in turn, has three and one-half times the population of the Connecticut portion. Thus, each of New York City's members represents five times as many people as Connecticut's—a major departure from the one man, one vote principle.

The commission has not encouraged local participation in its policy-making efforts. Local "cooperating committees" composed of local officials were part of the original intent but they were rarely convened and fell into disuse. Instead, Tri-State has maintained contact with localities through a "technical advisory group" composed of staff representatives of State, county, city, and Federal agencies. Despite the proximity of MRC as a 701-supported body, until recently there was no contact between the two agencies. Since 1970, MRC has received HUD grants through a sub-contractual arrangement with Tri-State and the professional staffs of the two organizations are now coordinating their planning efforts. Tri-State's revised compact legislation spells out its intent to work with "advisory committees and panels representative of citizens, and political subdivisions and other governmental agencies" in the region in performing its function and developing its plans, but the effect of this provision is uncertain. Tri-State's commissioners still have the final say in policy formulation and the region is actually too large and unwieldy to facilitate direct citizen input.

Until recently, Tri-State's work was heavily oriented toward transportation and transportation-related activities. Within the past few years, the commission has broadened its planning sights to cover further aspects of the physical environment like waste management and recreation.[8] These new areas of interest conform with its additional responsibilities under the amended compact legislation. This changed the commission's name, designated it the "official comprehensive planning agency of the party States for the compact region," and directed it to "conduct surveys, make studies, submit recommendations and prepare plans designed to aid in solving immediate and long-range . . . problems, including but not limited to plans for development of land, housing, transportation and other public facilities." To date, the commission has not published reports dealing with social and economic issues of regional concern; its housing reports, prepared in compliance with HUD requirements for a "housing element," have not yet been issued as public documents.

The commission's focus on transportation is not unexpected. Originally created as a transportation planning body, it has received more money from FHWADOT than from HUD in financing its annual planning budget. During 1971-72, the commission's budget for comprehensive planning studies approximated $2.8 million. The Federal share covers about two-thirds of the cost. The balance is derived from the States in the form of matching funds and is apportioned among the three states, New York, New Jersey, and Connecticut, on the basis of an assessment ratio of 45: 45: 10. The commission also receives Federal grants for demonstration projects which are matched by the State or States in which the program takes place.

Like MRC, Tri-State is largely unknown. Instead of seeking publicity for its findings or stimulating public discussion of its plans, it distributes its publications, quietly, to planners, public officials, and interested citizens and groups. The commission's insulation from the greater regional public appears to conform with its view of its initial role as a planner and researcher for operating agencies within State governments. In recent years, however, the commission has developed its substantial research capabilities into a regional resource, making available its abundant data base, analytical processes, and census-tape retrieval services to all of the region's communities and planners. Tri-State is now working more closely with subregional agencies in an effort to coordinate its own projections with theirs, to furnish technical assistance when required, and to perform its responsibilities of regional review and certification.

Despite Tri-State's great research strengths, its view of future regional developments has been found to be unduly cautious and bland.9 The commission has also been faulted for its failure to take positions with respect to controversial regional issues such as the creation of a fourth jetport or the building of a bridge over Long Island Sound. As with sensitive issues of social concern, troublesome issues have been sidestepped so as not to generate controversy among its members.

The representation of the three States on Tri-State's policy body quite naturally limits the commission's actions to those narrow areas which conform to each State's conception of appropriate planning concerns, and which respect statewide political considerations. This severely restricts the commission's flexibility and scope as a plan-generating body. The use of State-appointed officials to represent the interests of the States further limits the development of independent policy. As commissioners of operating departments within their respective States, each official tends to negotiate within the framework of specialized interests and to avoid programs which might conflict with his primary responsibilities.

Tri-State's impact on regional development is difficult to assess. On the one hand, its strong complement of State officials (which hinders it in carrying out its primary role as the region's planner) is useful in providing for an exchange of information and views among the three States and focuses the attention of State agencies on the compelling problems of the New York metropolitan region. And Tri-State's expanded contacts with local planning officials have served to secure greater coordination of regional and subregional planning efforts. On the other hand, the linkage between regional planning and regional decision making in the New York region is tenuous. In reviewing applications for Federal grant requests under the A-95 procedure, Tri-State wields advisory powers only and has no power to veto, or even delay, implementation. Although there is little hard evidence concerning the commission's influence over the distribution of Federal resources to local applicants or its impact upon the programs of the independent functional agencies, there are informal indications that the A-95 comments are useful to the Federal funding agencies: However, Tri-State, in common with planning bodies elsewhere, lacks the political base and the constituency to oppose programs of the powerful single-purpose agencies which do not conform with its own regional plans.10

Regional Plan Association. RPA is a private research and planning organization which seeks wide public exposure of its planning efforts. Consequently, its plans and proposals are better known than those of the publicly-supported bodies. In 1968, RPA formulated its *2nd Regional Plan,* calling for the creation of a series of new, relatively self-contained, metropolitan communities. The association has attempted to gain public support for these metropolitan sub-centers, holding a series of public hearings in different counties. RPA is currently preparing to present the issues discussed in the *2nd Regional Plan* and other regional planning documents to a large regional audience within a series of six one-hour television "town meetings" to be broadcast by every station in the region in the spring of 1973. It plans to organize listening groups and distribute a questionnaire for mass response; it hopes that a half million people will participate.

RPA's planning budget of approximately $800,000 per year is raised from membership dues, foundation grants, and special study grants from public and private bodies. It has a staff of 12 to 15 professionals and uses outside consultants as required. Its board is composed mainly of prominent business and civic leaders representative of different geographic areas and professional interests. Like the public advisory bodies, it is not representative of the region's low-income groups or the minorities.

It is noteworthy, however, that RPA is the only regional body which has issued a public document dramatizing the magnitude of the regional housing crisis. RPA's "Housing Opportunities: An Analysis and Presentation for the New York State Urban Development Corporation" (1969) described the increased racial and economic segregation in the region, emphasized the growing mismatch between housing and job opportunities, and suggested remedial measures. RPA has also acted as consultant to a National Committee against Discrimination in Housing study of employment and housing opportunities for racial minorities in suburban areas of the New York metropolitan region. It has supported the Urban Development Corporation's proposals to build low- and moderate-income housing in Westchester County.

As a private body, unhampered by the political constraints of State and local governments, RPA has been free to tangle publicly with the large functional authorities which abound in the region. It disputed the Port Authority's proposals regarding expansion of the region's commercial airport facilities, for example, contending that the immediate need was ground access to the existing airports. Recently, it has criticized plans for development of the Jersey Meadowlands, claiming that the office complex proposed by the Hackensack Meadowlands Development Commission would have a depressing effect on neighboring cities.[11] It has also taken public positions in such controversial issues as the lower Manhattan Expressway, the location of higher educational institutions, and the Long Island Sound bridge crossing. In certain instances, it has spoken out forcefully in support of its proposals, recently pushing hard for official acceptance of the Gateway National Recreational Area.

Presently, the private planning body appears to serve as the most visible generator of new ideas for guiding the region's growth and development. In performing this function, it relies heavily on the data and analytical documents prepared by Tri-State and the official contacts of MRC. If Tri-State were to present its plans to the public for consideration, RPA might be more useful in acting as a "regional gadfly" than as a comprehensive planner. In Tri-State's absence (and with its assistance) RPA has modified its role to serve as the regional innovator.

Major Functional Bodies

Some regional observers have suggested that general-purpose governments in the New York metropolitan region have lost control over the formulation of plans and the determination of priorities to single-purpose agencies which have the capacity to guide and effectuate long-range development. From this perspective, special-purpose agencies have evolved into planning and development agencies for the region, and general governments into the housekeeping units.[12] This observation seems to be particularly evident in the transportation arena where regional centers of activity are emerging. It is to these centers that we now turn our attention.

Port of New York Authority. The Port Authority is the oldest, largest, and richest of the single-purpose regional bodies. It was created 50 years ago by compact between New York and New Jersey to develop and operate terminal, transportation, and trade facilities within the Port of New York district—an area falling within a 25-mile radius of the Statue of Liberty—and to protect and promote the commerce of the port. Directing its effort primarily to the coordination and development of vehicular facilities, the Port Authority is now a multi-functional operation whose facilities presently include six interstate bridges and tunnels, four airports, two heliports, four motor vehicle terminals, six marine terminal areas, a world trade center, and the PATH commuter rail system.

The structure of the Port Authority was designed to provide continuity in decision making and program implementation. It is governed by 12 commissioners, six from New York and six from New Jersey, appointed by the governors of their respective states for six-year overlapping terms without pay. Four of the six commissioners chosen from New York State are resident voters of New York City and four of the six appointed by the New Jersey governor are resident voters within the New Jersey portion of the port district. The commissioners appoint the executive director, who is formally charged with implementing board policy. Compact provisions and traditions have helped to ensure longer tenure for port officials than for their appointing officers. This security enhances their relative freedom in policy making and helps to shield authority officials from political pressures.

The enabling compact denies the authority the power to tax or to pledge the credit of either New York or New Jersey to meet its financial obligations. The authority is authorized to issue bonds for the construction or acquisition of facilities and to liquidate them through collection of user charges. It tries to limit itself therefore to profitable ventures which can be sustained through user charges, tolls and fees, and to avoid involvement in mass transit operations which are traditionally deficit-inducing. Because of its heavy dependence upon the private investment market, the views of bondholders figure prominently in its policy decisions.

The current financial position of the authority is very strong. The port collected a record $279.9 million at its bridges, tunnels, airports, and terminals in 1971—a 9.6 percent increase over the previous year. Its total assets at the close of 1971 were $3.2 billion, a 12.6 percent gain for the year and more than 250 percent higher than its assets for 1961. The authority had an operating surplus in 1971 of $104.6 million, plus income of $34 million in interest on its investment portfolio.[13]

Despite its efforts to steer clear of mass transit responsibilities, the Port Authority has occasionally been forced to use limited portions of its resources in aid of commuter transportation programs. In 1960, for example, New York and the Port Authority agreed that the State legislature would loan $20 million to the port to help finance the purchase of new passenger coaches for use primarily by commuter railroads. The New York legislature also agreed to guarantee a bond issue of $100 million in authority bonds to finance the purchase of railroad equipment. In 1962, New Jersey officials compelled the port to undertake rehabilitation and operation of the bankrupt Hudson and Manhattan Railroad (Now PATH) as the price of New Jersey's approval of the authority's World Trade Center. As part of this bargain, the port succeeded in securing passage of bi-State legislation that would prohibit it from assuming any more unprofitable rail operations. Notwithstanding this provision, the port has recently agreed to work with New York and New Jersey in developing a $650-million program of mass transportation within the region.

Public supervision of the Port Authority's operation is limited. The major mechanism of accountability is a veto by each governor of the resolutions adopted by the authority within ten days of the meeting at which the resolutions were passed. The two States also require the authority to file an annual report and they possess the right to audit the authority's books and to conduct a legislative investigation. The authority must also receive bi-state legislative approval of its development plans in order to issue bonds. Once this authorization is received, the port can plan, finance, and operate its projects without further controls. Because of the intermittent nature of the supervision, the port possesses wide discretion in budgetary determinations and operating procedures, more characteristic of a private corporation than a public body.

Current issues concerning the port deal largely with its unusual autonomy in operations and finance. Opponents are particularly critical of the construction of the World Trade Center, two 110-story office buildings in lower Manhattan, which are viewed as questionable "civic improvement," inconsistent with the port's mandate to coordinate and rationalize transportation within the port district. Critics also fault the port's longstanding reluctance to assume additional responsibilities in mass transit projects and the covenant in the port's legislation which prevents the authority from using its revenues to fund deficit railroad operations beyond a limited amount.

Recent political developments indicate that the Port Authority may be required to redefine its responsibilities. Current straws in the wind include outspoken comments by both governors concerning the port's involvement in mass transit, new appointees to the port's board of directors, New York State legislative action designed to free the port's surplus funds for use in mass transit, and the recent resignation of the port's long-time executive director, who had been steadfast in his resistance to deficit-inducing activities. Furthermore, the practice of using revenues from profitable enterprises to support transit operations is gaining acceptance in the New York region. In 1969, the port's counterpart, the Triborough Bridge and Tunnel Authority, which was long regarded as inviolate, was taken over by the Metropolitan Transportation Authority, and its surpluses were used for the benefit of the subway rider.

Metropolitan Transportation Authority. MTA was created by New York State in 1967 with extensive responsibilities in rapid transit, surface transit, bridge, and rail commuter traffic. In addition to the Long Island Railroad, it serves as a "holding company" or "umbrella" agency over most metropolitan area transit, including the Triborough Bridge and Tunnel Authority (which operates nine toll bridges and tunnels in New York City), the New York City Transit Authority (which operates New York City subways), and the Manhattan and Bronx Surface Transit Operating Agency (which operates buses). Since its creation, MTA has acquired the Staten Island Rapid Transit Operating Authority and two general aviation airports, and has assumed responsibility for commuter service of the New York State sector of the New Haven division and the Harlem and Hudson division of the Penn Central Railroad. In its entirety, MTA is a giant transportation conglomerate which controls "the world's biggest subway system (720 miles of track, 7,000 passenger cars, 477 stations), the largest U.S. passenger railroad (the Long Island), 4,420 buses, serves 8,000,000 daily riders, . . . (and) operates on an annual budget exceeding $1 billion."[14]

MTA's governing board consists of a chairman and ten members appointed by the Governor for eight-year staggered terms. Only the chairman is salaried. The board of directors serves as the *ex officio* board of all agencies under its jurisdiction, and the MTA chairman is chief executive officer of these agencies as well. At least nine members must be residents of the transportation district and three of the members are nominated by the mayor of New York City. Unlike most of the regional transportation authorities which are emerging in different metropolitan areas throughout the Nation, local governments (aside from New York City) are not represented on its governing board.

MTA programs are financed in the main by users charges; State and Federal grants and special legislative appropriations constitute the major subsidies. Through 1971, MTA had received regular grants of more than $553.8 million from the State legislature and one time start-up appropriations of more than $61.8 million. Federal grants of over $116.6 million had also been made available.[15] MTA receives relatively modest amounts from mortgage tax revenues collected from the counties comprising the transportation district and railroad station maintenance and operation costs assessed against the localities. Capital programs for New York City's subways and public bus lines receive assistance from the city's capital budget. MTA is also authorized to issue revenue bonds to support its operations and New York State guarantees to shore up its reserve fund in the event that user charges do not produce sufficient income to meet debt service.

The new and significant feature of MTA's financial arrangements is the balancing of the operating surpluses accumulated by the profit-making Triborough against the deficits of the New York City Authority (CTA) and MTA's commuter railroad operations. MTA is empowered to transfer surplus funds from one of its constituent agencies to another and these can now be used for the payment of operating expenses of the recipients. MTA is also authorized to establish tolls and other charges to maintain the "combined operations" of the authority on a self-sustaining basis. Since the transit authority had been required to conduct its operations on a self-sustaining basis since 1953, this balancing means that subways no longer have to support their operating expenses solely by their fare structure.

Current criticisms of MTA deal largely with its exclusion of local communities from membership on its policy board, its high degree of autonomy over the setting of fares and tolls, and its less than regionwide jurisdiction. Local governments, both within and outside New York City, claim that they have limited capacity to influence or modify MTA's programs toward meeting the needs of their own residents.[16] And State legislators deplore the existence of another semi-autonomous public transportation body which is relatively free from budgetary review and legislative oversight.[17] Local and State viewpoints notwithstanding, MTA operates under closer public scrutiny than the self-sustaining Port Authority, its co-participant in the regional transportation field. Because of MTA's heavy dependence on public funds, its activities are reviewed by many different agencies at the Federal, State, and local levels. MTA also appears to work closely with its counterparts in the other two states, the Connecticut Transportation Authority and the New Jersey Department of Transportation, in dealing with common transportation problems.

Urban Development Corporation. UDC is a statewide public authority with strong powers to rebuild urban areas. It is included in this discussion of "regional" agencies because of its potential impact in stimulating housing development in the New York sector of the metropolitan area. UDC was created by the New York State legislature in 1968 to "acquire, construct, reconstruct, facilitate, or improve . . . industrial, manufacturing, commercial, educational and cultural facilities and housing accommodations for persons and families of low income . . . and carry out the clearance, replacing, reconstruction and rehabilitation of substandard and unsanitary areas. . . ." In addition to the customary powers adhering to a public authority, the corporation is given formidable powers to waive local laws, ordinances, zoning codes, charters, and construction regulations, substituting compliance with the State's building construction code when, "in the discretion of the corporation . . . compliance is not feasible or practicable." The enabling legislation calls for the corporation to "work closely, consult and cooperate with local elected officials" but it can overrule municipal disapproval by a vote of two-thirds of its directors.

UDC's governing board consists of four *ex officio* State officials, the Commissioner of Commerce, Superintendent of Banks, Superintendent of Insurance, and the director of the Office of Planning Services; and five directors appointed by the Governor, who serve for overlapping terms of four years each. The president, Edward J. Logue, is appointed by the Governor and is the chief executive officer of the corporation.

UDC is authorized to borrow up to $1.5 billion to finance its projects and has already sold a bond issue of $250 million. It has also received substantial appropriations from the State (almost $90 million) in the form of one-time start-up funds which must be repaid. It receives small amounts from municipalities for initial planning and development studies. Its projects are wholly or partially exempt from local real property taxes, except for assessments for local improvements.[18]

Through the use of tax exemptions on land, low interest rates, and Federal subsidies, the corporation proposes to induce private industry to produce housing within the economic range of middle- and low-income families. UDC's developments customarily provide a cross section of age and income levels, or 70 percent of all housing on a particular site for middle-income families, 20 percent for low-income families and 10 percent for the elderly.

Despite its relatively short life, UDC's programs reflect a recognition of the interdependence of different communities in the metropolitan area. In addition to agreements with individual cities, it is developing housing programs for Suffolk, Orange, and Rockland Counties, and has signed a

Memorandum of Understanding with Westchester County to initiate a countywide housing and development program.[19] It has established a particularly close working relationship with New York City, developing approximately 18 different projects in 1970. Because of its expertise as a packager and developer, and its ability to secure "236" subsidies, it is credited with stimulating one-third of the housing starts within New York City in 1971.

Since its creation, UDC has encountered strong resistance from local communities, who regard it as a threat to local integrity and municipal home rule. Several bills restricting its powers were passed by the State legislature in 1970 and 1971; all were vetoed by the Governor. In June 1972, UDC announced plans to build approximately 100 moderate- and low-priced units in each of nine towns in northern Westchester; most of the towns were zoned for single-family houses—with minimum lot sizes of up to four acres. This was the first time that UDC had publicly proposed using its power to override municipal zoning ordinances within the New York region. The opposition was so fierce that the corporation has voted to postpone its plans until the localities have had a chance to develop substitute proposals.

UDC's original intent embraced the creation of housing opportunities for the urban poor within suburban areas. It is now pursuing a countywide approach, seeking to improve housing conditions within each county. Although there are well-documented housing shortages in these areas, the corporation is encountering strong resistance from municipal officials and State legislators. It appears, therefore, that UDC's formal powers may be insufficient to counteract the formidable political obstacles which accompany any effort to alter the suburbs' exclusionary zoning policies.

Hackensack Meadowlands Development Commission. The Hackensack Meadowlands Development Commission was created by New Jersey legislative action in 1969 to sponsor and supervise development of a tract of about 18,000 acres of mostly vacant meadows, marshes, and salt water swamps, lying directly across the Hudson River from Manhattan. The commission was authorized to adopt and enforce a master plan for the physical development of the Hackensack Meadowlands and to promulgate and enforce codes and standards of land use, subdivision, and zoning regulations.

The commission consists of seven members, the commissioner of the New Jersey Department of Community Affairs, and six other members appointed by the Governor from Hudson and Bergen Counties. Its zoning and taxing powers transcend the municipal powers of the 14 municipalities included within its jurisdiction. A Hackensack Meadowlands Municipal Committee, consisting of the chief executive of each of the 14 municipalities, has review power over all improvement plans developed by the commission. If the Municipal Committee disapproves of a plan, the commission may override a municipal veto by a vote of five members.

The commission is empowered to issue bonds and notes to finance large-scale private and public investment. In turn, the participating communities will share in the increased wealth of the developed land through a complicated tax-sharing plan. Each of the 14 communities will be guaranteed its present tax income with the promise that existing high property taxes will be drastically reduced by additional wealth generated by the Meadowlands' development.

In 1970 the commission issued a preliminary plan for urban development which encountered resistance from local groups. The mayors of the municipalities wanted more industrial development than the plan called for and the environmentalists wanted less. RPA also recommended major changes which would relate the development of the Meadowlands to the surrounding area, particularly the nearby older cities, and leave more land in a natural state. In November 1972 the commission issued its revised master plan, which increases open space to about 6,200 acres, "more open space facilities than . . . any similar place in any other U.S. urban area," calls for residential construction for about 125,000 people, and limits office building construction.[20]

Interstate Sanitation Commission. The ISC was created by interstate compact among the three States in 1936 to provide for the abatement of water pollution in the region's tidal waters and to prevent pollution in the future. The commission is composed of five commissioners from each State (including, in each case, the State health commissioner) and has the power to set and enforce water quality standards within its geographic district. Despite early recognition of the problem by the three States, water pollution has become increasingly severe in the New York metropolitan region. Because of minimal and vague standards of treatment embodied in the initial compact, inadequate financial and political support over the years by the States, and a limited staff of technical and administrative personnel, the commission has been ineffective in enforcing and developing new standards of water treatment. In addition, the ISC has relied heavily on a program of "public education, persuasion and cooperation" throughout its existence and has been timid in enforcing compliance orders against recalcitrant municipalities and industrial polluters.[21] For all of these reasons, the commission appears to be playing a less significant role in recent years at the same time that Federal and State enforcement activities are gaining in importance.

The ISC entered the air pollution field in 1962 when New York and New Jersey authorized it to assume certain advisory responsibilities with respect to regional air quality. Connecticut became a participant in this aspect of the commission's program in 1969. In April 1970 the three Governors called on the commission to coordinate and plan air activities in the tri-state Air Quality Control Region, pursuant to the Federal Air Quality Control Act. In this capacity, the commission coordinates a regional air pollution warning system, maintains an answering service for citizen's complaints, and operates mobile monitoring units. Since the commission lacks enforcement powers in air pollution and has limited financial resources and personnel, its effectiveness as a regional air pollution control body is small.

PERFORMANCE OF MAJOR REGIONAL FUNCTIONS

Many of the functions performed by governments in the tri-state area involve important regional or subregional considerations. In a few functional fields, limited progress has been made toward relating and coordinating the activities of the various governing bodies; in others, fragmentation of decision making and operations is prominent. Not all observers agree, however, about the advisability of organizing governmental functions on a tri-state regional basis. Some planners believe that, in the absence of public pressure for change or a strong showing of regional need, existing governmental arrangements should be utilized to the maximum extent possible—and control retained at the lowest practicable unit of government.[22]

Transportation: Limited Progress Toward Regionalism

Transportation is the most regionalized of the public functions. Although no single agency exercises region-wide authority over all transportation functions and modes, two powerful agencies, the Port Authority and the Metropolitan Transportation Authority, dominate public transportation activities in most of the New York and New Jersey sectors. By their size alone, each agency achieves some coordination of policy making within its own jurisdiction.

In addition, the Tri-State Regional Planning Commission serves as a useful coordinating mechanism in transportation planning. Federal officials, State commissioners of transportation, and the chairmen of the MTA and the Connecticut Transportation Authority meet regularly as Tri-State commissioners, and the commission provides a channel for an exchange of information among their staffs. The commission also reviews local and state applications for Federal transportation grants. In 1971 it was given responsibility by the Urban Mass Transit Administration for allocating mass transit planning funds within the region. Tri-State has also undertaken a number of special projects involving the coordinated efforts of several agencies. For example, it supervised the establishment of a special express lane for commuter buses along Interstate 495 in New Jersey, bringing together the Port Authority, the New Jersey Turnpike Authority, and several other agencies.

A further degree of coordination is achieved through *ad hoc* cooperation between agencies in response to particular problems. During the early 1960s, for example, an Interstate Staff Committee, composed of representatives of New York, Connecticut, Westchester County, and New York City joined forces with representatives of Rhode Island and Massachusetts to petition the Interstate Commerce Commission for a Federal loan guarantee for the New Haven Railroad. New York and New Jersey worked together, to a limited extent, in obligating the Port Authority to purchase, modernize, and operate the Hudson and Manhattan Railroad in 1962. New York and Connecticut jointly worked out several programs of short-term aid for the ailing New Haven Railroad during the mid-1960s. In 1969 the MTA and the CTA concluded an agreement under which they now share responsibility for continued operation of the New Haven's commuter services.[23]

Finally, coordination is achieved through a series of overlapping directorates held by key transportation decision makers. For example, at the time this paper was prepared the chairman of the MTA was serving also as vice chairman of the Port Authority and as a commissioner of Tri-State. Similarly, the chairman of the New York City Planning Commission was serving as a member of the MTA board as well as a Tri-State commissioner.

Environmental Management and Land-Use Regulation: Limited State Initiatives

In the fields of environmental management and land-use regulation, the States have promoted regionalization within their own sectors of the metropolitan area. Each of the States has created a new department of environmental protection (called the Department of Environmental Conservation in New York). In 1972 New York State passed a $1.2 billion environmental bond issue which calls for expenditures for water and air pollution, solid waste treatment, and the purchase and development of sites of environmental concern. To date, related efforts of the three States have been small.

Solid waste disposal is probably the region's most critical environmental problem. Although communities are rapidly running out of landfill space, and cannot afford to upgrade old incinerators to meet new air quality standards, solid waste disposal is still an almost completely local activity. All three States, however, have taken some steps toward handling it on a subregional basis. New Jersey mandated the Hackensack Meadowlands Development Commission to find an alternative to the existing system of municipal landfills in the meadows area. The commission is now considering the construction of a huge incinerator—the world's largest—to eliminate the need for further filling. Connecticut provides special incentive grants to communities for development of regional solid waste disposal arrangements and has asked General Electric to develop a statewide management system for solid waste. New York's Environmental Facilities Corporation has taken over the operation of several municipal landfills in the New York region.

The Interstate Sanitation Commission has been concerned with the maintenance of water quality in the region since 1936, but water pollution still depends heavily on the treatment of sewage by local governments. Because of local inability to finance the needed improvements and a lack of substantial financial help from higher levels of government, the localities have made slow progress in upgrading their sewage treatment facilities. Within the past few years, there has been an increased trend toward sub-regional handling of sewage disposal at the county level in both the New York and New Jersey sectors of the region.

Under the Federal Clean Air Act of 1970, the States must adopt implementation plans for maintaining or achieving the national primary and secondary ambient air quality standards issued by the U.S. Environmental Protection Agency (EPA). The three States have not yet adopted uniform techniques, monitoring practices, and reporting systems for the sampling and analysis of pollutants in the tri-state Air Quality Control Region.

The great drought of the early 1960s increased public awareness of the need to plan carefully to meet the region's future water supply needs. New Jersey has built several large reservoirs to serve its northeastern counties and both Connecticut and New Jersey have encouraged consolidation of small water supply systems. New York is, in a sense, fortunate to possess the large New York City system, which draws heavily on upstate watersheds beyond the region's nothern border. It is possible that communities in Long Island and northern New Jersey, many of which now depend on small independent systems, will tap into the city system in the future.

Despite attempts by all three states to develop statewide, county (and, in Connecticut, regional) systems of land-use planning and regulation, these functions remain primarily local. Connecticut's regional planning agencies are voluntary bodies and lack enforcement powers. In recent years, both New York's Office of Planning Coordination and New Jersey's Department of Community Affairs have prepared comprehensive revisions of planning and zoning legislation which would make local decision on land use subject to review at higher levels. Neither State took affirmative action on the proposed reforms. Statewide planning in New York was significantly restructured during the State's 1971 budget crisis, when the Office of Planning Coordination was merged with several other agencies into the Office of Planning Services, and its budget was reduced by more than 50 percent.

While local governments retain firm control over land-use policies generally, all three States have enacted specialized legislation dealing with critical areas of environmental concern. A notable example of this is found in the power given to the environmental protection agencies to regulate development of the coastal wetlands.24 It is possible that environmental land-use controls of this type will be used in the future as major instruments of State influence over land-use development in and around the metropolitan region.

Law Enforcement and Health Services:
Limited Cooperation on a Substate Basis

Regional cooperation in law enforcement dates back to 1953 when New York and New Jersey created a bi-state Waterfront Commission Compact for the elimination of criminal and corrupt practices in the handling of waterfront cargo within the Port of New York. The States have also enacted an Interstate Compact on Juveniles (signed by New York and New Jersey in 1955 and by Connecticut in 1957) which established procedures for the supervision and return of juveniles, and an Interstate Agreement on Detainers (signed by New York and Connecticut in 1957, New Jersey in 1958), which facilitated speedy disposition of indictments, informations, or complaints filed against prisoners of one State by officials of another.

Pursuant to provisions of the Omnibus Crime Control and Safe Streets Act of 1968, the three States created law enforcement planning agencies whose responsibilities include the encouragement of regional arrangements in planning and operations. However, law enforcement is considered to be predominantly a local function to be handled by local and State governments, and the prospects for extensive regionalization of services in the New York metropolitan area are limited. Presently, the States evaluate requests for law enforcement facilities grants under the A-95 review system and the Tri-State Regional Planning Commission reviews law enforcement grants for operating purposes only. The Metropolitan Regional Council provides information exchange services for local police officials and conducts a narcotics intelligence program.

The Federal government has also encouraged regional planning in health services and provides funds for areawide comprehensive health planning agencies. Nine such agencies have been established in the New York region. Since most are still in an embryonic stage, it is difficult to evaluate them. As with law enforcement, health professionals view the tri-state region as too large for meaningful health services planning and consider county and substate regional planning bodies more appropriate units for this task.

Housing and Economic Opportunity:
Evasion of Regional Responsibilities

In recent years it has become clear that some of the most pressing social problems of the New York metropolitan region require regional responses. The regional housing problem provides a clear example. The need for low- and middle-income housing in the region is acute; almost one dwelling in six is substandard and more than 80 percent of the region's families cannot afford to buy a home at current prices.[25]

Suburban communities have been steadfast in their opposition to subsidized housing because they fear, with some justification, that new residents will consume more in increased local services than they will return in local tax revenues. Since basic services are financed primarily from local property taxes, each locality has a strong incentive to resist low- and middle-income residential development. As a result, moderately priced housing is scarce throughout the region. In the central cities, where public policy still supports low- and middle-income construction, land is used for housing which, for economic and environmental reasons, might be better used for other purposes.

The effects of local land-use and fiscal policies extend beyond the housing field. Economic growth in the region, particularly industrial growth, is increasingly a suburban phenomenon. The region's low-income population is increasingly concentrated in the cities, far from the available job opportunities. Transportation is poor from the city centers to suburban job sites, and homes in the suburbs are generally unavailable. This mismatch of people and jobs perpetuates problems of poverty and racial segregation, and denies economic opportunity to a large number of the region's residents. Except for the creation of the Urban Development Corporation by New York State, none of the region's many governments has responded to this challenge.

CONCLUSION

Assessment of Governmental Responses

Federal Thrust. Over the past decade, the Federal government has been supporting regional approaches toward the development of metropolitan areas. In the New York region, Federal efforts in support of regional planning have led to the creation of a regional planning commission and the rebirth of a COG. Both of these agencies are deficient in complying with comprehensive planning requirements and guidelines: they have a narrow representative base; they are relatively unknown; they skirt sensitive issues; they fail to assume regional leadership roles.

Furthermore, the region's planning efforts appear to have limited influence on regional decision making. The major areawide development programs, ostensibly the end product of the planning efforts, are being performed largely by State-created functional agencies whose programs are frequently not reviewed by the official regional review body. Federal requirements for "cross acceptance" of regional plans have generated dialogue between the regional planning agency and the subregional bodies (i.e., the counties and planning districts) in formulating and upgrading their own plans. However, the review body's authority to review regional decisions is limited to only those projects which are to be Federally assisted, and this authority does not include the power to suspend projects even when they may not conform with the review body's plans. Thus, the A-95 review process has minimal impact upon the coordinated development of the region as a whole.

The Federal thrust is weakened by its failure to utilize regional entities for Federal programs other than metropolitan and transportation planning. Although a large number of Federal programs have regional implications, Federal agencies make use of a variety of specialized agencies with the States and localities to channel funds and implement policies. In overlooking opportunities to reinforce regional mechanisms in the different functional fields, the Federal government in effect minimizes its regional impact.

More significantly, the Federal government is failing to provide regionally oriented remedies for New York's critical social and economic problems. Many of these problems are national in character and require Federal resources and solutions for their alleviation. Without a set of coherent urban policies and strategies to deal with sensitive regional issues, planners and policymakers in the New York metropolitan area lack a national frame of reference to guide their own efforts.

This oversight is aggravated by the tendency of the Federal government to treat all metropolitan areas alike: large or small, interstate or intrastate. New York's size and importance, its distinctive needs and attributes, and its tri-state character require special Federal efforts in promoting a regional approach. It is unlikely that a strong move toward regionalism will emerge without special attention from the Federal level of government.

State Thrust. New York, a strong urban-oriented State, has responded to the need for areawide services in metropolitan areas with the creation of public authorities, both statewide and regional in jurisdiction. The Housing Finance Agency, Metropolitan Transportation Authority, Urban Development Corporation, and Environmental Facilities Corporation are some of the recent authorities created by the State to deal with major metropolitan problems.

The deficiencies of the public authority approach to the handling of metropolitan service requirements have been well documented by urban observers and scholars. For present purposes, their most important disadvantages concern their relative immunity to political control, their diffuse responsibility, their independence from general-purpose governments, and their autonomy—which encourages functional and geographical fragmentation within the metropolitan area. According to John Bebout, a well-known urban scholar, New York's use of public authorities to implement regional plans has "encouraged the development of a rudimentary, regrettably unintegrated, *ad hoc* system of regional governance, for limited purposes."[26]

New Jersey and Connecticut, the other two States which comprise the region, assume fewer direct metropolitan responsibilities and play a less active role in regional matters. New Jersey has, of course, cooperated with New York in the creation and supervision of the Port Authority, and has created its own Hackensack Meadowlands Development Commission to oversee the development of a large underdeveloped area in northern New Jersey. Connecticut has formed the Connecticut Transportation Authority to negotiate with New York's Metropolitan Transportation Authority regarding the operation of the New Haven Railroad.

The region presently accommodates 66 percent of New York State's population, 75 percent of New Jersey's, and 52 percent of Connecticut's. Despite this mutuality of interests, none of the three States has incorporated a regional frame of reference within its thinking, programs, or policies. Like the Federal government, the States have not given special attention to the unique needs of the New York metropolitan region or treated it differently from other metropolitan areas within their own States. Aside from sharing common membership on the Interstate Sanitation Commission, the Tri-State Regional Planning Commission, and less important regional bodies, the States engage in common action only on an *ad hoc* basis when crises occur. The three States will probably continue to create their own institutions for policy coordination unless they are compelled to act in unison by a higher level of government.

Local Response. The 21 counties, six planning regions, and 600-odd municipalities in the New York metropolitan region remain parochial in outlook. They seem unable to adjust to a political environment in which problems are no longer "local." In a limited sense, some of the counties provide a "regional" perspective for inter-municipal planning and relate well to the Tri-State Regional Planning Commission. But, overall, the localities cooperate only when they perceive strong advantages from acting in unison, and they frequently refrain from joint action even when seeking a common end. City-suburban hostilities are intense and aggravate the difficulties of alleviating pressing regional problems.

There is little sense of regional consciousness among local governments in the New York metropolitan region and MRC has been ineffectual in promoting a regional community of interests among its diverse body of members. New York City, the most important local government, was noteworthy in promoting and sustaining a regional cooperative effort in the late 1950s and early 1960s; it has played a less prominent role in regional matters since that time.

Applicability to Other Metropolitan Areas

The issue of applicability can be approached from different vantage points. On the one hand, the New York region is so large and complex, and the socio-economic differences between central city and suburban areas are so sharp, that the problems seem unique and the constraints seem overwhelming. Hence John Keith, president of the Regional Plan Association, points out that regional planning in New York has more in common, in some respects, with that performed in Paris, London, or Tokyo than it has with planning in most domestic metropolitan areas.27 Regional planning and action programs by large counties in the New York area, equivalent in territory and population to whole metropolitan areas in many other parts of the nation, represent mere fragments of the total effort.

These features limit the applicability to the New York region of the more traditional mechanisms which are useful in smaller metropolitan areas like Portland, Nashville, Indianapolis, and Jacksonville. Metropolitan arrangements that are regarded as regional elsewhere are probably more appropriate for application at the subregional level in New York. If new institutional arrangements are desired, they may have to be devised for New York alone. Because of its size, diversity, and complexity, the New York region would provide a useful testing ground—and challenge—for new regional relationships, untried thus far in the American federal system.

On the other hand, it can be argued that New York's problems are essentially the same as those in other large domestic metropolitan areas and that they differ mainly in their size and visibility. From this perspective, public policies which would provide regionally oriented solutions to some of New York's socio-economic, political, and environmental problems would be equally useful elsewhere. Moreover, because of the enormity of New York's challenge, if solutions can be developed here, this would probably be a strong indication that they would be beneficial in other places as well.

Future Directions

A review of current trends toward regionalism in the New York metropolitan region leads one to believe that *ad hoc* measures—rather than permanent arrangements—will continue to characterize the local and tri-state responses to this region's metropolitan problems. The local governments lack the requisite financial and legal resources to solve regional problems and are unwilling to act jointly in matters of common interest. The three States occupy a central role in the development of new regional approaches, but they too are unlikely to act in unison short of a crisis affecting a major regional service. The States may be required to undertake major changes in land-use policy and the financing of education services in the future, as a result of court action, but even in these areas they will probably continue to preserve statewide perspectives and fashion policy individually for their respective state sectors, except in the most critical functions where interstate special districts have gained a foothold. It may be, therefore, that new areawide interstate approaches to the future development of the New

York metropolitan region, of a generalist nature, will emerge, as they have already begun to, largely as a response to strong Federal inducements for regional change.

NOTES

1. Letter from Charles D. Norton to Frederic Delano, November 24, 1921.
2. Forbes B. Hayes, *Community Leadership: The Regional Plan Association of New York* (New York: Columbia University Press, 1965), chaps. I-III.
3. Jameson W. Doig, *Metropolitan Transportation Politics and the New York Region* (New York: Columbia University Press, 1966), pp. 80-88 and 168-90.
4. The jurisdictional situation in the field of water pollution planning is particularly confusing. For many years, HUD was the only Federal agency which required regional sewerage plans to be developed by Tri-State and the sub-regional planning bodies. (The latter must submit their completed sewerage plans to HUD via Tri-State for certification in order for their areas to be eligible for HUD sewer grants.) Now that the Federal Environmental Protection Agency has adopted planning requirements for water quality management, two types of plans are required: water quality plans for river basins—to be prepared by a State sewerage agency, and a metropolitan sewerage plan—to be prepared by an areawide planning agency, as well as the on-going certification process. The new requirements alter existing HUD guidelines, set new emphases in water quality, and cause considerable uncertainty with respect to technical aspects and jurisdictional considerations.
5. *By Laws* of MRC, Inc. adopted March 3, 1967.
6. Robert C. Wood, *1400 Governments: The Political Economy of the New York Metropolitan Region* (Cambridge: Harvard University Press, 1961), p. 118.
7. The plan has been roundly criticized on this count by Beverly Spatt, former commissioner of the New York City Planning Commission, Paul Davidoff, and others. See NYC Planning Commission, *Plan for New York City: A Proposal,* "Critical Issues," p. 81.
8. e.g., *Managing the National Environment: A Regional Plan for Water, Sewage, Air and Refuse* (1970), and *Outdoor Recreation in a Crowded Region: A Plan for Selecting and Acquiring Recreation Lands* (1969).
9. See David E. Boyce, Norman D. Day, Chris McDonald, *Metropolitan Plan Making: An Analysis of Experience with the Preparation and Evaluation of Alternative Land-Use and Transportation Plans,* Monograph Series No. 4 (Philadelphia: Regional Science Research Institute, 1970), p. 403. Their analysis notes that the commission's *Regional Development Guide* was not a "dynamic force (even of persuasion) in guiding growth and upgrading the quality of life in the New York metropolitan region."
10. For further discussions of this point, see Melvin B. Mogulof, *Governing Metropolitan Areas: A Critical Review of Councils of Governments and the Federal Role* (Washington: The Urban Institute, 1971), particularly chap. IV, "The A-95 Process at the Metropolitan Level."
11. Regional Plan Association, "The Region's Airports: A Policy on Air Travel in the Region," *Regional Plan News,* July 1969, No. 89; "The Region's Agenda: The Real Airport Issues," Vol. I, No. 4, December 1970, and Vol. III, No. 4, May 1972.
12. Robert G. Smith, *Public Authorities in Urban Areas: A Case Study of Special District Government* (Washington: National Association of Counties, 1969), p. 258.
13. The Port Authority, *Annual Report,* 1971.

14. Metropolitan Transportation Authority, *Annual Report,* 1971.

15. NYS Office of the Comptroller, "Audit Report on Examination of Financial Statements MTA as at and for the Year Ended Dec. 31, 1971," Report No. NY-Auth-4-73, p. 3.

16. For further discussion of the local reaction to MTA see Joseph McC. Leiper, Clarke Rees, and Bernard Kabak, "Mobility in the City; Transportation Development Issues" in Lyle C. Fitch and Annmarie H. Walsh (eds.), *Agenda for a City: Issues Confronting New York* (Beverly Hills: Sage, 1970).

    With respect to the composition of MTA's governing board, the MTA chairman explains, "It was recognized that the agency had a regional task to perform and local representation could mean local vetoes of regional necessities." William J. Ronan, "The Crisis in Representation," address to Colgate University Political Science Department, Hamilton, N.Y., February 20, 1969, p. 3.

17. New York State Joint Legislative Committee on Transportation, *Transportation—A Blueprint for Mobility,* Legislative Document No. 14, 1969, pp. 12-13.

18. Much of the material in this section comes from UDC, *Annual Report,* 1970 and 1971, and NYS Office of the Comptroller, "Report on Survey of the Initial Financing and Operating Practices NYS Urban Development Corporation" Report No. NY-Auth-5-71.

19. It should be noted that nine of the smaller, more rural towns in Westchester are resisting the UDC plan and testing UDC's ability to use its local override authority.

20. *The New York Times,* November 9, 1972.

21. Harvey Lieber, "The Politics of Air and Water Pollution Control in the New York Metropolitan Area," (unpublished Ph.D. disseration, Department of Political Science, Columbia University, 1968), p. 319. The assessment of the ISC's effectiveness in water polution control is based largely upon chap. VI, "The Interstate Sanitation Commission: The Solution that Failed," pp. 284-373.

22. e.g., Richard S. DeTurk, Deputy Executive Director, Tri-State Regional Planning Commission.

23. Doig points out in *Metropolitan Transportation Politics,* chap. IX, "State Leadership and Partial Remedies," that this era of "State dominated leadership" was characterized by "a few key actors who devised solutions through relatively private investment and negotiation . . . sought to define the problem narrowly in order to minimize cost and the use of political resources . . . (and) tried to construct programs within a relatively self-contained State framework, not in terms of the regional needs of the interstate New York area," pp. 192-93.

24. New Jersey has recently passed legislation controlling flood plains areas which authorizes the adoption of land-use regulations for flood hazard areas within the State.

25. RPA, "Housing Opportunities: An Analysis and Presentation for the NYS Urban Development Corporation," June 5, 1969, and National Committee Against Discrimination in Housing, "Jobs and Housing: Final Summary Report on the Housing Component," March 1972.

26. John E. Bebout, *Regional Planning Issues,* Part I, Hearings before the Subcommittee on Urban Affairs of the Joint Economic Committee, 91st Congress, 2nd Session, 1970, p. 131.

27. John P. Keith, *Regional Planning Issues,* Part 4, 92nd Congress, 1st Session, 1971, p. 715.

THE WHY'S AND WHEREFORE'S OF COUNCILS OF GOVERNMENTS

Gary Helfand
Director of Academic Affairs,
Criminal Justice Programs
New York Institute of Technology

In reviewing Joan Aron's article on the "New York Interstate Metropolis," it is easy to see that the theoretical benefits that abound when one contemplates the use of a regional planning body are not so easily realized in practice. However, in an attempt to stimulate regional cooperation among local governments, the Council of Government (COG) concept was developed and then implemented in virtually every metropolitan area (SMSA) in the United States.

Simply stated, a COG is a VOLUNTARY association of officials who hold significant positions in local governments within a particular metropolitan area. These officials come together periodically (at the weekly, bimonthly, or monthly "COG meeting") to discuss mutual problems, explore *joint* application and funding proposals for state and especially federally sponsored projects, and, in general, to share differing views regarding the expansion of and improvement in the delivery of a variety of functional services (e.g.: health-care, transportation, pollution control, emergency services, etc.). In short, the COG is a clearinghouse for the sharing of information and additionally functions as a vehicle for the coordination of grant proposals among local governments. In this way, projects and programs with a regional focus may have a chance of getting off the ground. As so vividly described in an Urban Institute report, a COG "is not a new level of government. It is a Council *of* governments, a governmental *conference,* an *association* of governments . . . a coming together of governments—but not a government in itself."

In reviewing the role of New York's COG, it is easy to see that its failure to implement anything approaching true regional planning is due to the highly fragmented and confusing array of local governments that exist side-by-side in the New York SMSA. On the other hand, the Association of Bay Area Governments (San Francisco's COG) has been extremely successful in encouraging interlocal cooperation because of the very real powers it has been given throughout the past several years to actually make binding decisions relating to regional planning and the construction of major capital projects.

It should be realized by all students of metropolitan government that if necessity is the mother of invention, then governmental fragmentation is the mother of COG's. In other words, in metropolitan areas where local governments have been legally consolidated into a METRO government, the COG is not needed. In Jacksonville, for example, regional application for federal aid, regional planning, and regional project construction is, by definition, uniformly implemented. The same is true with regard to the Toronto Metro.

COG's-vs-FRC's

So as to minimize the confusion that presently exists in relation to the operations and functioning of various regional governmental and quasigovernmental planning and policy-making organizations, a word about Federal Regional Councils (FRC's) is appropriate at this point.

In the late 1960s, the Federal Government began to get nervous about the lack of coordination among its own grant-giving organizations, particularly in relation to categorical grants given out in the nation's SMSA's where upwards of *fifty* different components of the federal bureaucracy were simultaneously charged with such responsibility. In an attempt to insure that the right hand knew what the left was about, officials within the Office of Management and Budget, the General Accounting Office, and both chambers of Congress were looking to create a coordinating mechanism to avoid or at least minimize duplication and waste in the administration of more than 900 categorical grants. These newly created mechanisms were known as Federal Regional Councils. Their membership would typically consist of the Regional Directors of the major domestic cabinet level Departments and top level officials within appropriate (to the region) agencies. While the Federal Regional Councils have not been able to overcome all of the criticisms that have been aimed at the categorical grant system, they at least comprise a very important first step in increasing the degree of internal coordination that should exist within the federal bureaucracy.

In contrasting Councils of Government with Federal Regional Councils, it can now be seen that the former are concerned with maximizing *interlocal* cooperation and joint project planning and project implementation, while the latter consist of federal officials (whose membership is *ex officio*) who are chiefly concerned with maximizing *intrafederal* communication regarding the allocation of federal grants-in-aid within a particular SMSA.

The Future of COG's

In trying to assess the future role of COG's, two questions need to be answered. First, how are COG's *likely* to function over the next couple of decades? Second, in ideal terms, what role *should* COG's take on?

To answer the first question, it seems almost inevitable that, as city and suburban areas become increasingly polarized due to radical differences in the racial and socioeconomic characteristics of their respective populations, the COG will find it increasingly difficult to encourage *regional* cooperation or the joint implementation of area-wide programs. If past performance is any indication of the future, it can be confidently stated that Councils of Government will succeed in giving a sense of regional identity to local governments in only a handful of metropolitan areas. More often than not, the COG will function as it has within the New York SMSA—as an ineffective quasigovernmental body given nebulous status by members and nonmembers alike, and having a consistent record of failure or nonperformance.

In pondering the second question, it seems (to this writer at least) that the true role of COG's is actually synonymous with its stated purpose. In other words, a COG SHOULD encourage interlocal cooperation; it SHOULD provide a device for the sharing of information in order to facilitate the solving of problems common to the region; it SHOULD enable local governments within an SMSA to jointly apply for categorical grants. What, then, has stood in the way of COG's realizing these goals?

Referring back to the definition for COG's given at the beginning of this article, it is this author's contention that the fatal weakness up to this point has been the fact that membership by local governments is on a voluntary basis. While mandatory membership opens up a variety of legal and even constitutional questions, it nevertheless would be the first step in giving some teeth to the COG's coordinating role. With metropolitan wide membership thus assured, the COG would in fact encompass the entire area. In addition, if membership fees could also be mandated, the COG would have operating revenue needed to actively engage in comprehensive regional planning. Finally, the COG should be given more legitimate status. This could be accomplished by gearing state aid to COG review in the metropolitan areas within the state. For those SMSA's which transcend state boundary lines, interstate cooperation would be vital and might be achieved by amending state constitutions or by the enactment of special acts by the state legislatures concerned.

Having examined the past performance of COG's and explored their probable versus their desired future role, the reader should attempt to propose some feasible alternative. If not COG's, then what other mechanism might be devised to facilitate cooperation and regional planning within the nation's SMSA's? To date, the answer has not been found.

Introduction

Consolidation of law enforcement agencies into a single, metropolitan wide Police Authority is the subject of Ed Powers' thought-provoking work dealing with the New York SMSA. While a metropolitan authority falls far short of the radical consolidation that occurs with the creation of an actual METRO government, it is, as the title suggests, a first step toward regionalization in the delivery of police services.

*Before one can lightly dismiss Powers' normative conception for rearranging the policing function, it must be realized that the enormous gains achieved in policing in the Toronto region came about only **after** creation of a Metropolitan Police Department which administered the police function **without regard for the boundaries of local jurisdictions.** Above all, Powers is concerned with overcoming the problems associated with fragmentation of the police function. His plea for taking a chance in changing the status quo is provocative if not eloquent.*

A NEW YORK METROPOLITAN POLICE AUTHORITY: FIRST STEP TOWARDS REGIONAL POLICING

Edward Powers
Director of Criminal Justice Programs
New York Institute of Technology

A NEW YORK METROPOLITAN POLICE AUTHORITY FIRST STEP TOWARDS REGIONAL POLICING

At the present time there are approximately 20,000 police departments in the United States, ninety percent of which have less than 10 men. Over 400,000 men engaged in policing throughout the country have had varied training and experience.

It would seem that a citizen should be assured of the same treatment by a policeman, whether he be in New York City or Sioux City. The fact is, however, that while there are over 250 Standard Metropolitan Statistical Areas (SMSA's), in only a handful of these is there any semblance of region wide coordination of policing. This article will therefore suggest that a region wide Police Authority be created in the New York SMSA. It would have jurisdiction over all of Nassau and Suffolk counties, New York City, Westchester county, and the few counties in New Jersey and Connecticut that complete the metropolitan area.

Current Status of Things

In one relatively small area, Nassau County (which takes up approximately 350 square miles), 32 incorporated villages have opted to create small police departments which are costly and not able to effect professionalization because of the restrictiveness of their work locale. There is a love affair that exists between the individual citizen and the notion of having his "very own police department." When specialization is required, such as forensic laboratory work, detective investigation, case preparation, computer research, physical training facilities, police academy, custodial

Reprinted with permission of Edward Powers, Director of Criminal Programs C.A.P.P. New York Institute of Technology, Old Westbury, N.Y.

care of prisoners, and so on, the local agencies must establish a relationship with the larger jurisdiction (Nassau County Police Department). In addition to these scattered village police departments, the two cities of Long Beach and Glen Cove also operate (and pay for) separate police departments. Finally, the county itself completes the picture with a full-time complement of 3,800 police personnel. This fragmented pattern is repeated in Suffolk County and New Rochelle, and is typical of the make-up of policing in many small sections of this SMSA. It should also be noted that the New York City Police Department and various policing agencies (e.g.: F.B.I., U.S. Park Police, Port Authority Police, etc.) may have concurrent jurisdiction with up to six other police agencies! If the agencies having jurisdiction in a particular area have developed an effective intercommunicative network, effective policing MAY result. As a corollary, police jealousy, lack of trust in another jurisdiction, and interlocal resentment will cause the citizen to be cheated of the police service he is paying for. We must remember that the public is paying for *all* police agencies and has the right and responsibility to know what is being offered for the money that goes into the tax pie. In addition, this proliferation of police jurisdictions has the deleterious effect of further confusing the average citizen attempting to make some sense out of the hodgepodge of police officialdom.

Police service is sought because of real and usually urgent needs such as:

the committing of a crime
injured person(s) in need of an ambulance
lost adult or child
deceased body in public, etc.

The person seeking aid wants a policeman to respond and doesn't care to know the name of the agency the policeman works for or any jurisdictional problems the police officer may have in dealing with the situation. The victim (or those close to the victim) is interested in service and is ENTITLED to service. A complete revision of the present geopolitical arrangement would improve the *quality* of service.

The Change: Proposed Structure

It is suggested that one police jurisdiction be set up with boundaries that are coterminous with the entire New York SMSA. It would be structured into various subdivisions on the basis of geography and topography, demographic characteristics, and any other relevant factors. These subdivisions would be termed "precincts" (as is now the case in many jurisdictions). For purposes of supervision and control, a specific number of precincts can be included in a "district." Several districts would encompass the entire SMSA, all under the control of ONE governing body.

Governance of the Metropolitan Police Authority

It is proposed that the governing board be composed of thirteen members, one from each of the thirteen districts that the SMSA would be divided into. Since the SMSA now contains approximately seventeen million people, each district official serving on the Board would, in effect, represent an area containing about 1.6 million people, a substantially smaller constituency than that of the New York City Police Commissioner.

A simple majority vote would determine day-to-day policy. Long-range policy would, however, require a two-thirds majority of a twelve-person quorum. This would insure responsiveness to local conditions and requirements while maintaining stability and continuity over a longer period of time. Inasmuch as these are elective positions, each member of the Board is, DE FACTO, an ombudsman for his constituency.

Selection of the Governing Board

It is proposed that the Missouri Plan for choosing state judges be incorporated in the selection process of the Governing Board. Consequently, it would work in the following way:

1. A task force consisting of representatives of all criminal justice agencies, prisoners (e.g.: Fortune Society), insurance companies, the local and national Bar Associations, A.C.L.U., the League of Women Voters, groups such as the Urban League and even certain radical groups—would compile a list of candidates (three for each of the thirteen districts) who would then run—BY DISTRICT—at the regular election time.
2. The term of office would be set at four years, with no restrictions for reelection (except that fifty percent of the districts would hold elections on alternate years—this would mean, in effect, that for the first term only, seven of the Board of Governors would serve two-year terms).
3. Upon taking office, the Board of Governors would select a Metropolitan Police Administrator, who would, in turn, nominate thirteen individuals who would act as line commanders for the thirteen subdivisions.

Financing

It is the author's opinion that to insure equality of police performance between affluent suburbs and financially ailing cities, the cost of the newly created Police Authority should be borne by the Federal Government under a revenue-sharing scheme. Legislation such as the *1972 State and Local Fiscal Assistance Act* could provide for special revenue-sharing funds to pay for this new service. Each of the existing local governments would be required to give up the portion of the revenue-sharing allotment it *would* have used for policing. The assumption is, of course, that the Federal Government would encourage such an arrangement by allowing this sort of transfer of funds. If this were done, there would be no legislative impediments to the formation and implementation of a metropolitan-wide Police Authority, at least in terms of the Federal Government. The final requirement, then, would be that the State Constitution would not prohibit such a restructuring if the authority concept were to be ratified by a regional referendum of all those who would reside within the boundaries of the Metropolitan Police Authority.

Probable Outcomes

Bearing in mind the public's fear of centralization of police power as a first step towards the evolution of a police state, it must be remembered that even if a Police Authority were to be created in EACH of the nation's SMSA's, there would still be over 200 separate, completely antonomous, locally responsive police jurisdictions. However, several possible advantages would result. First, there would be standardization of selection, training, and performance. Secondly, through increased centralization, increased specialization would become economically feasible (e.g.: lie detection, dactylagraphy, forensic labs, and the like). A third advantage would relate to the economies of scale that would result with regard to purchasing (in greater volume) and construction of physical facilities. Fourth, since all local law enforcement personnel would be a part of the same jurisdiction, internal communication would be enhanced in terms of both speed and accuracy. Finally, information gathering would become more comprehensive throughout the region regarding the collection, tabulation, and uniform dispersement of police statistics.

Since no metropolitan area anywhere approaching the size of New York has ever regionalized the delivery of police services, the previously proposed outcomes remain speculative. How, then, may we assess the outcomes *before* resorting to such a radical change in structure? The only honest reply is—we can't. To coin an old phrase, in order to be a gain, there must first be a venture. The sooner the venture is undertaken, the sooner we'll know the answer. . . .

Introduction

*The restructuring that has taken place in Dade County, Florida, combines two different approaches to metropolitan reorganization. On the one hand, there is the concept of the **Urban County**, which has been strengthened by creation of the position of a professional county manager who is given broad-based administrative and fiscal authority. The county manager, in turn, reports to a county Board of Commissioners which has been authorized to provide many of the services previously performed by the cities located within Dade County. The Urban County, then, functions as the central or area-wide level of government, with the municipalities located within the county representing the lower- or grass-roots level of government.* Consequently, added to the notion of the powerful urban county is the concept of two tiers (levels) or government, each providing certain types of service to the populace.*

*As is the case everywhere within the nation's SMSA's, a formal decision to create a METRO would have to be approved by the residents of the entire metropolitan area. In the past, there has been a great deal of opposition to the radical restructuring of metropolitan government, especially on the part of the white middle-class suburbanites who live close to, but **not within** a major central city. This suburban opposition is frequently the chief obstacle to the creation of a METRO. How then, was this opposition overcome in 1957 as regards the Miami/Dade experiment? To answer this question, the reader should focus attention on such factors as the variety and level of services being offered to the unincorporated areas of Dade County prior to 1957, provisions for retention of zoning powers by the municipalities after the reform occurred and the assurances given to local government employees to insure continuance of their jobs after the reorganization was to take place.*

---

*Except in the case of the half-million Dade residents who live within the unincorporated areas of the county. For these people, the County acts as both a first *and* a second tier government since no other multipurpose local jurisdiction exists. Indeed, this is one of the major differences in the way the two-tier concept was utilized in Toronto, as opposed to Dade County.

METROPOLITAN DADE COUNTY

Aileen Lotz
Staff Consultant
Joint Center for
Environmental and Urban Problems
Florida Atlantic University
Florida International University

For the purpose of this paper, Dade County, Florida, is defined as a "region" comprising over 2,000 square miles and containing approximately one and a quarter million permanent residents, roughly 20 percent of the State's total. It is a diverse area ranging from extensive agricultural interests in the southern part of the county to the highly sophisticated, tourist-convention atmosphere centered on Miami Beach. Dade County hosts over seven million tourists a year and is a major international air transportation center with extensive central office and aircraft maintenance facilities. The black population is 15 percent of the total and the unique influx of Cuban refugees during the Sixties has led to a permanent Latin population of 299,217 (1970) or 23.6 percent of the total. Dade County was designated a standard metropolitan statistical area after the 1960 Census.

Although most of the present discussion will be confined to the geographic boundaries of Dade County for the purpose of describing the effects of a general purpose governing body (the Board of County Commissioners) on a "region," it is recognized that the region, under more traditional definitions, includes additional area. The southern part of Broward County to the north, and the Gold Coast area comprising Dade, Broward, and Palm Beach Counties are often considered a region. The tri-county area is that covered by a joint transportation technical study administered by the Dade County Department of Traffic and Transportation, but is not the region identified for other purposes. The South Florida Regional Planning Council, an outgrowth of the jetport planning activity, comprises seven counties in south Florida.

The government of Dade County was substantially changed in 1957 when a home rule charter was adopted, pursuant to a 1956 Dade County home rule amendment to the State constitution. The amendment gave the Board of

From: *Regional Governance—Promise and Performance: Substate Regionalism and the Federal System.* Vol. II—Case Studies, May, 1973, p. 6.

County Commissioners power to become a "central metropolitan government"[1] usurping, as will be discussed below, many functions previously performed exclusively by the 26 incorporated municipalities within the county.

Dade County's metropolitan government can best be described as a modified two-tier government conforming in large measure to the Committee for Economic Development (CED) recommendations of 1970.[2] For more than half the city-resident population; the two-tier description is accurate, but to the 530,000 residents of the unincorporated area there is only the Board of County Commissioners to serve them. Special taxing districts have been utilized for a variety of purposes. They have no separate autonomy, however, and are administered by the county Public Works Department. Further reflecting the CED bias against parochial bargaining, cities in Dade are not represented on the County Commission. Area representation, however, is assured by the division of the county into eight districts for election purposes. The nine-member commission is composed of a representative from each of the eight districts elected at large. A county mayor is elected at large and presides over the commission meetings but otherwise has no powers other than those of a member of the commission.

"Metro," headline shorthand for the Metropolitan Dade County government, did not emerge overnight, but rather was a product of trends which began to emerge more than a decade before the effort which resulted in restructuring. As far back as early 1940s the county was considered a "region" for numerous political, economic, and social purposes. In part, the State government began to identify counties in Florida as the appropriate unit of government for some State-related purposes. In 1943, a countywide public health system was created (supplanting municipal health agencies) pursuant to an enabling act of the State legislature. Two years later, county voters approved a countywide school system. (In 1947 State legislation converted all school systems to county systems.)

Additionally, the move to restructure the government grew out of the declining dominance of central city Miami. New municipalities were incorporated in the mid-Forties and population growth began to take place in the unincorporated area of the county, particularly during the Fifties. Miami's position relative to the entire county declined from 64 percent in 1940 to 31 percent in 1960, a trend which continues today. However, as the central city in a relatively undeveloped area, the City of Miami had developed services and facilities which were being utilized by residents of the *greater* Miami area. One such was the public hospital, which proved too costly for the City of Miami to maintain for the residents of the region. It was transferred to the county in 1949. The city also gave up operation of the airport and through State legislation it was transferred to a Dade County Port Authority created primarily to operate the airport.

The trend towards the shifting of governmental services to countywide jurisdiction was also reflected in civic and social institutions, most of which existed as countywide organizations. The forerunner of the United Fund of Dade County was a countywide organization as were the Red Cross, the League of Women Voters, church federations, etc. With few exceptions, the population growth in most of the municipalities was recent enough that strong loyalties to the municipal institution had not developed.

Prior to the 1957 reform, the governmental jurisdictions, in addition to the county government, included 26 incorporated municipalities, a countywide school district governed by an elected Board of Public Instruction, the Miami Housing Authority, and the Dade County Port Authority, comprised of the County Commission—all in all, a comparatively simple organizational structure. Services were unequally provided by cities and increasing numbers of residents in the unincorporated area were virtually unserved by any but the most rudimentary services.

Charter Issues

Dade's governmental reform plan grew directly out of the near success of an effort to consolidate the Miami and Dade County governments in 1953. Several earlier efforts had been made without success. Proponents and opponents alike recognized the inevitability of some kind of reorganization and banded together to form the Metropolitan Miami Municipal Board, comprised of city and county officials and citizens. The board's efforts resulted in a study by Public Administration Service,[3] which recommended that a constitutional home rule amendment be adopted, that the existing county government be given additional areawide authority, and that services be divided between the cities and the county. This concept was generally supported by city officials, the Miami-Dade County Chamber of Commerce, the League of Women Voters, and the press. County officials were generally lukewarm if not hostile. Although the concept increased the power of the county government, it threatened individual "kingdoms" which had been built up over the years. The groups which supported the concept then successfully campaigned for its adoption both countywide and statewide. Following the adoption of the amendment, a Charter Board went through the charter-drafting process and the resulting charter was passed by a slim majority of Dade voters.

Although the margin of approval of the amendment both in Dade County and statewide was substantial, the small margin of success in the Dade County vote for the charter resulted from issues raised and compromises made during the charter-drafting process. Provision for major services such as central traffic control, water and sewers, and planning on an areawide basis were generally accepted as desirable, as were usually controversial issues such as non-partisan elections and the manager form of government.

However, a major conflict between the consolidationists and the municipal autonomy advocates erupted during the charter-drafting period and has not been completely resolved to the present time. From the consolidationists' viewpoint, the major compromise was a section guaranteeing the continued existence of municipalities as long as desired by the voters of the municipality and providing that each municipality could enact higher standards of zoning, service, and regulation than provided by the county. [4] Other issues revolved around the number of county commissioners, their method of election, and the protection of municipal employees performing services transferred to the county. The original charter resolved the commission issue by providing part district and part at-large elected commissioners. (This provision was changed in 1963 to provide for nine commissioners, all elected at large.) The employee issue was resolved by providing a partial guarantee of employment in the event of a transfer of services. [5]

Supporting adoption of the charter were the members of the Charter Board, members of the Dade County State legislative delegation, the Miami-Dade County Chamber of Commerce, the League of Women Voters, the Dade County Research Foundation, various University of Miami officials, and the media. Opposition was led by city officials both independently and through the League of Municipalities, groups of city employees, local chambers of commerce, and in particular, various civic organizations (with one exception) on Miami Beach. Labor groups did not play any significant role due to their relative lack of strength in this service-oriented community.

To what extent these groups highlighted the issues for the general public can only be inferred. Media editorial support meant that the charter issue was well covered in the press. However, the 26 percent turnout was less than the 40.8 percent turnout for the 1953 consolidation attempt or the 48.7 percent turnout for the later, more controversial "McLeod Amendment" vote in 1961. This amendment, in the form of a completely new charter, was a desperate attempt to abolish the manager form, to reinstitute various elected offices which had become appointive, and in general to recreate the pre-"Metro" governmental structure. The low voter turnout may have indicated a lack of awareness, but more probably reflected the large number of new residents who had moved to Dade County in the mid-Fifties who had not yet gained a grasp of local political issues.

The reorganization of the traditional local government pattern in Florida has had some results of considerable significance. Most important in the long run is the spreading of the tax base to an entire metropolitan area and the expansion of expensive services to a metropolitan base. In this way, central city Miami has escaped the serious financial problems of many other central cities, impotent in the face of taxable bases streaming to suburban areas. Although far from perfect equity, indications are that detailed analysis will confirm that the cost of most metropolitan services is spread more evenly throughout the Dade metropolitan area than is the case elsewhere except possibly where central city-county consolidation has taken place.

City officials have the authority to transfer to the metropolitan government on a timely basis those services, costly to maintain on a local level, which can qualify logically or legally as metropolitan services. This flexibility is one of the unique features of the Dade County charter, which can at least provide basis of contrast for the advocates of a rigid division of functions between two levels of government. Not only did the charter give flexibility to the cities for the transfer of services to the county, the charter gave to the county commissioners nearly unlimited powers to perform municipal government services. In the early years, city officials had fought for a division of services between the two tiers of local government out of fear that they would be swallowed up by the larger government.

As a result of city pressures, the county Planning Department prepared a report which attempted to allocate functions along criteria suggested by the Advisory Commission on Intergovernmental Relations and by department staff.[6] The report met with support by municipal officials who claimed they could not plan capital improvements until they knew which services they were to retain and which were to become countywide. Ironically, only four years after the report was published, the City of South Miami became the first city to transfer its fire department to the county, although fire service had been identified in the report as one best handled at the municipal level. The report, although the subject of continuing discussion, particularly by city officials, largely has gathered dust and cities have continued to take the initiative in the expedient transfer of services. However, the recent study commission which recommended a strong mayor form of government also recommended that the study be updated.[7] There has been no discernable public interest in such recommendation.

The initial, overriding purpose for the reorganized Dade County government was "efficiency, economy and elimination of duplication." This generally meant provision of areawide services by an areawide government which would eliminate separate provision of such services by individual cities. It was assumed that the elimination of duplication would also bring economies which, in fact, it did in individual instances discussed below. In addition to the efficiency-economy argument, there existed a general recognition among community leaders, particularly in the early Fifties, that a countywide planning agency was imperative if the debilitating effects of a fragmented approach to urban growth were to be avoided. A department of planning was one of only four departments specifically required by the 1957 charter.

The drive towards the metropolitan basis of providing services was perceived almost entirely within the community leadership and pre-dated by several years the Federal emphasis on a regional approach to urban problems. Creation of the Dade County Department of Housing and Urban Development in 1965, however, was a direct response to the earlier creation of the U.S. Department of Housing and Urban Development in a conscious effort to capitalize on the Federal philosophy and funding. Although encouraged at the Federal level, it was to be more than a decade after Dade's reorganization that the State of Florida began to recognize the need for new approaches to regional governance. In most functional areas in which the Federal government has encouraged a regional approach, Dade County serves as the region, *e.g.,* comprehensive health, manpower, anti-poverty. A Federally financed transportation technical study, however, was expanded as a result of pressure from Federal and State governments to include two counties to the north of Dade.

Areawide and Local Functions

One of the significant characteristics of the Metropolitan Dade County government has been the gradual increase in functions and services. The limited purpose county government of pre-1957, based on rural notions of another century and providing little more than caretaker services, is a far cry from the sophisticated "municipal" government of today. The county charter gave Dade County Commissioners virtually every power needed by a major municipal government. Not every power has been fully exercised nor is it anticipated that all functions authorized will ever be provided. The county has the power but does not, for example, provide and operate rail and bus terminals, gas, light, power, and telephone service. The power to provide central records, training, and communications for fire and police protection is only partially exercised to date. Most significant of powers not yet exercised is the power to enforce comprehensive plans as they pertain to land use. Insofar as zoning is used to enforce comprehensive land use planning, the county has not chosen to administer zoning laws within cities. In some instances, additional functions were mandated by the charter, such as unified property assessment and tax collection.

Sometimes the adoption of an ordinance effective countywide resulted in a major increase in function. The adoption by the County Commission of the traffic code in 1958 resulted in assumption of a major responsibility by the charter-ordained Metropolitan Court and the subsequent abolition of all municipal traffic courts. Air and water pollution control, sub-division control, landscaping (parking lots), and tree removal ordinances are illustrative.

However, the majority of services which have accrued to the metropolitan government came as a result of the transfer of services, on the initiative of city governing bodies, to the areawide government. In some instances there has been a total assumption of functions previously performed by cities. First was the transfer of traffic engineering functions by the City of Miami and several other cities which had staff for this purpose. Traffic engineering thus became a metropolitan function performed solely by the metropolitan government. In other cases, services have been transferred on a piecemeal basis. In some instances the impetus for transfers was a particular city budget problem; in other instances the logic of countywide operation probably overshadowed the monetary issue in the eyes of city officials. In this fashion several of the medium-sized cities have transferred their fire departments to the county although the City of Miami has not. Originally, the county fire department served only the unincorporated area, doing little more than putting out brush fires. As a modern, well-equipped department, it now serves not only the unincorporated area, much of which is highly urbanized, but 15 cities as well. In addition to the traffic engineering staff, the City of Miami has transferred to the county its seaport, crime laboratory and some other specific police functions, its minimum security stockade, five arterial bridges, a park, the harbour patrol, trade standards division, its neighborhood rehabilitation division (housing code enforcement), arterial street lighting, and miscellaneous other functions. The bus system, achieved early through the consolidation under the county of several private companies, operates countywide with the exception of those areas served by the Coral Gables municipal system.

One major community policy decision which resulted in the metropolitanization of a function revolved around urban renewal. As the community began to grasp the implications of renewal programs, controversy arose over whether this was the responsibility of the City of Miami, where the first renewal project had been identified, or whether it was a function with implications beyond city boundaries. The issue was resolved through public debate in favor of the county with its larger tax base. This decision later enabled the county through appropriate legislation to absorb the functions of and actually abolish the Miami Housing Authority and to create a Department of Housing and Urban Development. This department now administers not only the housing program, virtually on a countywide basis, but is administering a Federally financed neighborhood development program (NDP) with projects in four cities and in several sections of the unincorporated area.

Public library service is another example of a service which illustrates the flexibility built into the metropolitan system. The City of Miami, along with a number of other cities, opted to become part of a county-operated system based on the Miami system. Through the device of a special taxing district, the system serves the unincorporated area and 17 cities. However, nine cities have, for the present time, opted to keep their own libraries and not become part of the system. The option to stay out has also been exercised by a small number of cities for other services which are provided to a majority of cities: voter registration, occupational licensing, and certain police functions.

Metropolitan planning is another mixed bag. Although the general land use master plan was prepared by the county Planning Department and adopted by the County Commission, the county has not yet chosen to face the political battle which would undoubtedly arise over forcing the cities to conform to the plan through some control over zoning power still retained by cities. The plan has been utilized to highlight public issues which might result in violation of the intent of the plan. Some control over municipalities exists, however, as a result of a countywide subdivision control ordinance which provides for county approval of all subdivision plats whether in the cities or in the unincorporated area. The county Planning Department serves as the A-95 review agency and has a local planning services division which provides, on a cost basis, detailed planning at the request of municipalities. The A-95 review function has less of an impact on other agencies, and particularly on the municipalities, than may be the case in other areas. The principal reason for this is that the county government itself is the applicant for the vast majority of Federal funds and those applications which are prepared are generally done so with the full knowledge of the Planning Department and of the necessity to conform to both local and A-95 review requirements. The Planning Department has developed fairly good communication with the various cities and is often consulted prior to the preparation of applications; in some cases it actually prepares them. However, on a few occasions, the review function has served to notify the Planning Department and therefore the county of intentions of the city governments which may be in conflict with overall county planning objectives. In such cases the city is immediately informed of the conflict. The Planning Department is routinely performing A-95 review functions for FHA, for some LEAA applications processed through the Governor's Council on Criminal Justice, and for the State Department of Transportation.

Metropolitan Financing

Dade, as a traditional county government up until 1957, was limited substantially to the property tax for the financing of its services, a limitation continued by the home rule constitutional amendment. Over the years, however, the sources of funding have become diversified. The proposed budget for 1972-73[8] shows the property tax as 53.1 percent of the general fund revenue. This figure is misleading, however, as many revenues, including most Federal funds, are not included in the general fund. The program budget for 1970-71[9] provides a more realistic picture of total revenues. Estimated revenues for that year show the property tax accounting for 33 percent of total revenues, with the second largest source of funds, State and local grants, amounting to 20 percent of total funding. Disregarding hospital receipts derived from private patients and bus fares, the largest user fee revenues come from the garbage collection fees charged in the unincorporated area. User fees are also levied in special purpose districts, created largely to provide residential street lighting in the unincorporated area. The county does not wholesale services to the cities and therefore derives no revenues from them.

Capital projects financing has been accomplished in Dade primarily on a pay-as-you-go basis, although there is no limit in State law on bonded debt for counties other than the requirement that bond issues be approved by the voters. Revenue bonds have also been used to a limited extent.

By the terms of the charter, property assessment is a unified function performed by the county rather than a separate municipal function. By State law and court dictum, assessments are theoretically on a "full value" basis, and a recent study by the State auditor indicates that Dade is at 94 percent of market value. In addition to providing the tax base for the cities, the county assessment also serves as the millage base for the School Board, the Central and Southern Florida Flood Control District, and the Florida Inland Navigation District. The county prepares a single tax bill showing all relevant taxes, collects all taxes, and distributes them to the various units of government in accordance with the established millages.

Dade County Performance

Has metropolitan government in Dade County achieved its objectives? The original objectives included home rule power and the elimination of the "local bill evil" in the State legislature; economy, efficiency, and elimination of duplication; provision of services to residents of the unincorporated area; provision of major services on a unified, countywide basis, particularly water and sewers, transportation, and planning. A conflict of objectives between the consolidationists and the municipal autonomists can be read as both success and failure. The consolidationists saw the governmental structures as outlined in the charter only as a stepping stone towards total consolidation of all governmental units in Dade County, which has not happened. City officials and some civic leaders, however, were dedicated to preserving the autonomy of the incorporated cities within the larger structure of the county government, which is the case today.

The first of the above objectives, eliminating local bills, was accomplished with the passage of the Dade County home rule constitutional amendment. The State legislature is now precluded from enacting legislation affecting only Dade County. As a result the Dade County legislative delegation has gained a reputation for being better informed than others on statewide problems.

There has been considerable elimination of duplication through the unification under the county of property assessment, tax billing, and collection; traffic engineering and traffic courts; elections registration (only a few cities remain outside the central system); and tourist publicity. Other partial functional consolidations have been discussed earlier. Purists complain that "we still have 27 police chiefs." They ignore however, the piecemeal transfer of services which has been proceeding steadily for 15 years which in fact reduces duplication. The existence of the metropolitan government undoubtedly has prevented duplication of functions in those activities which were assumed by the county after charter adoption which were not previously being performed by any unit of government.

Although not one of Dade's initial objectives, the reapportionment of the State legislature became a major objective in the early 1960s. A study prepared by the Government Research Council of the Miami-Dade County Chamber of Commerce illustrated the inequity in State provision of services and facilities and in the distribution of formulas for State aid to the largest county in the State.[10] County and council officials subsequently joined hands in court challenges which resulted in equitable reapportionment. Significantly, Senate Bill No. 1, introduced by a Dade County legislator in the reapportioned legislature of 1967, called for the equitable redistribution of a portion of the State gasoline tax. In the first year after passage of the bill, Dade County received over $1 million in additional gas tax returns for highway construction.[11]

Efficiency and economy, although popular objectives, remain objective concepts in the absence of effectiveness measures. Although nearly universal objectives of reform, it is a mistake to believe that a reorganization of local government will reduce costs and lower taxes. Governmental costs in Dade County were rising before the government was reorganized and have continued to rise since then. Per capita cost of county government rose from $10.97 to $46.22 in the 15 years prior to the adoption of a metropolitan government and from $50.90 in the first post-Metro year to $111.90 15 years later.[12] During the earlier period, the county budget increased from $3,458,127 in 1944-45 to $38,940,563 in 1957-58, the last pre-Metro budget year. Although the millage was actually reduced from 17.0 mills to 15.9 in the first budget year after reorganization, the budget was increased to $45,241,870. Fifteen years later it had risen to $144,910,632.

What cannot be known, of course, is what the cost would have been had the government not been reorganized. Any attempt, however, to come to conclusions about the cost of the Dade County government would be specious without an analysis of the change in the expenditures of the city governments within Dade County. Such a comprehensive study has not been made in Dade and is unlikely to be undertaken for two principal reasons: the complexity of the shifting patterns of service provision along with the increases in extent and quality of services, and the fact that such a study could do little more than illustrate complexity.

Individual instances of savings and economies of scale always can be identified. At the time of the transfer of traffic engineering staffs from Miami and several other cities, the total expenditure for traffic engineering by the several cities and the county was $1,057,180.[13] Under a unified and expanded operation at the county level, the total expenditure dropped to $926,569 and it was two years before the total cost rose to the pre-change cost. The City of Miami saved a quarter of a million dollars as a result of the transfer but, as is often the case, other revenue losses and expenditure increases negated the savings.

The establishment of central purchasing and competitive bidding saved the county in its first year of reorganization a reported 40 percent on printing and furniture and 15 percent on food purchases.[14] When Dade County pioneered in the area of cooperative purchasing, cities were delighted to take advantage of real savings through the use of the county contracts. One city reported savings of 10 percent on the cost of automotive batteries, another a savings of 4 cents per gallon on gasoline, another small city $300 on a police car, etc.[15]

Overall cost of the metropolitan county government, however, has increased. The reasons for the increase are many. First among these was the need to upgrade the county government itself. The original county government structure lacked business-like organization and its financial adminstration was "marked by its dispersion and general inadequacy."[16] Forty percent of the county equipment was identified as obsolete. Salaries of county employees were low and non-competitive with community salary levels. In the first year under the new system, 50 key promotions were made and $1,690,000 in additional funds were expended on increases in pay levels and new services.[17]

In addition to cost increases and decreases attributed to reorganization and modernization of structure, other cost increases have arisen as a result of factors which pre-dated the change and because of metropolitanization. The latter has occured through the transfer of services from cities to the county, the extension by the county of its original services to meet areawide needs of a growing population, and the provision of new metropolitan services or facilities. In a report to the county manager on increased budget costs of $20,493,909 during the first four years of metropolitan government, the Dade County budget director stated that a $12,319,066 increase resulted from bond issues and increased operational costs resulting in capital improvements approved prior to the reorganization; a $2.2 million increase in salaries as a result of state legislation; a $2 million appropriation for construction of a new seaport; and other similar expenditures.[18] The seaport appropriation is illustrative of the shifting of financial burden. With an old port site literally falling into the bay, the City of Miami transferred Dade's only seaport to the county in 1960. Through its countywide taxing power, tax funds amounting to $14 million over a seven-year period were utilized along with revenue bond funds to construct the most modern port in the nation.

On top of the shifting of cost from the lower to the higher unit of government, population increase played a major role in spiraling costs in Dade

County. In reporting to the county manager on the population increase of 88.9 percent in the decade of the Fifties (it was 310 percent in the unincorporated area where the biggest service need existed), the budget director pointed out, "These new residents (439,963 of them) did not bring with them their own policemen, firemen, health officers, judges, welfare workers, juvenile officers, etc. Their appearance also meant that the local government had to undertake an extensive capital improvement program to provide roads, hospitals, health clinics, jails and other essential facilities." [19]

Today's half million-plus residents in the unincorporated area are receiving a relatively high level of services that is apparently sufficiently satisfactory that no attempts at annexation or incorporation involving developed areas have been successful since Metro's inception. Residents in the unincorporated area are now receiving most essential municipal services. The principal inadequacy is perceived to be the need for more police protection, better transit services, and sewer service. Vast areas of the county are still served by septic tanks, but considerable progress has been made in the past six years. Not only has the county constructed $32 million worth of water and sewer projects, but an agreement recently entered into will convert the Miami Water and Sewer Board to a county agency to operate the beginning of a unified system.

Recreational programs in the unincorporated area were non-existent prior to Metro. Using utility tax revenues derived from the unincorporated area, parks were acquired, developed, and programmed. Prior to 1958, the Dade County Park Department maintained a few fine regional parks, all on the ocean or bay. Today, park and recreational services have been expanded to include 47 neighborhood parks in the unincorporated area and a few in Miami, nine regional parks, 13 wayside parks, 13 specialized facilities including a rifle range, a zoo, an art museum, a science museum, five golf courses and four marinas, along with 51 tennis courts and a multitude of other related facilities serving the entire area. This area is certainly indicative of the increased cost of providing services on an areawide basis. The 1957-58 County budget provided $2.8 million for parks with no recreation appropriation. Today more than $10 million annually is being expended.

It is safe to say that all citizens have benefited to some degree from the improvement in the quality and extent of services. City residents, particularly those in Miami, have benefited as a result of certain facility costs being spread across the county tax base. However, persons in the unincorporated area gained most in services. At the time of the charter adoption most cities provided at least a minimal level of municipal service. However, police, fire protection, garbage and trash removal, sewers and water, libraries, neighborhood parks, etc., were either totally lacking in the unincorporated area or provided on such a minimal basis as to be essentially ineffective. Today there is a relatively high degree of service equity in the unincorporated and incorporated areas. Minority groups, particularly blacks, are the ultimate beneficiaries of the regional approach to housing which now serves disadvantaged areas outside the city. The $9-million annual Model City Program and the largest neighborhood development program (urban renewal) in the southeast also serve generally the black disadvantaged.

Aside from cost changes resulting from restructuring there is another important factor: the ability of the restructured government to compete for Federal and State funds. In a study of the effects of Dade's metropolitan government, Parris Glendenning concluded that "Dade County has increased its share of state funds since 1957 at a greater rate than have other (Florida) urban counties." Also, "the combination of home rule and areawide planning powers has helped Metro secure federal redevelopment funds, and one may infer that it has helped in other areas as well."[20] This prediction of further success in obtaining Federal funds has been proved correct. A status report on Federal funds being used by Dade County as of June 30, 1972, showed that $133 million in Federal funds were currently under contract.[21] It is unlikely that the separate municipalities could have aggregated such a level of funding.

Economic and social disparities between the central city and the suburban areas are relatively unimportant in Dade County. They do exist between the have and have-not areas throughout the metropolitan area. With some exceptions, corrective programs, largely financed by Federal funds, have not been funneled just to the central city, but allocated throughout the metropolitan area with no significant regard to municipal boundary lines. One NDP area, for example, includes both part of the City of Miami and part of "suburban" Coral Gables. The Model City area spans the Miami city boundary and includes a large, densely populated urban area which is unincorporated.

Citizen participation (not including Community Action and Model City programs) is of a fairly traditional nature, generally consisting of participation in public hearings before the County Commission and service on the numerous advisory boards appointed by the commission. However, steps have been taken in recent years to facilitate citizen business with the county government. For the past decade the Building and Zoning Department has had north and south county sub-offices. Early in 1972 the first of several planned regional subcourthouses was opened in south Dade to serve the population center furthest from downtown. More recently, a citizens information and referral service has been established with four neighborhood offices. Dade County has not generally addressed itself to the question of decentralizing resources and policymaking except through the Community Action Agency and the Model City organization, both of which function as divisions of the county manager's office.

Minority Involvement

Dade County's minority populations, black and Latins, are distributed unequally throughout the county, although the largest concentrations of both occur in the central city. However, the school desegregation decision, followed a decade later by urban renewal displacement, has resulted in a large concentration of blacks in northwest Miami and the adjoining unincorporated area, the area designated generally as the Model City. Population maps prepared on the basis of 1970 Census figures show Latins scattered from the north county line down to the southernmost urbanized area.[22] Blacks are concentrated in nine small areas throughout the county in addition to those areas mentioned above.

These areas are also identified in the Community Improvement Program study as those areas with a concentration of low income and high unemployment. Dade's historic segregated housing pattern has resulted in a high economic mix within the limited areas in which blacks could reside. In recent years, this pattern has slowly changed and affluent blacks now have somewhat greater choice of residence. Although areas with high concentrations of Latins have some of the same characteristics as the black areas, they are somewhat more economically viable. It is generally recognized that the influx of the Cubans in the Sixties resulted in the rescue of a number of declining commercial and residential neighborhoods in the City of Miami.

Minor racial disturbances have flared up in most of the black areas of the county, but the only major disturbance occurred in conjunction with the Republican convention in 1968 in the Liberty City area in northwest Miami. Although not on the scale of many northern riots, the National Guard was called out and the Dade County Public Safety Department was called in to end the violence. Two years later another disturbance occurred in the Brownsville section of the Model Cities area and there was intermittent gunfire for several days.

Prior to the adoption of metropolitan government in 1947, there was no black representation on the County Commission or on any of the city commissions. However, in recent years, blacks have become somewhat visible in local politics. In 1965, a female black funeral director and civic leader was named to fill a vacancy on the Miami City Commission and subsequently won election in a citywide vote. In 1968, a black insurance agent won election to the nine-member County Commission in a countywide vote. To date, Latins have not been quite as visible, but with the increasing number of Cubans who have become United States citizens, it is anticipated that they will be an important factor in future politics. A Cuban was recently named to fill a vacancy on the Miami City Commission.

Black leaders generally have supported district as opposed to at-large elections when the issue has been brought up by other community groups, but there is no contained push to change the present at-large system among either blacks or other groups. It should be noted, however, that blacks have in fact been elected in countywide votes, including the election of two black members of the Dade County legislative delegation.

Dade County's success in attracting Federal funds is in sharp contrast to its experience with the State of Florida. Traditionally, Dade County, the State's largest county, containing approximately 20 percent of the State's population and historically providing more than its per capita share of the State's revenues, has been given the short end of the stick. Although the State legislature gave the Board of County Commissioners extensive municipal powers in the Dade County home rule constitutional amendment, it neglected to provide any additional sources of revenue, creating serious fiscal limitations. Had Dade's economic growth not been so rapid during this period of time, it is doubtful that metropolitan government could have survived.

Up until the first attempt at reapportionment, when Dade improved its relative strength in the legislature somewhat, the largest county in the State had not a single State institution or facility. Dade was not alone, however, for the populous southeast coastal area generally was heavily discriminated against by the "pork chop" legislature.

As other urban areas turned to the Federal government for assistance in meeting mounting urban problems, so did Dade. During the past six to eight years, Dade County has met all appropriate Federal guidelines for Federally funded programs. The Johnson Administration emphasized a metropolitan approach, and there is no question but what Dade County was favored because it was a general purpose government serving the metropolitan area, because it had a competent county planning organization, and because it had established a county Department of Housing and Urban Development. In more recent years greater emphasis has been placed on a broader regional approach, particularly under the Safe Streets Act. Dade County became part of a four-county planning district for the purposes of LEAA funding and was designated by the Governor's Council on Criminal Justice as the administering agency for funds involving the district. It is doubtful that such inter-county cooperation would have occurred by State fiat in the absence of Federal guidelines. However, in recent months the regional approach for LEAA funding, particularly as it affects large urban areas, has been reevaluated and the regional planning concept has been abandoned in favor of a metropolitan planning agency, of which Dade will be one. Although the regional approach has some obvious advantages, there are practical problems when a relatively sophisticated county such as Dade attempts to develop a joint project with a small, relatively primitive (governmentally speaking) county such as Monroe (Key West).

Dade County's emphasis on metropolitan planning, however, predated the Federal emphasis. By the time the Federal open space program was passed in 1961, Dade County had begun the metropolitan planning process and was accordingly the first jurisdiction in Florida to be awarded funding. Recent requirements for planning certification for water and sewers and open space programs have thus been treated routinely in Dade.

Throughout this discussion of metropolitan government in Dade County, the metropolis has been considered a region. It matches other regions in size and diversity if not in jurisdictional complexity. Dade County has become a strong areawide general purpose government through which major services and functions are performed, financed by a tax base which coincides with county boundaries. The areawide government operates at this level while municipal governments, performing differing combinations of largely local services, function to serve their residents. Is it successful? The answer to this question depends upon the measures of success. If the measure is whether all the region's residents are served by public water and sewer systems, whether the region's canals are free of sewage and other harmful nutrients, whether the public transportation system has solved the region's traffic congestion, the answer must be no. If, however, the measure is tax equity and service equity among all residents, the answer must be more affirmative. Since its inception, the regional government has provided an increasing number of services on an areawide or virtually areawide basis. A variety of devices have been used to achieve tax equity, including special taxing districts with flexible service areas.

The decision-making process was built into Dade's metropolitan government by the terms of the constitutional amendment which identified the County Commission as the governing body. County commissioners in Florida have long had a countywide constituency and have been elected at large. State legislative delegations, historically, have also been elected at large, thus solidifying the metropolitan nature of the political process. These factors, however, are not without their problems. Professional staff within the county government develop plans for improvements on a priority basis countywide. Often these priorities fail to satisfy the citizen or councilman from Miami Beach, who feels that a Miami Beach project should have the highest priority although it may be low on the countywide totem pole. County officials must constantly walk a narrow path between taking those actions which can be justified on a countywide basis with those actions requested by city officials, county commissioners, and neighborhood residents.

Inter-Local Antagonism

Relationships between the county and the municipalities have ranged from good to bad to worse. In the past six years, bitter city-county feuding has marked the establishment of basic county policy on sewer construction. However, today an integrated system is nearer reality as a result of agreement on a long-sought means of marrying the Miami Water and Sewer Board with the county. City-county agreements have been hard to come by; but they have come, one by one. On the less controversial side have been the numerous voluntary and conflict-free transfers of services and the utilization of county services.

Given the predominance of the manager form of government at the city level in Dade County, most controversies have been resolved at the administrative rather than the political level. County managers (with the exception of the present manager) have been city managers before coming to Dade and a professional relationship pre-existed which, in spite of battling at the political level, often resulted in compromise and concensus being reached at a professional level. True brokerage politics, however, has not emerged. It existed for a time at the civic level when the Government Research Council of the Miami-Dade County Chamber of Commerce established in the early days of Metro an inter-governmental committee which included some of the most vocal anti-Metro city politicians along with pro-Metro civic leaders. The research council provided a forum for the discussion of differences, largely those associated with the issue of division of services. A concensus was actually hammered out and resulted in a joint statement by the League of Municipalities and the Government Research Council. The two groups also cooperated on the financing of a report prepared by the University of Miami on city-county finances.[23] Although concensus was reached, little happened to change the course of events. But tempers were blunted for a time. The *Miami Herald,* which could have acted as a broker, rarely did. Its position was to decide most issues in favor of the county.

One continuing problem for the metropolitan government has been the frequent antagonism of city officials. In the early years this manifested itself in vehement public expressions of hostility, attempts to amend the charter through referendum, and challenge of the charter in the courts. In more recent years, the antagonism has been reflected by the difficulty of working out agreements for particular services. There has also been a tendency on the part of city officials to use Metro as the scapegoat in explaining away their own lack of ability to provide adequate services.

Although numerous attempts have been made to alter the structure of Dade's metropolitan government, it remains substantially today as it was created by the 1957 charter. The most recent attempt to change the structure dealt not with boundary lines or service responsibilities, but with the nature of its executive direction and the method of electing the County Commission. Had the proposal been successful, it would have substituted a strong mayor for a county manager and district elections for the present at-large elections.[24] The proposal was defeated by a two-to-one vote. The proposal had been developed by a committee appointed by the County commission to study and recommend improvements in the county charter. Business and civic leadership was divided on the issue, but a vigorous campaign launched by the opposing group was successful. The proposal was supported principally by city officials who felt they might have more influence with district-elected commissioners and an elected chief executive. Blacks generally supported the proposal but made no all-out effort on its behalf.

It is anticipated that there will be continual changes in the relative authority of the county government *vis a vis* city governments in functional areas. A trend towards a fragmentation of the unified government may also be emerging. In recent months proposals have been made for a transportation authority and an independent airport authority. The authority concept for water and sewers is inherent in the transfer of the Miami Water and Sewer Board. Such proposals generally have the support of business leaders. The transportation authority concept originated at the State level to facilitate transit funding; at this writing the specifics have not been worked out. An independent airport authority, proposed in 1962 by a group of businessmen, was defeated at the polls. The recent resurrection of the concept was initiated by a businessman-appointee to the County Commission and has the support of the Greater Miami Chamber of Commerce. At this writing, the proposal has not yet been adopted. At present, the County Commission functions as the Port Authority. A county Water and Sewer Authority, with which the Miami Water and Sewer Board was merged in October 1972 by charter amendment, was proposed originally by the Chamber of Commerce. Authority proposals are generally supported by the *Miami Herald,* but otherwise arouse little interest outside of the Chamber of Commerce. Such proposals generally draw opposition from some county commissioners who recognize the tendency towards fragmentation.

Inter-county regionalism will also become an increasing factor. Dade County officials have spearheaded several moves in this direction, as discussed earlier. It is not considered likely, however, that Dade County will in the near future be a party to any super-governmental body. It is more likely that Dade will enter multi-lateral agreements on individual services.

Dade County's form of metropolitan government may not be as easily accomplished in other metropolitan areas where the central city is the only incorporated area of significance within a single county, and where a city-county consolidation can readily be recommended. However, other single-county metropolitan areas which contain a number of cities of substantial size would do well to consider the Dade County experience. Thus, the county government would be strengthened in order to create a mechanism for providing regional services while at the same time allowing the constituent cities to maintain decision-making authority in relatively non-metropolitan functional areas. Where the central city government has greater competence than the county government, the Dade experience may be adapted with a modified consolidation of city and county with similar guarantees for the continuance of the other cities for the provision of non-metropolitan services. The objective, however, should be the achievement of an areawide tax base to finance services which serve all area residents.

NOTES

1. State of Florida, *Constitution*. Art. III, Sec. 2.
2. Committee for Economic Development, *Reshaping Government in Metropolitan Areas*, February, 1970.
3. Public Administration Service, *The Government of Metropolitan Miami* (Chicago, 1954).
4. Metropolitan Dade County, Florida, *Charter*. Art. V.
5. Metropolitan Dade County, Florida, *Charter*. Art. V. Sec. 4.05D.
6. Metropolitan Dade County Planning Department, *Municipal Boundaries in Metropolitan Dade County—Problems and Recommendations*, September, 1962.
7. Dade County Metropolitan Study Commission, *Final Report and Recommendations*, June, 1971.
8. Metropolitan Dade County, *Proposed Budget*, Fiscal Year 1972-73.
9. Metropolitan Dade County, *Proposed Program Budget*, Fiscal Year 1970-71.
10. Government Research Council, Miami-Dade County Chamber of Commerce, *County-State Financial Relationship*, March 1, 1963.
11. Porter W. Homer, *1967-68 Budget*, Memorandum to Board of County Commissioners, September 18, 1967.
12. Metropolitan Dade County, *Proposed Budget*, Fiscal Year 1971-72. These and other figures taken from table "Schedule of County Budgets, Fiscal Years 1940-41 Thru 1971-72."
13. George H. Kunde, *Metropolitan Regulation of Traffic*, Memorandum to O.W. Campbell, County Manager, August 21, 1959.
14. County Manager's Office, *Metro in the Making*, June 1, 1959, unpublished report.
15. John Berger, *County-Wide Contracts: Cooperative Purchases*, Memorandum to Irving C. McNary, County Manager, April 4, 1964, and attached letters from municipal officials.
16. Public Administration Service, *The Government of Metropolitan Miami*, p. 49.
17. O.W. Campbell, *First Annual Report on the Progress of Metropolitan Dade County*, undated.
18. Dennis I. Carter, *Why the County Budget Has Increased $20,493,909 Since 1957-58*, Memorandum to County Manager Irving G. McNary, July 28, 1961.
19. Carter, *Why the County Budget has Increased $20,493,909 Since 1957-58*.
20. Parris N. Glendenning, "Metropolitan Dade County Government: Examination of Reform" (Unpublished Ph.D. Dissertation), Department of Government, Florida State University, August, 1967, p. 150.
21. R. Ray Good, *Federal Grants Report*, Memorandum to Board of County Commissioners and Attachment, July 21, 1972.
22. Metropolitan Dade County Community Improvement Program, *Profile of Selected Ethnic & Economic Characteristics*, May, 1972.
23. University of Miami, *Municipal Finance in Dade County for the Fiscal Year 1960*, A Report by the Committee on Municipal Research, Department of Government, submitted to the Miami-Dade Chamber of Commerce and the Dade League of Municipalities (Coral Gables, June, 1961).
24. Dade County Metropolitan Study Commission, *Final Report and Recommendations*.

Introduction

The metropolitan reorganization that was implemented in Nashville-Davidson County represents what is known in the literature of metropolitan government as "City-County Consolidation." In effect, the city combines with the county into a SINGLE, stronger jurisdiction.

In each of the two case studies to follow, it will be seen that the city council and county legislature have been replaced by a county-wide council which is the main policy-making vehicle for the METRO.

In both Nashville and Jacksonville, the chief factor that led to the consolidation movement was a serious and, in certain areas, critical deterioration of local government services. The mixing of human excrement in the Nashville water supply and the danger of loss of accreditation of the Jacksonville school system are only two of a multitude of examples that could be mentioned.

*The two case studies, while similar in several ways, are different in one important respect. Namely, the consolidation that occurred between the city of Nashville and Davidson county encompassed only about three-quarters of the SMSA. With regard to Jacksonville and Duval counties, however, the consolidated government has boundaries that are coterminous with the entire SMSA. The reader should bear this in mind when assessing the relative successes and failures of the two METRO's in administering to **regional** needs.*

THE METROPOLITAN GOVERNMENT OF NASHVILLE AND DAVIDSON COUNTY

Robert E. McArthur
Associate Professor of Governmental Research
and Political Science
University of Mississippi

The 13 counties of upper middle Tennessee surrounding the capital city of Nashville contain over 800,000 people. They are organized for regional cooperation in two organizations with interlocking administration: the Mid-Cumberland Council of Governments (M-C COG) and the Mid-Cumberland Development District (M-C DD).

Within this 13-county district lies the Nashville metropolitan area. In 1970 the Nashville SMSA contained the counties of Davidson, Sumner, and Wilson; the Nashville planning district included the additional counties of Williamson and Rutherford. The five-county district had a 1970 population of over 630,000.

This report describes the operation of the central unit in this complex, the Metropolitan Government of Nashville and Davidson County (Metro), one of the most successful examples of city-county consolidation in the United States in this century.

History

Following World War II the problems caused by metropolitanization in the Nashville area rose in public visibility, especially the core city's difficulty in planning for its orderly growth, the absence of sanitary sewers in the suburbs, the inadequate private-subscription fire and police protection in the fringe, and the county's failure to provide parks and playgrounds for the outlying districts.[1] As dissatisfaction with these and other deficiencies grew, there was continual buck-passing between the city and county governments, with officials in each blaming the other for most of the dilemmas facing the area. Although numerous community groups studied these problems and proposed various solutions, alleviation was not forthcoming.

In response to the demand for some areawide authority to meet the situation, the 1951 Tennessee General Assembly authorized the creation of a

From: *Regional Governance—Promise and Performance: Substate Regionalism and the Federal System,* Vol. II—Case Studies, May, 1973, p. 26.

Community Services Commission for Davidson County and the City of Nashville. That commission's report, issued in June 1952, recommended, among other things, extensive annexation by the central city, county assumption of countywide functions, and city and county home rule.[2] These halfway measures would not have provided the areawide solution which the frustrated civic and business leadership sought. In response to their urgings, the mayor of Nashville and the Davidson County judge (the chief executive in Tennessee counties), both newly elected, came to support in varying degrees the idea of governmental change through city-county consolidation.

To aid Nashville and other Tennessee areas facing similar problems, the General Assembly submitted to the electorate Amendment 8 to Article XI, Section 9, of the Tennessee Constitution, authorizing the legislature to provide for city-county consolidation. The amendment was ratified by the State's voters in November 1953.

During the next three years, in response to requests from the public and private sectors, the Advance Planning and Research Divison of the joint Nashville and Davidson County Planning Commission studied the problems confronting the area and considered alternative forms of consolidation. In June 1955, County Judge Beverly Briley urged in a Rotary Club address that a single areawide government be established. This was the first public statement in support of Metro by a local political leader and added impetus to the work of the planners. In October 1956, they submitted a proposal for the creation of a single metropolitan government to replace the existing city and county structures.

With the planners' proposal in hand, consolidation supporters moved to the legislative halls in an attempt to persuade the General Assembly to authorize a metropolitan charter commission. Starting with a base of support in the Davidson County delegation, proponents sought help among the other metropolitan county delegations and among rural representatives. These efforts were strengthened greatly by the persuasiveness of Judge Briley, then president of the Tennessee Association of County Officials.[3]

The resulting 1957 consolidation law authorized the creation of a 10-member charter commission. The mayor and county judge each appointed five members. The body examined problems of the Davidson County area, mainly the need to provide for orderly planning and metropolitan growth. The commissioners developed a metropolitan charter under which the city and county would consolidate governmental structures but continue to deliver services and levy taxes through two districts, one corresponding to the former city and the other encompassing the entire county. The urban district would expand only as it became able to provide full urban services in the areas to be annexed.

While there were no avowed consolidation opponents on the charter commission, the group was aware of latent opposition in the community. In addition to traditional suburban and rural suspicion of efforts to expand the city, the commission had to contend with the possibility that central city residents, especially blacks, would consider city-county consolidation a threat to their political development.

The campaign for the adoption of the charter was similar to other unsuccessful consolidation attempts in the United States:

> The 1958 Nashville referendum appeared to be much like other referenda on governmental integration. The actual proposal was put forward by such typically reformist groups as a taxpayers' association, a chamber of commerce study committee, a special "community services commission" established by private act of the state legislature, and by city and county planners. It was then supported by numerous civic associations, by businessmen and young lawyers, and by the central city mayor in a largely amateurish, upper-class, good-government campaign. . . . The opposition concentrated on the county area and stressed such issues as higher taxes and city dictatorship.

> The outcome was a typical "yes" vote in the city and a "no" vote outside.

> There was, in short, nothing very different about the Nashville referendum of 1958.[4]

In addition to the typical suburban suspicions and the fears of many officials that their political futures might be threatened by Metro, another analyst felt that "the whole consolidation proposal lacked a crucial issue to arouse the interest of the citizenry."[5] In the absence of such a bread-and-butter cause, the proponents relied on good-government arguments and were completely unprepared to answer the anti-Metro propaganda which flooded the community during the last week of the campaign. They overcame much Nashville opposition, but the majority of the suburban and rural voters remained unconvinced. The plan which the commissioners prepared was rejected in a June 1958 referendum, receiving approval in the city but losing in the county precincts.[6]

After the failure of consolidation, the city council, in an effort to meet the problems created by Nashville's stagnant boundaries, pressed a vigorous annexation program, adding in two years' time nearly 50 square miles containing over 87,000 people. These annexations were made without referendum and created widespread resentment in the suburbs which had voted against Metro and wished to remain outside the corporate limits of the central city.

In January 1960, the county governing body called for a new charter commission, but this time the city council refused to join the effort. The council majority apparently felt that Nashville had gained enough from its extensive annexation program and would profit little from a new consolidation campaign.

It was precisely because of annexation, however, that suburbanites demanded another vote on Metro. After the courts upheld the right of Nashville to annex without referendum, voters outside the city saw that "it was only a matter of time" before they too would be annexed. Many felt that immediate consolidation would at least give them a voice in a new government, instead of annexation at some uncertain future date determined by a city council in which they were not represented.

In the August 1960 legislative primaries, most victorious candidates promised Davidson County another chance to vote on consolidation. A major obstacle was existing State legislation which required that charter commissions consist of both city and county appointees. Because of the city council's opposition to a new commission, consolidation proponents were forced to seek authorization in the 1961 session. As with most acts affecting only one locality, the legislature seemed willing to defer to the judgment of the Davidson County delegation. The 12-member group was almost solidly behind a new commission. Despite the persistent objection of one member, the General Assembly approved the private legislation which amended the 1957 legislation to permit the creation of a new charter commission, subject to approval by vote of the people. Such creation was approved in August 1961 by majorities in both the city and the suburbs.[7]

Eight of the ten members on the new commission had served on the first body—a prominent attorney and civic leader who was chairman of the 1958 commission; a woman attorney who served as commission secretary in 1958; an attorney who frequently represented labor interests; the principal of an elementary school in a lower-income neighborhood; a former State senator; a retired black druggist; a businessman who had served as president of the Nashville Chamber of Commerce; and a popular black member of the Nashville city council. The 1958 legal counsel was retained. Both Mayor West and Judge Briley were entitled to fill one vacancy each on the new commission. West, who had reversed his 1958 stand and now opposed consolidation, appointed the city's finance director. Briley, in a move indicating his firm support of consolidation, named a young attorney who had been active in the renewed consolidation movement.[8]

Given the second commission's composition, it was not surprising that the second metropolitan charter was similar to the first. Apparently the only close vote came on the question of an appointive metropolitan school board; the commission voted 6 to 4 in favor of giving such appointive power to the metropolitan mayor.[9] The major changes were provisions for a higher salary for the metropolitan mayor; a larger metropolitan council (41 rather than 21 members); and a method whereby two-thirds of the metropolitan board of education could force a referendum on any school budget reduced by the metropolitan council.

Observers are agreed, however, that Metro's success in the second campaign was attributable largely to changes not directly related to charter revisions. The main factors were more determined organization (on both sides) and more specific issues. According to one commentator, "the struggle for Metro—which had been a reasonably polite and friendly contest in 1958 . . . became an all-out political war with the in-fighting sometimes assuming vicious proportions."[10] While the Metro forces retained the bulk of their good-government adherents, the city mayor and his partisans (including one of the two metropolitan newspapers) defected, arguing that Metro was a dead issue and was now being used by the mayor's opponents to oust him from power. The county judge who had supported Metro in 1958 intensified his support, and his followers (including the more "liberal" metropolitan newspaper) saw him as the likely beneficiary in any new government resting on an all-county constituency.

The campaign was organized much more broadly than in 1958. Almost every precinct had groups actively working on either side. "On both sides, it was as if the professionals and the politicians had taken over from the amateurs and do-gooders."[11] The issues of the campaign were much more specific; the hotter contest made both sides more articulate, and the public responded by choosing sides:

> In 1958, the situation lacked urgency. The question was nebulous and hinged on the desirability of adopting an abstract solution to real and anticipated problems. In 1962, the issues were critical and clear-cut, though they varied for different groups.[12]

In his analysis of the 1962 Metro campaign, Brett Hawkins placed the issues in two categories, those in defense of the status quo and those in assault upon the status quo.[13] Defenders of the existing governmental structure agreed that despite its shortcomings the existing system was preferable to a metropolitan structure which was "novel, untried, untested," and whose constitutionality had not been ascertained. Some alleged that Metro would raise taxes; others contended that it would centralize governmental power under the control of liberal forces; and some even feared the scheme would undermine States' rights. For their part, the pro-Metro forces concentrated, as in 1958, on many of the customary reformist issues, e.g., the elimination of city-county bickering over schools, an end to duplication of offices and personnel, more economy and efficiency, and improvement of suburban services.

The proponents' crucial arguments, however, had developed since the 1958 vote on Metro. The city's insistence on expansion through annexation without referendum had infuriated suburbanites and created thousands of Metro converts in the annexed suburbs and in the fringe areas just outside Nashville. Closely related to annexation was the notorious Nashville "green sticker," a $10 wheel tax on all motor vehicles using Nashville streets for 30 days or more, which had been adopted by the city council in 1959 following the defeat of consolidation to force commuters to contribute to the cost of city services they used daily.

While it was possible for the city to present rational arguments for both annexation and the wheel tax, both devices were viewed by many suburbanites as power grabs by an unrepresentative city government. The dissatisfaction over these two matters was seized by pro-Metro forces and made the basis for the new campaign. City officials, especially the mayor, were vilified as power-hungry opponents of progress.

The vigorous campaign resulted in approval of the new charter in June 1962 by majorities in both the city and the suburbs. Interestingly, the anti-Metro city administration succeeded in defeating Metro in the old city territory, but the newly annexed precincts voted overwhelmingly for the change and thus delivered the city for the new government. Although the rural precincts continued in opposition, the fringe adjacent to the annexed areas produced Metro majorities large enough to carry the country outside the city.

Metro opponents made their last stand in the Tennessee courts. In April 1962, they had initiated a suit contending, among other things, that the 1957 act authorizing creation of charter commissions in Tennessee was an unconstitutional delegation of legislative power; that the charter, through its two-district service-taxation mechanism, violated the State constitution by authorizing taxation which would not be uniform throughout the new government's territory; and that the charter unconstitutionally abridged the terms of office of all Nashville officials. In August 1962, the chancery court rejected these challenges and upheld the constitutionality of the Metro legislation. The Tennessee Supreme Court affirmed that decision in October 1962.

In November 1962, a metropolitan mayor, vice mayor, and enlarged council were elected. Thus, after 12 years, a State constitutional amendment, passage of two public and one private act by the General Assembly, two exhausting Metro referenda, and challenge in the courts, officials of the new government were inaugurated on April 1, 1962, and the experiment was underway.

Despite the local controversies which were so important in their campaign for the adoption of the new government, the primary concern of most supporters of Metro remained the need to establish an enlarged system which could provide services and guide the growth and development of Davidson County through control of the urbanizing territory surrounding Nashville. The hope was that a consolidated government covering the county's 533 square miles would produce significant improvements by economies of scale, areawide service delivery systems, and increased accountability and responsiveness to a truly metropolitan community.

Structure

Metro Nashville operates under a mayor-council form of government. The metropolitan mayor is elected to a four-year term and may not serve over three consecutive terms. The vice mayor, who presides over the metropolitan county council, is also elected by the citizenry for a four-year term. The county council, elected every four years, is composed of 40 members, 35 selected from single-member, equal-population districts, and 5 elected by the county at large.

The consolidated government has all the powers of a municipality and all the powers of a county under Tennessee law and is thus eligible for increased amounts of State aid because of its enlarged population as both a city and a county.

The government comprises two service districts. The general services district (GSD) consists of the entire county. The smaller urban services district (USD) still consisted in 1972 of the area of the former city of Nashville. Each district has its own tax rate to support the services provided. Residents of the USD pay both USD and GSD property taxes. The USD may be expanded whenever the metropolitan county council determines that a given area needs urban services and that the government can provide such urban services within one year after the USD tax rate is levied upon property in the area.

The functions performed by the GSD comprise the following services:

General Administration	Airport
Police	Urban Redevelopment
Courts	Planning
Jails	Building Code
Assessment	Housing Code
Health	Transit
Welfare	Beer Supervision
Hospitals	Fair Grounds
Housing for the Aged	Public Housing
Streets and Roads	Urban Renewal
Traffic	Electrical Code
Schools	Plumbing Code
Parks and Recreation	Electricity
Libraries	Refuse Disposal
Auditorium	Taxicab Regulation

Residents of the USD receive the following additional services:

Additional Police Protection	Street Lighting
Fire Protection	Street Cleaning
Water	Refuse Collection
Sanitary Sewers	Wine and Whiskey
Storm Sewers	Supervision

Although the city and county were consolidated, six suburban municipalities existing in 1962 were allowed to retain their incorporated status and to continue to function, although they may not extend their boundaries. They may contract with Metro for the administration and handling of any of their governmental services, and they are part of the GSD just as they were part of Davidson County. Their residents thus pay taxes to the metropolitan government based on the GSD rate, and Metro is obligated by its charter to furnish them with the same services received by the rest of the GSD.

Finance

City-council consolidation has had a considerable impact on the financing of local government in the Nashville area, mainly because the new structure furnished a much more diversified tax base. Some of the major changes are discussed below.

(1) **Sales tax.** In the first year of Metro a one-cent sales tax was approved by the voters and earmarked for educational services. One-half cent has since been added to the levy and is also used for education. Following Nashville's lead, many other counties in the region have adopted similar sales taxes.

(2) **User charges**. Metro has increased user charges on many of the services it provides. Water/sewer charges were adopted not only to relieve the property tax, but also to provide a way for the rapid extension of sewerage facilities into the areas which had been annexed to Nashville before consolidation. Charges for permits, hospital fees, and other services have also been raised.

(3) **Automobile regulatory fee.** A $15 fee was tried in 1967-68 and made permanent in 1970-71. Enforcement of a similar charge by the former city of Nashville had been virtually unenforceable because of the city-county division. Most other counties in the area now collect similar fees, following Metro's example as in the case of the sales tax.

(4) **Bonds and interest**. Before Metro the city of Nashville was approaching its statutory bonded debt limit. The consolidation has relieved this threat and has made it much easier to identify and invest surplus funds. For example, Metro realized approximately $1,000,000 from interest earned from investments of temporary fund surpluses during Metro's first fiscal year; this was approximately $400,000 more than the interest earned by both city and county from short-term investments during the last year of divided government.

(5) **Property tax**. This levy supplies a large portion of local revenues in American municipalities, and Metro is no exception. Perhaps the best assessment of the impact of consolidation on the area's property taxation has been given by a Nashville banker:

Metropolitan Nashville is the only major Tennessee city which has been able to stabilize its property tax rate over the last eight years [to 1968]. In

1960 [before Metro] the rate of the old city was $5.33 and in 1968 it was $5.30. It has been estimated that if Metro had not been approved, the rate in Nashville would have increased by at least 50 cents and possibly $1.00. Experience in other cities confirms this belief. In the same period of time the property tax in Memphis and Knoxville has increased 9 percent, and in Chattanooga, 37 percent.

The general services levy, which applies to the entire county area and would be the only tax paid in the general services district outside the old city limits, has gone up. Between 1960 and 1968 the rate increased 26 percent in Davidson County compared to 23 percent in Hamilton County [Chattanooga], 20 percent in Shelby County [Memphis], and 19 percent in Knox County [Knoxville]. The metropolitan government is responsible for some of this higher tax burden outside the old city because it forces those taxpayers to pay a part of countywide services like the auditorium, the airport, and parks which were formerly paid for entirely by city taxpayers. Many taxpayers outside Nashville, therefore, complain that they are now paying more taxes and receiving no new services. Actually they are now paying for services which they formerly received free. [14]

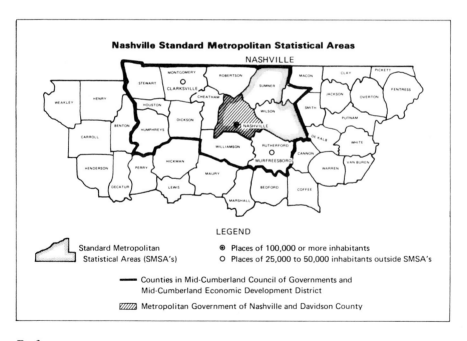

Nashville Standard Metropolitan Statistical Areas

LEGEND

Standard Metropolitan
Statistical Areas (SMSA's)

◉ Places of 100,000 or more inhabitants
○ Places of 25,000 to 50,000 inhabitants outside SMSA's

—— Counties in Mid-Cumberland Council of Governments and
Mid-Cumberland Economic Development District

▨ Metropolitan Government of Nashville and Davidson County

Performance

After nearly a decade, it is interesting to consider the accomplishments of Nashville Metro in selected areas. [15]

Decision Making. Metro proponents claimed that the new government would eliminate city-county buckpassing and help fix political responsibility for decisions. Opponents alleged just as forcefully that Metro would create a more centralized government which would be less responsible and less accessible to the people, expecially to core-city blacks, who constituted over 37 percent of the city of Nashville's 1960 population.

It would seem that the proponents' predictions were more nearly accurate. Metro has indeed provided a framework for more comprehensive problem-solving and program implementation. In the decade before Metro, hundreds of citizens in the Nashville area had worked extensively on some 54 studies of local problems, but there was a frustrating lack of an implementing device to effectuate their findings and recommendations. Metro provided an effective unit by merging two large governmental organizations and providing a means for the representation of suburban citizens on metropolitan boards and commissions.

This change in decision making was enhanced by the election of Beverly Briley as the first metropolitan mayor. Having served as Davidson County judge since 1950, Briley had built an image as representative of the entire county. Perhaps no other individual could have been better selected to head a new government which had to consider simultaneously the needs of the core city, the suburbs, and the rural fringe. His stature was invaluable in convincing others of the need for regional decision making and compromise in the new government.

Surveys of voter attitudes since 1963 indicate that citizens are generally pleased with the decisions Metro has produced. In 1964 respondents were asked, "Are you generally satisfied with the way 'Metro' has worked in its first year of operation?" The responses indicated that, except for voters in the outlying areas, most citizens felt the new government was performing well. [16]

In 1965 a closer look was taken at the fringe dwellers in the outlying areas, where greatest Metro opposition was centered. [17] Surprisingly, in light of their earlier opposition in both consolidation referenda and in the 1964 survey, it was found that nearly 68 percent of the respondents agreed that Metro was "generally more efficient than city and county governments were before Metro was adopted." [18] Strong refutation was provided to the prediction that Metro would dilute the access of this "least urban" portion of the population. Over 63 percent agreed with the statement, "Under Metro it is easier to know whom to call or see when you have a problem than it was under separate city and county governments." [19] Further, when asked, "Now, how do you feel about the effect of Metro on your personal ability to get an attentive hearing from the responsible officials when you feel a problem exists in the community?", 50 percent thought that Metro had

TABLE 1.1
Opinions on Nashville
1964

Area	Actual Vote in 1962 Percent Favorable to Metro
"Old City" of Nashville	45
1960 "annexation area"	72
Unincorporated suburbs	63
Six incorporated suburbs	47
Rural area	34

Area	1964 Survey Percent Favorable to Metro
"Old City" of Nashville	80
1960 "annexation area"	85
Unincorporated suburbs	63
Six incorporated suburbs	42
Rural area	38.5

made an attentive hearing easier to obtain, 30 percent felt it had brought no change, and 20 percent believed Metro had made it more difficult.[20]

Metro has provided partial refutation to those who claimed that metropolitan consolidation would inevitably result in dilution of black political influence. The black leadership of Nashville was carefully cultivated by Metro proponents, and two of the ten members of the charter commission were black. Provisions for the metropolitan council were subjected to a kind of racial gerrymandering to assure the election of several blacks to the council, and the first council contained five black members.

As for black voters in general, in surveys in both 1964 and 1965 they expressed slightly greater satisfaction with "the way Metro has worked" than did white voters.[21]

Significantly, in the most recent councilmanic elections, seven blacks were elected, despite the fact that the black percentage of the metropolitan population remained virtually the same between 1960 and 1970 (19.6 percent in 1970 as compared to 19.1 percent in 1960). Even more noteworthy is the fact that two black council members were elected to represent districts with white majorities.

Administration. Many Metro supporters promised that the consolidation would eliminate duplication of administrative effort, provide greater specialization and professionalization of personnel, and promote more economical government. The first year was devoted to extensive studies and surveys, 17 in all, designed to establish a starting point and to provide the base for building the new government. The administration initiated studies to determine the economic potential of the community and explored various avenues for financing programs and services. They were especially fruitful, both because Metro held advantages as a city/county for State-aid purposes and because the new government was inaugurated at the beginning of new Federal efforts to aid urban areas.

Metropolitan consolidation created a more efficient "funnel" for the collection and dispersal of governmental funds, resulting in dramatic increases in aid for various metropolitan programs. In the first metropolitan budget in 1963, slightly over $20 million in revenue came from other agencies; by 1970 income from this source was estimated to be over $37 million. In the area of governmental expenditures consolidation produced significant gains for central city residents, especially the black poor, since most of the Great Society programs which Metro was able to tap were aimed at this segment of the population.

The merger also reduced the amount of housekeeping duplication and competing functions. Eight hundred positions were eliminated, and 1,500 job titles were lowered to less than 700. An extensive program of retraining through various technical and adult education programs encouraged employees to find job slots in the new service expansion areas of the government. Through these efforts the educational level of metropolitan employees was increased markedly.

New Directions in Community Services. The metropolitan government seemed to provide a general boost to the spirit of Nashville and Davidson County. Just as the proponents argued, the new government was able to create "a progressive community image in the national spotlight," and wide attention has been given the Nashville experiment.[22]

As many citizens came to believe the public-relations claims that Metro was a "dramatic break with the past" heralding a new day in the life of the community, public expectations escalated. The "booster spirit" caused government and people to look more and more at what other metropolises in the United States and abroad were doing. This produced an increased responsiveness to innovation, and some "soft" services, which many citizens in beleaguered cities elsewhere consider too expensive or impractical, received new attention under Metro. Services improving the urban environment became important goals. Governmental reorganization released resources from housekeeping functions to be used in improved policies concerning education, criminal justice, health, culture, recreation, and public works. It was especially timely that this innovative spirit came just as Federal grants-in-aid were moving in similar directions.

City-Suburban Service and Financial Disparities. Advocates of Metro had argued that the new government would equalize services on a "single community" basis and assure through the two taxing districts that citizens would pay only for those services which they actually received. In addition, it would be a "truly progressive solution" to the universal problem of how to plan and guide urban growth in the metropolitan fringe. Opponents countered that Metro would only raise taxes while providing little or no additional benefit to rural residents.

The most significant reduction in city-suburban disparities came in public education. Consolidation gave a lift to the education delivery system through merger of the city and county school organizations. Serving approximately 95,000 students, the new network had the total resources of the community behind it and was able to undertake extensive administrative reorganization in aid of its educational objectives. Salaries were equalized, teacher transfers were made easier to obtain, and a flexible rezoning of school service areas made possible the transfer of many former county students to previous city schools, and vice versa, saving considerable amounts in construction costs which would have been required under the former divided system of education.

Consolidation of law enforcement agencies took place rapidly. City and county patrols were merged and many actions were undertaken to improve the image of municipal police operations. The establishment of the county-wide professional police system resulted in a 7 percent decrease in Nashville's major crimes in 1965, compared with a 5 percent increase nationally.

The administration of road maintenance was improved. The metropolitan Department of Public Works was able to purchase specialized equipment which neither the city nor county alone could have justified before consolidation. General service expenditures increased markedly in the rural areas.

Parks and recreational facilities became a general service to be provided throughout the Metro area, giving rural residents access to a service previously denied them. A park board was established with authority to acquire parkland in advance of urban development. Priority systems were established, and park and school facilities at 68 locations were combined to provide optimum recreational facilities to all residents of the area. Seventeen new park sites were added, with an aggregate of 1,086 acres, contributing to a metropolitan total of 5,500 acres in 1972.

In a similar manner Metro extended health, hospital, welfare, and branch library services into the old county area, and street lighting was extended to the county line on all major arteries. Labor-saving devices, including computers, central purchasing, central labor sources, and task-force interagency pools for solution of short-term problems were all used.

In these and other service areas the new government focused administrative and political responsibility for the entire county. It reduced the financial burden of the core city by spreading the cost of countywide services throughout the area. Although first-year Metro expenditures increased about 7 percent, property tax rates for core-city residents decreased 1 percent, in marked contrast to the rate for rural residents, which increased more than 34 percent.[23]

These changes in services and taxation did not go unnoticed in the fringe, the area of greatest inital opposition to metropolitan consolidation. Surprisingly, in light of the marked increase in their tax burden, fringe dwellers were generally supportive of the new government. A 1965 survey indicated that more than 65 percent of the respondents were satisfied with each major service provided by the all-county General Services District, i.e., schools, streets and roads, parks and recreation, and police protection.[24] Over 83 percent said they were satisfied with all local services "considered as a whole," and more than 67 percent agreed with the statement, "Metro is generally more efficient than the city-county governments were before Metro was adopted."[25]

Although 61 percent of the respondents felt that taxes were too high, over 57 percent agreed with the statement that "the tax burden is more fairly distributed under Metro than it was before Metro was adopted."[26] To secure service and tax satisfaction—or lack of dissatisfaction—in the fringe on such a scale after only three years' operation was a significant achievement for a government controlling 533 square miles.

Regional Leadership. The consolidation undoubtedly strengthened Nashville's position as the developmental leader of middle Tennessee. The characteristics of the metropolitan mayor, Beverly Briley, probably more than any other single factor, enhanced this role. As a former county judge, the mayor possessed strong ties with other county executives throughout the region. As the chief executive of a government serving core-city, suburban, and rural constituents, he could claim to understand the needs of all geographical interests, and this position made him a better salesman of urban causes to the small towns and rural areas in the counties surrounding Nashville.

This stature was enriched by the mayor's election to the presidency of both the National League of Cities and the National Association of County Officials. As a member of several Federal advisory agencies, including the Advisory Commission on Intergovernmental Relations, the Federal Hospital Council, the President's Commission on Crime, and several other governmental task forces, the mayor gained important Washington knowledge and influence which made him a valued spokesman for Metro and the middle Tennessee region.

Metropolitan Nashville, in keeping with its increased regional responsibility, has begun to think about the future of its leadership structure. Mayor Briley's generation provided strong leadership during the period following World War II, and persons who served with the mayor as "back-benchers" in community affairs before the war moved to positions of directorship in the legislature, the chambers of commerce, and other civic and economic organizations during the 1950s and 1960s. This group is now concerned with the preparation of another leadership group for the 1980s and 1990s. Such organizations as the Middle Tennessee Regional Conference, a project of the Nashville Area Chamber of Commerce, are working diligently to train younger men and women to assume responsibility in metropolitan and regional affairs. Much of this training will come through increasing participation in the activities of such agencies as the Mid-Cumberland Council of Governments.

Future Directions

One of the major challenges confronting Metro in the future will be its relationship to the surrounding region. Just as urban growth spilled outside the former city of Nashville into the suburban areas of Davidson County in the 1940s and 1950s, it continued to accelerate in the 1960s throughout the adjoining counties and along the Interstate highways which radiate from the Metro core.

As Federal pressures for cooperative planning in the region increased, Metro officials sought to have the Metropolitan Nashville-Davidson County Planning Commission designated the A-95 regional review agency. When this was rejected on the grounds that the entire metropolitan area should be represented, Metro attempted to establish a multi-county planning commission encompassing the Nashville SMSA. The suburban counties rebuffed this initiative, apparently fearing they would be swallowed up by cooperation with Metro. A *modus vivendi* was achieved by the establishment of two cooperative organizations composed of 12 outlying counties and Metro. These organizations seem to be in keeping with Tennessee's goals in substate regionalism and the Federal insistence on a truly regional approach to planning and development.

The Mid-Cumberland Development District (M-C DD) is an organization composed of the 13 counties and 45 incorporated cities and towns in the upper Tennessee area. The organization was formed in accordance with the Tennessee Economic Development District Act of 1965, as amended, and Executive Order No. 17 (Oct. 14, 1968, as amended on June 23, 1970). The sister agency of the M-C DD is the Mid-Cumberland Council of Governments (M-C COG). It encompasses the same counties as M-C DD and is a voluntary association of local governmental units organized in accordance with the Tennessee Interlocal Cooperation Act of 1968. As is typical in similar organizations, M-C COG and M-C DD have power neither to legislate nor to tax, nor do they supplant any authority or jurisdiction. They merely provide a means whereby local public officials, working together, may coordinate programs and projects for maximum efficiency and economy.

The two organizations now do together what each sought to do separately when they were created. The organizations serve as a clearinghouse for Federal projects (including A-95 review), information, and regional planning activities, and promote cooperative arrangements and coordination of action among members. The membership of M-C COG is made up of the county judges and mayors in the 13 counties. The membership of M-C DD consists of county judges, mayors, and another representative from each county appointed by the county judge. The two organizations have the same officials and the same professional and clerical staffs.

They are financed from local dues paid by the counties and municipalities. These dues are matched by the State of Tennessee—with certain exceptions—and by grants from the Federal government. The Middle Tennessee Regional Conference has also contributed funds to the areawide operations.

Since Nashville Metro accounts for over one-half the people in the 13-county region, it seems inevitable that the government will play a leading role in the two Mid-Cumberland units. At this stage, however, the scope of Metro's eventual participation is uncertain, and only some of the positive and negative aspects of the Metro-regional relationship can be described.

On the positive side, the relationship is off to a good start. Although Mayor Briley keeps a rather low profile in the regional organizations, as county-judge-turned-metropolitan-mayor he can and frequently does take varying positions on urban, suburban, and rural questions facing the region. This flexibility enhances his influence with the varied interests represented on the COG and the EDD.

Furthermore, Metro, with its well-developed and knowledgeable bureaucracy, together with a business community which is aware of the need for regional cooperation in economic development, has been able and willing to provide much technical assistance to the staff and membership of the Council and district through workshops, seminars, grant application preparation, in-kind contributions, and computer services.

Through planning and consultation the region is achieving more program coordination. Metro is encouraging land-use studies through the COG which will promote economic expansion and development through nucleated growth with a minimum amount of environmental damage. Utility district water plans are being scrutinized closely by the regional organizations. In these and other fields, Metro is not directly perceived as "core-city," including as it does such a large suburban and rural fringe, and a healthy spirit of reciprocity usually prevails. In relations with State and Federal agencies, there is evidence that Metro and the COG tend to stand together on most matters.

Metro has affected the region in other ways. Emergency employment funds have been channeled through the COG, and salaries of the regional organizations have been tailored to Nashville pay scales. These actions have made Metro's adjacent counties more aware of standards and higher pay scales, creating a regional labor market for government employees. Federal requirements that the national prevailing wage be paid in Model Cities and other programs have raised Metro wages; this increase has gradually spread to other parts of middle Tennessee. Labor communications have improved and various occupational groups and unions in the area have been brought closer together.

Much like a well-organized core city surrounded by rapidly growing suburbs, Metro must prepare for the day when even closer cooperation, perhaps even consolidation, with its neighbors will be required. Thus far, Metro has lost little political or administrative muscle to the emerging regional movement; indeed, as has been shown, there has been commendable cooperation in substantial areas. There are still spheres, however, where "regional thinking" is not complete.

There is some evidence of occasional friction between Metro officials and the COG staff, the staff responding to Federal guidelines, the Metro representatives demanding "more attention to local agencies"—which, because of its preponderant size in the region, usually means Metro. Since the COG depends upon the local matching funds and in-kind contributions supplied by Metro, core-county officials have great leverage in any showdown on such matters. Indeed, there is a gentlemen's agreement in the COG that when there is disagreement on a question, there must be a "division of the house" and the population represented by each vote must be shown on the final policy position. Since Metro contains more than half the regional population, this presumably gives comparatively greater power to Metro representatives, power which may one day lead to suburban resentment and conflict between Metro and the outlying counties.

Two areas of potential controversy are highways and Federal grants for water and sewer development. In all likelihood Davidson County will continue to push for priority development of arteries which lead into Nashville, while rural and suburban counties will demand more attention to their road needs. As Federal water and sewer grants become scarce, a regional question will arise concerning which parts of the 13-county region need them most. As with most core cities, Metro will claim that its environs need greatest attention. The small towns and rural areas may feel otherwise. As one Metro official frankly noted:

Davidson [County] will be for greater concentration of the "goodies" and decentralization of the problems. Rural and suburban counties will be for the opposite.[27]

Ironically, Metro may come to behave more and more like the Nashville city government it supplanted in 1962, protecting its interests against the restive suburbs and opposing areawide control in many fields.

This is not to portray Metro as the villain in the regional scenario. An auspicious beginning has been made toward coordinated planning and development with a view toward the encouragement of nucleated growth in the 13-county Mid-Cumberland region, and Metro officials have been crucial to this movement. Whether middle Tennessee will continue the intensification and expansion of its regional efforts may be the challenge for the embryonic regional leadership now developing. If the youngsters have the foresight and persistence shown by the Metro founding fathers, they may break some new regional ground themselves.

NOTES

1. These and other pre-Metro problems are discussed in Daniel R. Grant, "Metropolitics and Professional Political Leadership: The Case of Nashville," *Annals of the American Academy of Political and Social Science*, CCCLIII (May 1964), pp. 74-75.
2. The commission did not recommend city-county consolidation because it was believed that such a merger would require two taxing districts, action deemed violative of the Tennessee constitution.
3. See Brett Hawkins, *Nashville Metro: The Politics of City-County Consolidation* (Nashville: Vanderbilt University Press, 1966), p. 42, and Daniel J. Elazar, *A Case Study of Failure in Attempted Metropolitan Integration: Nashville and Davidson County, Tennessee* (Chicago: National Opinion Research Center of the University of Chicago, 1961), pp. 23-25.
4. Hawkins, *Nashville Metro*, pp. 56-57.
5. David A. Booth, *Metropolitics: The Nashville Consolidation* (East Lansing: Institute for Community Development and Services, Michigan State University, 1963), p. 2.
6. The poor county showing was somewhat puzzling in view of the public support of Metro by County Judge Briley, considered a leading spokesman for suburban interests. Indeed, some observers felt that Briley's political machine was not fully committed to this first Metro campaign because of the fear that Nashville's mayor, Ben West, might be elected the first metropolitan mayor, denying Briley the areawide leadership position which he sought. Booth, *Metropolitics*, p. 64; Hawkins, *Nashville Metro*, pp. 46-47.
7. Several of the newly annexed areas which had opposed Metro in 1958 voted for the new commission by margins of more than eight to one.
8. Hawkins, *Nashville Metro*, pp. 71-72.
9. Hawkins, *Nashville Metro*, p. 74.
10. Booth, *Metropolitics*, pp. 83-84.
11. Booth, *Metropolitics*, p. 85.
12. Booth, *Metropolitics*, pp. 86-87.

13. Hawkins, *Nashville Metro*, pp. 82-90.
14. T. Scott Fillebrown, "The Nashville Story," *National Civic Review*, LVIII (May 1969), p. 199.
15. A very useful comparison of predictions and actual performance under Metro during its first two years appears in Daniel R. Grant, "A Comparison of Predictions and Experience with Nashville 'Metro,' " *Urban Affairs Quarterly*, I (September 1965), pp. 34-54. The following treatment is based upon a fusion of Grant's categories of analysis.
16. Daniel R. Grant, "Opinions Surveyed on Nashville Metro," *National Civic Review*, LIV (July 1965), p. 376.
17. Robert E. McArthur, *The Impact of Metropolitan Government on the Rural-Urban Fringe: The Nashville-Davidson County Experience* (Washington, D.C.: U.S. Department of Agriculture, 1971).
18. McArthur, *The Impact of Metropolitan Government . . . .* p. 20.
19. McArthur, *The Impact of Metropolitan Government . . . .* p. 27.
20. McArthur, *The Impact of Metropolitan Government . . . .* p. 26.
21. Grant, "A Comparison of Predictions," p. 53.
22. Since Metro's inauguration, some 1,000 groups and individuals have visited Nashville from all over the world to investigate the new government. Metro officials in the summer of 1972 were offering assistance to approximately 25 groups concerned with metropolitan problems.
23. In Metro's second year, the government's revenue sources were expanded through the adoption of a 1-cent sales tax and a user charge for water-sewer financing. These changes made possible a reduction in the property tax rate for the all-county general services district.
24. McArthur, *The Impact of Metropolitan Government*, p. 19.
25. McArthur, *The Impact of Metropolitan Government*, pp. 19-30.
26. McArthur, *The Impact of Metropolitan Government*, p. 23.
27. Interview with a Metro official, July 5, 1972. Other officials characterized this view as far too pessimistic.

THE CITY OF JACKSONVILLE: CONSOLIDATION IN ACTION

John M. DeGrove

The present consolidated City of Jacksonville includes the former County of Duval, the old city of Jacksonville, and four small municipalities. Consolidation made Jacksonville the largest city in Florida, the largest city in land area in the United States (841 square miles) and moved it up to 23rd in population of the Nation's cities. The questions to be examined in this paper are how and why did it happen, and how has it worked.

Background to the Merger

In 1940, Jacksonville-Duval County had a total population of over 210,000; some 170,000 in the city and 37,000 in the rest of the county. From that point to 1965, county growth outstripped the declining city, so that the county outside Jacksonville rose rapidly to an estimated 327,000, while the city fell below 200,000. Projections to 1980 showed the county with 885,000 and the city remaining almost static with 211,000.

These population shifts had important age, race, income, and education characteristics that contributed to the sense of crisis fueling the fires of the consolidation movement. By 1960, Jacksonville was over 41 percent black, the third highest percentage in the Nation among cities over 100,000. The county outside the city was only about 9 percent black. During the 1950s in the city the black population increased over 14 percent, while the white population decreased over 10 percent. During the same period, the old city was becoming more and more the residence of the very old and the very young, with the economically productive 20-64 age group down by 15 percent during the 1950s. The over-65 group was up over 36 percent to a total of just over 9 percent, while the under-20 group increased 17.5 percent during the Fifties. By contrast, the over-65 group in the county totalled only 3.8 percent. The contrast carries through to income and housing. In the old city in 1960, 31 percent of the population was below a poverty level of $3,000, while the comparable figure in the county was 15 percent. Thirty percent of the houses in Jacksonville were deteriorated or dilapidated, while the county figure was 13 percent. In education the average years of schooling of adults over 25 was 9.5 in the city and 11.5 outside the city.[1]

The picture is not an unfamiliar one. It shows a central city in decline, loosing its most productive citizens, at least in economic terms, gaining citizens disproportionately in the very old and very young categories; and well below its relatively affluent suburbs in income, housing, and education. While these trends undoubtedly supported the consolidation movement, their presence in dozens of other cities where consolidation movements have not developed makes it clear that they are not sufficient to explain the success in Jacksonville.

Jacksonville's governmental structure was a bizarre hodgepodge of overlap and duplication. The city had a nine-person city council elected at large and presided over by a president. The council was the major legislative authority. The administrative power was located in a city commission of five members elected at large, each of whom headed up the city's services in a particular functional area or areas. A mayor-commissioner presided over this group. In addition, city voters elected a recorder, a municipal judge, a treasurer, and a tax assessor. Thus, a structure defended in the name of checks and balances was in fact a maze of duplication, and gaps in authority characterized by buck-passing and inability or unwillingness to cope with emerging problems. When widespread corruption was added to these disabilities, another link in the consolidation chain was forged.

The county structure featured a commission form with five commissioners elected at large who served as both administrators and policymakers for the county. In addition, voters elected several administrators such as the sheriff. The system was designed for another age. By the mid-1960s the pressures for urban services in the suburbs had been strained to the breaking point. Home rule was not available to either the city or the county until a new State constitution was adopted in 1968. The fragmentation of local government was further assured by the existence of an expressway authority, a Port Authority, a Hospital Authority, a Housing Authority, the Air Improvement Authority, and the Jacksonville-Duval Planning Board. These authorities were essentially autonomous single-purpose districts that did not share central services and were not subject to budgetary or other coordination.

By the mid-1960s, Jacksonville and Duval County could be described as a central city with a fancy facade of new buildings downtown, and deepseated social, economic, and political problems just beneath the surface. The suburbs were booming, with no governmental structure capable of meeting their service needs. Perhaps most important, the school system had reached the critical stage in its steady decline from mediocrity to disgrace. The countywide school district was faced with a steadily weakening property tax base as thousands of homes built for families in the suburbs were kept off the property tax rolls by a low assessment ratio (estimated in the 20 to 50 percent range of market value) and a $5,000 homestead exemption. A taxpayers' group estimated that 60,000 of 93,500 homesteads in the entire county were not on the tax rolls.[2] Finally, the Southern Association of Colleges and Schools removed accreditation from all of Duval County's 15 high schools.

In addition to schools, a broken-down city sewer system discharging raw sewage into the St. Johns River, inefficient package sewer plants or septic tanks in the suburbs, lack of adequate police and fire protection in the suburbs, the soaring cost of Jacksonville's city government in the face of a declining population (from 1950 to 1965 per capita costs of services rose more than 400 percent, from $116 to $479), an increasing air pollution problem—these and other issues set the stage from which the consolidation movement emerged.[3]

The Consolidated Government Plan

Reform of the local government system for the area had been an issue for many years. The most recent effort to cope with the emerging problems had involved a massive annexation plan to extend the limits of the city throughout most of the county's urbanized areas. The annexation case was weakened by suspicion of the central city by suburbanites, easy to understand in the face of the statistic that Jacksonville "had the largest number of full-time employees and the highest monthly payroll in the nation" for a city of its size.[3] In the 1963 election, city voters supported annexation by more than 3-to-1, but the proposal to add 66 square miles and over 130,000 people to the city was turned down in the suburbs with 16,000 votes against and 12,000 votes for. A similar proposal was defeated the following year.[4]

With annexation as a solution not acceptable, the forces for consolidation became active in early 1965 when Claude Yates, retired Southern Bell executive and president of the Jacksonville Area Chamber of Commerce, called a meeting of civic and business leaders. After several hours of discussion it was decided to ask the legislative delegation to allow the preparation and submission to the voters of a consolidated form of government for Duval County. The legislative delegation subsequently approved the proposal, which, when submitted as a local bill, meant automatic approval by the legislature. The bill actually named the 50-person group, with provision of a 17-person executive committee. No person holding public office was eligible to serve. Four blacks and five women were included. The group was chaired by one of Jacksonville's leading civic and business leaders, J.J. Daniels. It hired an executive director and adopted a budget of some $60,000, one-third of which it had to raise, with the remainder mandated from the city and county. The commission divided itself into task forces, and over the next 15 months drafted, held hearings on, and presented to the legislative delegation a consolidated plan of government for Duval County.

The "Blueprint for Government" abolished completely the old city and county governments, and all other governmental units within the boundaries of Duval County except several authorities.[5] It substituted a single government structure composed of a mayor with full administrative powers, a 21-member council elected from districts to serve without pay, and a non-partisan school board of seven members elected from districts formed by combining three city council districts.[6] The proposal was a bold one, and it was boldly defended by its creators, but a legislative delegation, expanded from eight to 16 members by reapportionment, had to approve it before the people could vote on the charter.

As described by Martin[7], Representative George Stallings, who anchored the right wing of the House delegation, led the fight to assure defeat of the proposed charter. The center of opposition to the plan was in the House delegation. In the final key vote on the proposed modifications, Stallings led a majority of the House delegation in opposition to placing the charter before the people in a legally defensible form, while all senators voted for the modified plan. The critical issue within the delegation was whether to put the charter to the people with a questionable judicial article attached, or whether to modify the charter in this and other ways so as to assure its legality and strengthen acceptability to the voters. No legislators supported the study commission proposed charter without modification. After much political maneuvering and sharp delegation in-fighting, the charter was approved, but not without substantial modifications. The major changes included the restoration to elected status of administrative officers of the old county government (sheriff, tax assessor, tax collector, and supervisor of elections); the reduction of the council to 19 members, 14 to be elected from districts and five at large; and *ad valorem* tax limitation; an option for the four small municipalities to join or not join the consolidated government; added pension and other employee protections; and a provision for an elected Civil Service Board.[8]

While most of these changes weakened the purity of the consolidation proposal, it was still a bold and far-reaching plan. The fight for adoption was carried on with as much enthusiasm as had been displayed in drafting the proposal. The leaders were the same people from the business, civic, and professional community who had initiated the consolidation drive. Proponents formed themselves into Citizens for Better Government, raised about $40,000, and waged a strong campaign. Claude Yates chaired the group and Lex Hester, study commission executive director, served as referendum coordinator. They had the full support of the Chamber of Commerce; the media; most other business and professional people; and many other groups such as the League of Women Voters, the Duval County Medical Society, and the bar association. More unusual perhaps, they had the support of many key black groups, including the Jacksonville Urban League and the Voters League of Florida. Most civic clubs endorsed and worked for the proposal. On the "con" side was a group called Better Government for Duval County, the Central Labor Union and its city and county affiliates, some of the suburban press, some black leaders, two black newspapers, certain members of the legislative delegation, and some extremist groups who branded the proposal as communistic. The supporters stressed economy, efficiency, responsible government, and the ability to deal with problems; the opposition denied economy, raised the spector of unresponsive government, and most of all, raised the ghost of a "communist plot."9

The support of black leaders was jeopardized in mid-campaign by the apparently inadvertent adjustment of council district lines so as to pit two incumbent black councilwomen against each other. The resulting cry of "foul" from the black community led to a quick adjustment of the boundaries. Ms. Sallye Mathis, one of the councilwomen affected; Clanzel Brown; and Earl Johnson were the key leaders in rallying black support for consolidation. Ms. Mathis was an educator, active in a large number of civic organizations, including the Urban League and the NAACP. Brown was executive director of the Jacksonville Urban League. Johnson was a lawyer, widely recognized in both black and white communities as one of the most effective leaders in the area. He was later elected to an at-large seat on the Consolidated Government Council, and still holds that seat. Dr. W.W. Schell, vice president of Greater Jacksonville Economic Opportunity and president emeritus of the Jacksonville Urban League, headed a group of blacks for consolidation in which Ms. Mathis served as treasurer, and Wendell Holmes, later elected to the School Board, served as secretary.

Black opposition was largely composed of old-line black leaders satisfied with the status quo, many of whom had been active in support of former Mayor Hayden Burns' political organization. A different kind of opposition came from Ms. Mary Singleton, an educator who operated a restaurant. She took the position that consolidation was a white move to dilute black political power. Blacks in the old city constituted about 40 percent of the vote, a figure that would drop to about 20 percent with consolidation. Ms. Singleton was later elected to the Consolidated Government Council and in 1972 was elected to the State Legislature.10

Probably the most optimistic supporter of consolidation failed to anticipate the size of the victory in the August 8, 1967, balloting. Of the 86,000 voters who went to the polls, over 54,000 voted in favor of consolidation. Every section of the county favored the proposal, even the small municipalities, which opted in a separate ballot to stay out of the new government.

Only the rural sections of the county favored the status quo. In the old city, consolidation proponents won by more than two to one. In the county, the margin was almost two to one in favor. Blacks in both the city and the county favored consolidation, though by narrower margins than the overall vote. Upper income voters supported the change by five to one; the issue carried among lower income voters, but by a narrow margin in the county, more comfortably in the city. Voters in the densely populated urban fringe around the old city gave the heaviest majorities to consolidation—six to one.[11]

The question remains why Jacksonville citizens went against the tide and approved a radical restructuring of their local government, providing in one sweeping change the machinery for a unified, regional approach to urban problems. Some factors that built support have been named. The school crisis and the inability of either the city or county governments to keep up with service demands surely were a factor. Strong media, business, and professional leadership was undoubtedly important. But most of these conditions had been present in many other metropolitan areas that were unsuccessful in attempting to change their local government. Was there a multiplier factor in Jacksonville to put the issue over the top? The answer is yes. The indictment of two out of five city commissioners; four out of nine city councilmen, the city auditor, the city recreation head, and the resignation of the city tax assessor under a cloud provided the extra added ingredient needed to mobilize and sustain public support of change. In short, things seemed to have sunk so low that almost any change would have been welcome. The grand jury began its work in May 1966, after television station WJXT launched a series of exposures pointing toward various kinds of corruption in city government. By the time the Local Government Study Commission released its findings, counts of grand larceny, bribery, and perjury had been brought against no less than eight city officials.[12]

Organizational and Fiscal Structure

The Local Government Study Commission recommended a fully consolidated government, excepting only the School Board, which the commission lacked authority to change, certain court officials mandated by state law, and several authorities.

With regard to the authorities, the study commission recommended that the Expressway, Port, and Planning Authorities continue, and also proposed a new authority, the Jacksonville Electric Authority, in place of an old department of city government. The study commission recommended that the Air Improvement Authority, the Housing Authority, and the Hospital

Authority be abolished. The recommendation was not followed in the case of the Hospital Authority. The boundaries of all these authorities were county-wide. The authorities and the School Board were subject to budget, purchasing, personnel, and other central service powers of the Consolidated Government. As enacted, all the small municipalities were given the option of coming in or staying out of the consolidation. Though not a complete consolidation, the new government still represented a sweeping move from fragmentation to unification.

The major fiscal feature of the new government was a differentiated property tax arrangement featuring an Urban Services District (USD) and a General Services District, the latter covering the entire area. The purpose was to promote an equitable property tax system, linking services to property taxes paid. The great bulk of all services provided by the city fell into the General Services District category, including such things as fire, police, health and welfare, recreation, public works, and housing and urban development. The Urban Services District was confined to street lighting, garbage, street cleaning, and debt service. The charter provided that no new USD could be established, nor could an existing one be expanded, unless all these services could be furnished within one year. The old city of Jacksonville and the four smaller municipalities constitute the five Urban Services Districts established to date. Some of the peculiar aspects of the USD system with regard to the smaller municipalities will be discussed below.

One striking feature of the new fiscal system was that a large part of total spending takes place in agencies not wholly within the control of the Consolidated Government. A financial summary for 1971-72 shows, in a budget of almost $286 million, 34.6 cents of every dollar is spent by the School Board, 21 cents by the Jacksonville Electric Authority, and varying lesser amounts by other authorities. Thus, about two-thirds of total spending in the City of Jacksonville is carried out by independent agencies subject to little control from the Consolidated Government. Furthermore, a substantial part of the General Services District funds are expended by elected administrators such as the sheriff. Thus, the effectiveness of the City of Jacksonville as a unified government may depend on how meaningful the budget control powers of the mayor and the city council are (or can be made to be) over independent agencies.

Performance: An Assessment

All local government structural and functional changes tend to be promoted, and often oversold, on the grounds that major economies and efficiencies will occur because of the proposed change. This has been especially true of consolidation proposals. The "Blueprint for Improvement" did stress economy through eliminating duplication, although some care was taken to link the quality and quantity of services to the economy and efficiency claims. The question remains: Has the Consolidated Government of Jacksonville yielded major savings in service costs for the people of Jacksonville?

The question must be answered against a background of at least 20 years of neglect in meeting many basic service needs of the area. A Consolidated Government special report, issued after two years of operation, did not overstate the problem when it noted that "prior to Consolidated Government, Jacksonville was a community in crisis with disaccredited schools, indicted public officials, inefficient and wasteful local governments, disgraceful pollution and innumerable other problems with no hope of solution."[13] Against this background, the accomplishments of the new government in expanding services to areas that had never had them, especially the suburbs, is impressive; old programs have been upgraded, some drastically; new programs have been launched. Expanded service has cost more money. The always sensitive property tax rate declined slightly in each of the first three years of consolidated government, from 31.98 mills in 1968 to 29.72 mills in 1970. The rate in the three years prior to consolidation had ranged from 40.58 to 41.85 mills. The cost to an average taxpayer owning a $15,000 home declined almost $60 per year even after accounting for increased service charges on water and the imposition of a sewer charge. Taxpayers in both the former county and the former city benefited.

If taxes have been reduced while services were improved, where has the money come from? The question cannot be given a definitive answer, but several sources are obvious. The Consolidated Government has maintained an aggressive program of attracting Federal funds. The lower millage rates have produced more property tax dollars as the tax roll has risen, from $1.7 billion in 1968 to $2.5 billion in 1971. Some increases in State funds have been realized. For instance, the establishment of the entire county as a city qualified the Consolidated Government for additional cigarette tax aid amounting to some $2 million in the first year.

An examination of new services and improved quantity and quality of old services will help clarify the picture. A comparative study of old and new government programs, revenues, and expenditures completed by in-house staff in 1971 gives some basis for assessment. The study compared the last year of the old city and county governments (1968) with Consolidated Government revenues and expenditures in 1969, 1970, and 1971. The figures include all general government funds, but exclude agencies such as the school system and authorities. Over this period spending rose from $56.2 million in the last year of the old government to $57.6 million in 1969; rose to $73.2 million in 1970, and increased further to a budgeted figure of $80.2 million in 1971. Thus, spending rose most sharply in the second year (21.4 percent) and increased 8.8 percent in the third year. Where and why did the increases occur?

Almost $8 million of the total $24 million increase took place in new programs, the largest single category being urban renewal and other Federal program areas. A widely praised new service was a Rescue Service System that in 1970 handled over 18,000 patients with an average response time of 4.2 minutes. The added cost was $600,000. A street lighting program, mainly benefiting the suburbs, had added almost 8,000 street lights by 1970, with 9,000 additional lights projected for 1971. The added cost was $700,000.

Major increases in existing programs included the addition of over 200 firemen that allowed staffing all formerly volunteer fire departments in the old county with at least two full-time firemen; some 200 additional police, allowing a drastic upgrading of police service in the suburbs; and a complete overhaul of the child services program where children had been "kept in a condition of filth, abuse, neglect, and apathy."[14] These and other improvements in the quality of programs were estimated to total over $13 million by 1970.[15]

In specific examples of saving, one report cited "nearly a half-million dollars saved through Central Services purchasing of patrol cars."[16] A special study of savings brought about by having all agencies use the Legal Division of the Consolidated Government showed total government legal expenses dropping from $576,586 in 1966-1967 to $494,967 in 1970-1971. The head of the Legal Division commented that "the real value of the Legal Division has been its ability to provide coordination and liaison between agencies . . . and to provide full-time career legal talent whose sole responsibility is to the taxpayers."[17] It was further noted that the cost reductions came in the face of a significant increase in duties. An added area of dramatic savings cited was in validation and approval of over $100 million in bonds, where costs were cut to less than half those of pre-consolidation days.[18] Improved investment practices, which raised the percentage of city funds invested to 96.2 percent, increased such earnings by over $800,000, of which $600,000 was attributable to better investment practices.[19]

The picture that emerges from this assessment is one in which costs did in fact go up after consolidation, but the quality and quantity of services to the public was substantially increased. The suburbs benefited especially from better fire and police protection and the equalization of utility rates. A major water and sewer program also promised large benefits in the future. For the old central city, the first priority in the sewer program was to reconstruct collapsing lines in the old city areas. By 1972 that program was complete. Consumers benefited from a new Division of Consumer Affairs that handled over 11,000 complaints in 1971. Recreation programs have been expanded, largely with Federal funds. The Consolidated Government seems to be moving on many fronts to launch new and upgrade old services, with tangible and substantial benefits to central city and suburb, black and white, and to the region as a whole.

The Limits of Consolidation

The favorable consolidation vote in 1967 abolished the old county and city governments, but it did not produce complete consolidation in the strict sense of that term. The several categories of governmental units with some degree of independence from the Consolidated Government include: (1) elected administrators (sheriff, tax assessor, tax collector, supervisor of elections, and county clerk); (2) the small cities (Jacksonville Beach, Neptune Beach, Atlantic Beach, and Baldwin); (3) authorities (electric authority, Port Authority, Hospital Authority, Beaches Public Hospital Board); (4) the School Board; (5) the Area Planning Board; (6) the Civil Service Board; and (7) Federally encouraged areawide agencies in areas such as health, poverty, and crime. None of these units are completely independent of the Consolidated Government, but neither are they subject to its full control.

The elected administrators' independence has been substantially curtailed, in that they are subject to budget control by the mayor, and must operate through the Department of Central Services in purchasing, personnel, and legal services. A study of the effect of the election of these administrators on the operations of the Consolidated Government revealed little or no operating problems between the mayor and the elected administrators. However, both the study and most of the city councilmen and administrators interviewed for this study felt that the elected status interfered seriously with efforts to pinpoint responsibility and accountability. In addition, there was a widespread feeling that the lack of friction and operating difficulties to date was due largely to the eagerness of both the mayor and the elected administrators to get along, and that the potential for operating difficulties is always there. This concern was expressed with special emphasis regarding the law enforcement function, where the mayor has the responsibility, at least in the eyes of the people, but does not have operating control over the elected sheriff.[20]

The former small cities, technically Urban Services Districts under the new charter, were seen by most Consolidated Government officials as a minor irritant that sooner or later should be removed in the process of perfecting the consolidation plan. The cities offer not only Urban Services District functions such as garbage collection and street lighting within their boundaries, but have to date continued to offer General Services District functions such as fire and police. Since they are restricted by the Consolidated Government to the USD millage rate of 6 mills, they pressed for the right to levy a full 10 mills, as other Florida cities do. This was refused by the Consolidated Government, but it has agreed to a kind of revenue sharing system in which money is given to Urban Services Districts two through five (the former small cities) to compensate them for General Services District functions they perform within their boundaries. The Consolidated City stands ready to take over these services at any time, but has not forced the issue. The small cities are clearly a source of irritation and discontent for the central government. However, their total population and budgets constitute only about five percent of the total, and fiscal pressures seem to be moving them more and more into the orbit of the Consolidated Government.

The independent authorities constitute a different, and perhaps in some ways more serious, limitation on the power of the Consolidated Government. On the positive side, several persons interviewed defended the authorities on the familiar grounds that they are performing "business-like" functions that demand flexibility and imagination that might not be present if they were a regular department of the city. Conventional wisdom has it that such functions as the production and distribution of electricity, or the operation of a transit system, is hampered by the inflexible bureaucracy assumed to be characteristic of regular departments. On the negative side, others felt that the authorities constitute a fragmentation that weakens the effectiveness of the new government, and support their abolition. In operational terms, there have been problems of coordination, but none that seem major. One example was cited by the head of the Department of Housing and Urban Development, whose department had not been consulted in Downtown Development Authority plans for reshaping the central city. The two agencies were thus deeply involved in planning major changes in the same area without effective coordination. In addition, the mere existence of authorities sets up a constant tug-of-war between the authorities and the Consolidated Government as the authorities press for more autonomy and the Consolidated Government for less.

One thoughtful assessment of the authorities from a man who generally favors them stressed the need for strong mechanisms to coordinate their programs with the rest of the Consolidated Government. He cited the following controls as necessary to keep them in orbit: (a) full use of the mayor's appointment and the council's confirming power; (b) making them fully subject to central services controls in the budget, personnel, and purchasing areas; (c) strong budget review by the council; and (d) a firm requirement that all their activities should be reviewed and approved or rejected in the light of an overall development plan. This student of the Consolidated Government felt that where there was one Consolidated Government, authorities could be kept in line.

While at least one top staff member and some council members feel strongly that the authorities should be converted to regular departments, or at least drawn more tightly into the fabric of the Consolidated Government, there seems to be limited support for such a move. Legislative delegation backing of such a move, critical to its support, is not in evidence. In terms of the greater (multi-county) region, there has been no link-up as yet between the authorities and the emerging council of governments.

The School Board might be thought of as a special authority with an elected board. It uses the Department of Central Services, and it is subject to Consolidated Government review of its budget. Given the fierce independence of school districts generally, even this much control was no small achievement. The Civil Service Board has been forcefully condemned as unsound by almost every person interviewed in or out of the new government structure. It has been called "the worst compromise we made" by one observer. Several feel that its elected status and full range of personnel powers make true management responsibility impossible in the personnel area. The general recommendation is that it be an appointed board with strictly advisory powers, with the personnel function turned over to management. Every top administrator interviewed stressed the difficulty of weeding out decades of deadwood, given the resistence to such efforts by the elected Civil Service Board. Finally, the Jacksonville Area Planning Board operates more or less as an independent authority, with board members appointed by the mayor. A recent management efficiency study recommended that the planning function come under a regular department, abolishing the independent Area Planning Board.

A variety of Federally encouraged districts exist in the Jacksonville area, some with countywide and some with multi-county jurisdiction. Whatever their functional merits may be, they add an element of further fragmentation to the consolidation picture. Law enforcement, health, manpower, and community improvement agencies are included in the list.

The Law Enforcement Regional Planning Council originally encompassed a seven-county region, but more recently, one-county metropolitan regions have been substituted in several of the State's metropolitan counties, including Jacksonville. The governor appoints these boards, and the effort under Governor Reuben Askew has been to broaden the representation on the board from a former heavy emphasis on police chiefs and sheriffs. Bureaucratic inertia often approaching the paralysis level has characterized the program statewide. Jacksonville has probably fared better than most areas, with some 36 projects funded, but the problem of effective coordination with the Consolidated Government remains.

In the area of health planning the Community Health Facilities Planning Council has been designated by the State for Hill-Burton Act "sign-off" authority. It operates outside either the Consolidated Government or the Area Planning Board, and the mayor enjoys no appointment power with regard to it. One highly placed Consolidated Government official felt that the council had not done a good job of setting community health priorities, partly because of internal disputes and conflicts that seem to characterize its functioning.

The Manpower Planning Council, appointed by the mayor with countywide responsibilities, operates out of the mayor's office, so it does not constitute a coordination problem. It has had very few operating dollars other than Emergency Employment Act funds.

The community action programs are controlled by a 45-person board made up of one-third public officials, one-third poor, and one-third citizen members. The CAP program involves some $7 million annually and 400 employees. Coordination problems with such Consolidated Government agencies as the Housing and Urban Development agency exist, although the City of Jacksonville has some input through the one-third public official members.

The existence of the Federally encouraged and typically single-function agencies just described do tend to further limit the inclusive authority and responsibility of the Consolidated Government. They are in that sense typical of the host of catagorical grants-in-aid programs that have generated in recent years increasing objections to the resulting "vertical functional autocracies" that, whatever else their merit may be, weaken the capability of governments of general jurisdiction to allocate scarce resources within a comprehensive planning and implementing framework.

In assessing the limits of consolidation, it is first clear that Jacksonville is not a case of pure unified government. There is still some fragmentation involved. At least up to now, this fragmentation has not been a serious handicap in the operations of government. All units are subject to some degree of control by the Consolidated Government. Yet the problems, immediate or potential, are viewed as serious enough by most of those interviewed so as to call for further tightening of the consolidation plan.

The Emerging Political System

The abrupt and far-reaching structural changes accomplished in Jacksonville also brought abrupt and far-reaching changes in the political system. First and perhaps obvious, the old leaders of the pre-consolidation days, thoroughly discredited by the grand jury findings, for the most part lost their power and have not come close to regaining it. Hayden Burns was a symbol for the old-style politics, in which he headed a political organization that, in the eyes of many, assured corrupt and inefficient government for the area. The reform fervor swept in a different breed of politician, personified by the new mayor, Hans Tanzler. Tanzler was viewed by every person interviewed as a good mayor. His own view of his political style conforms essentially to the assessment of others interviewed. Tanzler noted that he was not a good politician in the old "boss politics" sense. He has not made patronage appointments; he has not built up a political machine, nor made any effort to do so. His style is essentially one of a non-partisan approach in which he goes to the people through the media for support on key issues.

The mayor is not without his critics, but they are for the most part friendly critics. The strongest criticism concerned his lack of forcefulness as an administrative leader. Some also felt he was not aggressive enough as a policy leader. Yet these same critics admitted that he had tackled some tough, potentially unpopular issues, such as the need for a sewer fee to help support a pollution control program. One thread of criticism picked up at several points concerned the mayor's unwillingness to use his political clout to pull together more forcefully the threads of administrative fragmentation discussed above.

The 19-person council in the Consolidated Government has had forceful leadership of its own, rather than simply the lead of the mayor to follow. The mayor does not seem to have an identifiable working majority that cuts across issues; he must put his majority together on each succeeding policy matter. Every person interviewed, including five incumbent council members, like the mixed at-large/district arrangement. The single exception was a black council member who would prefer all district elections. The feature most often mentioned by council members and others as helping the council perform effectively was the council's auditor. This office has functioned with a small staff to give the council the background on which to base policy/administrative initiative.

The place of blacks in the post-consolidation political system is viewed by both black and white leaders as a vast improvement over pre-consolidation days. A black leader and council member who opposed consolidation on the grounds that its central purpose was to dilute the power of blacks in the old city now feels that it has not had that effect. She feels that "blacks have more political power than ever before under consolidation." She noted, as did others black and white, the sharp increase in jobs for blacks under consolidation. Blacks have been added to the fire department for the first time, and more blacks have been recruited in the law enforcement area. All leaders interviewed stressed the great success in drawing blacks into the political system by appointing at least one black to every advisory board.

On the always delicate subject of blacks and law enforcement, one black leader held that while the sheriff was a good person, blacks felt that he was not a strong leader, did not really run the department, and thus left many things to racist old-regime law enforcement officers. Many blacks, including the two interviewed, would support the appointment of the sheriff so that he could be controlled by the mayor, who is perceived as a strong friend of blacks. A current cooperative effort between the Urban League and the sheriff to recruit more black policemen was praised by both black leaders interviewed.

The black council member elected at large felt that blacks definitely have had a greater input under consolidation. His view was that blacks struck a bargain in supporting consolidation by "opting for representation now rather than waiting to get the whole central city." He noted that if the latter course of action had been chosen, "I might have been the black mayor, but I would have been only a referee in bankruptcy." This same black leader felt that leadership generally among blacks was getting stronger, and viewed the political future of blacks under the Consolidated Government as good.

The single problem with regard to the political system in the eyes of most Consolidated Government supporters interviewed was the area's legislative delegation. In Florida, local bills put through the legislature by a local delegation can often override local home rule powers. Consolidation supporters expressed the view that the Duval area delegation did not fully understand and often were not sympathetic to the Consolidated Government. This in turn meant that discordant elements such as the small cities had a potential ally in attempting to weaken the power of the Consolidated Government. It was also widely felt that lack of understanding and sympathy prevented further strengthening of the new government.[21]

The Jacksonville SMSA is surrounded by small, rural- and small-town-oriented counties that at first glance have little in common with the Jacksonville "giant." Very little urban development lies outside the boundaries of the new city, so the region in terms of dense urban development is almost wholly encompassed within the new city. In spite of this, there has been action to extend the scope of the region on a voluntary basis by forming a council of governments in the area. Mayor Tanzler has supported the move, but the chief architect of the Florida Crown Conference of Local Governments is Walter Williams, a councilman from the small town of Baldwin, in the western, rurally oriented part of the City of Jacksonville. All eight counties in the area around Jacksonville have joined. The board of directors consists of sixteen members: each county commission selects one representative, while the cities within each county designate one member to represent them.

Intergovernmental Cooperation

Williams stressed the delicate problem of constantly assuring the neighboring cities and counties that consolidation had nothing to do with the COG effort. He reported that the interest of the smaller counties and cities stemmed from their growing concern about slipshod development as Jacksonville tightens its zoning, subdivision, and building codes. Regional planning and an A-95 review process have been discussed, with considerable sentiment in favor of such a move. The main program to date is a regional emergency medical system which extends the excellent Jacksonville system to the surrounding areas in the Gold Crown COG. This regional emergency health program has received Federal support in the form of a $3 million grant. Telephone consulting services for doctors in the rural and small-town areas, and fast, efficient movement of patients from such areas to the Jacksonville Medical Center, are part of the operation. The Florida Crown Conference is just beginning, but it does signal a broadening of the regional outlook from the one-county SMSA to an eight-county region. As the Jacksonville metropolitan area continues to grow into the surrounding counties, the importance of the COG will increase. The A-95 review process has been confined to the City of Jacksonville, and until very recently very little has been done to use it effectively as a coordinating planning tool. Persistent pressure from the mayor's office on the semi-autonomous Area Planning Board to use the A-95 review process more effectively as a management tool finally resulted in a strengthening of the process during the last six months of 1972. The use of the review and comment power up to that point had been virtually dormant.

A parallel, and probably more significant, development has the potential for major strengthening of intergovernmental coordination in the Jacksonville area. A Federal chief executive review and comment grant will support an expanded staff in the mayor's office for review and comment on all aid proposals from local governments to Federal, State, or other sources. Thus, the authority of this new unit is much broader than the A-95 review powers. The extent to which the Federally encouraged areawide agencies such as CAP will be drawn into this review process is not yet clear, nor is the exact relationship between the mayor's office review and comment activity and the parallel A-95 responsibilities of the Area Planning Board.

In the eyes of consolidation leaders in Jacksonville, State and Federal governments are contrasted sharply in assessing support for the Consolidated Government. The opinion of one top Jacksonville administrator is stronger than most, but reflected the general attitude toward the State when he said that "the State has not helped very much; the Department of Community Affairs is hopeless; the LEEP program seems bogged down in bureaucratic impotence; and the State bureaucracy generally is very poor, highhanded, inefficient, and has little concept of the needs of local government." A two-year wait for a State assistance program in the sewer bond area accounted for a good part of the negative attitude toward the State.

The Federal government, on the other hand, was generally viewed as having given strong support to the Consolidated Government. A Federal programs coordinator had been successful in vigorously seeking Federal funds in areas such as housing, urban renewal, and recreation, in sharp contrast to the indifference or hostility toward Federal help that characterized the old government.

Consolidation and the Future

Jacksonville's Consolidated Government met its first clear test of public reaction in 1970 when Mayor Tanzler ran for election against the prime symbol of the old city politics, former Governor Hayden Burns. The new government passed with flying colors, with Tanzler winning by a wide margin. No serious effort to dismantle the new approach has emerged. Only the small cities persist in seeking to regain some or all of their past autonomy, and so far they have not succeeded. There is considerable talk among consolidation supporters about further strengthening the existing structure. The charter provides for the appointment of a charter review committee to recommend needed changes in the Consolidated Government, and such a group is being organized. Several persons interviewed thought the committee would give high priority to considering (a) how to bring the former small cities more fully into the consolidation scheme; (b) how to tighten Consolidated Government control over the independent agencies and offices; and (c) how to alter the role of the Civil Service Board so as to provide for a vigorous, positive approach to personnel administration. All three considerations promise to be highly controversial.

NOTES

1. The statistics for this section are taken from Local Government Study Commission of Duval County, *Blueprint for Improvement*, 1966, especially pp. 10-17.
2. Richard A. Martin, *Consolidation: Jacksonville-Duval County*, Jacksonville: Crawford Publishing Co., 1968, p. 39.
3. Martin, pp. 39-40.
4. Martin, pp. 44-45.
5. The authorities that were continued from the old to the new government included the Expressway Authority, the Hospital Authority, the Port Authority, and the Area Planning Board. In addition, the new Jacksonville Electric Authority was created. The Expressway Authority was later broadened to a Transportation Authority.
6. Martin, p. 68.
7. Martin, Chapter 6.
8. Martin, Chapter 6, especially pp. 123-134.
9. Martin, Chapters 7, 8, and 9.
10. Martin, Chapter 7.
11. Martin, pp. 224-26.
12. Martin, Chapter 4.
13. City of Jacksonville, Department of Central Services, *Bold View*, Vol. 3, No. 1, March, 1971, p. 7.
14. Consolidated Jacksonville In-House Memo, December, 1970.
15. In-House Comparative Study, 19.
16. *Bold View*, March, 1971, p. 21.
17. Annual Report, Legal Division, Exhibit B, 1970-71.
18. Annual Report, Legal Division.
19. In-House Memo, Investment of Funds, December, 1969.
20. William D. Talbot, *The Impact of Independently Elected Officials on Jacksonville, Florida's Consolidated Government*, Unpublished Master's Thesis (Florida Atlantic University, 1971).
21. A preliminary assessment of changes in the delegation resulting from the November 1972 elections indicate that the new delegation will be much more friendly to the Consolidated Government than the old delegation.

Introduction

The most famous and most successful metropolitan government ever created became a reality in 1954 in the Canadian province of Ontario. Unlike the American political system, which requires a public referendum or voter approval before a METRO can be formed, Canadian provinces can simply mandate the creation of a METRO by enacting appropriate legislation. While this system is certainly less democratic than the one used in the United States, it has the obvious advantage of expediting the creation of a METRO, while preventing organized interest groups from actively seeking to develop obstacles that would impede governmental reform.

Prior to the creation of the metropolitan wide government in 1954, the Toronto region consisted of thirteen separate municipalities, each continuing on in their own way in the provision of local government services. While their bureaucracies developed in thirteen different directions with virtually no coordination, they were alike in one important respect. Without exception, each was experiencing an increasing degeneration or breakdown of functional services approaching crisis proportions.

*When the METRO was formed, it was decided by the Ontario Municipal Board that all thirteen municipalities should be consolidated into one larger form of government. This newly consolidated government would, however, be federated—in other words, there would be two tiers or two levels of government. METRO's residents would thereafter receive certain public services of an area-wide nature (air pollution abatement, property assessment, regional parks, subways, expressways, etc.) from the top or central tier of the METRO, and other services would be administered by the lower, or **borough** level (after 1966)—services such as local road repair, garbage collection, fire protection, local recreation programs, etc.*

That the rest of the world has paid homage to METRO Toronto's incredible record of success is evidenced by constant repetition of the supreme compliment—cities all over the globe have sent study teams to Toronto for extended periods of time to see "what they've done right. . . ."

THE METROPOLITAN
TORONTO EXPERIENCE

Research and Policy Committee, C.E.D.

The Municipality of Metropolitan Toronto, with a population of more than 2,000,000, is the focal point of one of North America's most economically vital regions. Metropolitan Toronto contains almost 10 percent of the total population of Canada, and its 241 square miles contain approximately 11 percent of all Canadian employment. While, in terms of population, it is not of the magnitude of a New York or Los Angeles, Metropolitan Toronto does approximate the size of a Cleveland, Pittsburgh, or St. Louis. In fact, today it is one of the 20 most populous urban areas in North America.

Metropolitan Toronto has been termed a "boom town" and rightly so. The population of the metropolitan area has grown by about 75 percent in the last 15 years, and the increases of nearly 55,000 persons per year represent an annual growth rate of over 4 percent, one of the highest such rates among major metropolitan areas on the continent. Most of this development in the past several years has taken place in three large suburban municipalities—Etobicoke, North York, and Scarborough. In 1953, the City of Toronto had 57 percent of the total population in the metropolitan area compared with 43 percent in the suburbs. By 1969 the situation was reversed; the city had only 35 percent of the total metropolitan population and the suburbs 65 percent. During this period, Etobicoke's percentage increased from 6 percent to 14 percent, Scarborough's from 7 percent to 15 percent, and North York's from 9 percent to 23 percent.

This remarkable growth has not occurred without its problems and crises. Yet such matters are not unique to this area but rather are indicative of the problems associated with urban growth and expansion now facing *most* urban areas in North America. However, the approach to dealing adequately with these problems *is* unique. Indeed, it represents a major breakthrough in governmental structure. Hopefully, the Toronto ex-

Committee for Economic Development, *Reshaping Government in Metropolitan Areas,* "The Metropolitan Toronto Experience," pages 70-83. New York, 1970.

perience—modified to suit the needs of individual areas—can serve as a guide to metropolitan governmental reform in the United States.

THE TORONTO REGION:
ITS EVOLUTION AND DEVELOPMENT

As the population of the Toronto region grew during the last half of the 19th century, many small towns and villages developed outside the city proper but in close proximity to it. The city met this urban expansion on its borders in a customary fashion—by annexing these suburbs. Beginning in 1883 there was an annexation every few years of one of these suburbs. This procedure of absorbing adjacent areas continued almost unabated until the start of World War I.

In 1928, the Toronto City Council enunciated its unwritten policy which had existed since 1914: that there would be no further annexations of suburban lands. This announcement heralded a new type of political development on the urban fringes; for as areas contiguous to the City of Toronto became urban in character, they did not look forward, as they once did, to annexation by the city. Instead they developed their own municipal structures. By 1930 there were 13 independent and separate municipalities in the Toronto area—the central city (Toronto), five townships (York, North York, East York, Etobicoke, Scarborough), four towns (Leaside, Weston, Mimico, New Toronto), and three villages (Forest Hill, Long Branch, Swansea).

During the period of the 1930s, 1940s, and early 1950s, the 13 municipalities, while in close proximity to one another, went their separate ways with but a few exceptions. However, rapid growth and development, which was occurring particularly in the suburbs, affected all. The whole metropolitan area grew haphazardly with the suburban population growing almost five-fold in 20 years. With no comprehensive regional development plan, each municipality sought to provide development geared to a locally conceived plan.

Indeed, the area exhibited most of the now all-too-familiar urban problems facing North American metropolitan areas today. These include: (a) an inability to plan regionally because of governmental fragmentation; (b) the inadequacy of water and sewage facilities for a burgeoning population; (c) the inability to develop modern coordinated public transportation systems; (d) the inability of individual jurisdictions to finance reasonably major projects and programs; and (e) problems dealing with all aspects of the urban environment from the provision of education to the prevention of pollution.

It was plain that in order for the municipal governments in the Metropolitan Toronto area to function effectively a different form of governmental organization would be required.

METROPOLITAN GOVERNMENT—PHASE I

In 1947, the Province of Ontario's first Minister of Planning and Development (now Minister of Municipal Affairs) established the Toronto and Suburban Planning Board. It was the responsibility of this Board to study the problems of water supply, sewage disposal, transportation, the provision of education on an equitable basis, and the establishment of parklands in the Toronto area. Under the chairmanship of Frederick G. Gardiner, this Board (subsequently renamed the Toronto and York Planning Board) issued a report in 1949 recommending the progressive amalgamation of the 13 municipalities.

Two years earlier, in 1947, the Town of Mimico had applied to the Ontario Municipal Board[1] for the creation of a board to administer throughout the area of the 13 municipalities many of the basic public services which were inter-municipal in character. This application would have maintained the separate identity of the 13 established municipalities.

While the Mimico application was before the O.M.B., the City of Toronto adopted the recommendation of the Toronto and York Planning Board and applied to the Ontario Municipal Board for an order that the 13 municipalities be progressively amalgamated into one municipality. This application was supported by the Town of Mimico, but it suggested that, should Toronto's application be refused, its own application should be considered. The other 11 municipalities opposed Toronto's application in extensive hearings held before the Ontario Municipal Board under the chairmanship of Lorne R. Cumming.

The Cumming Report

After over two years of taking evidence and deliberating, the O.M.B. handed down its decision on January 20, 1953. The landmark decision, known as the Cumming Report, recommended a federal system of government for the Toronto area. It advocated a federation of the 13 municipalities, each retaining its local autonomy while passing over to the metropolitan government the responsibility for major regional services and other matters of common concern.

Shortly after the release of the Cumming Report, a bill to institute the recommendations of the report was introduced in the Ontario Legislature by the Prime Minister of the Province of Ontario. In this way the provincial government threw its full support behind the proposal for a metropolitan government. Less than three months later, on April 15, 1953, the Ontario Legislature passed "Bill 80" or the Municipality of Metropolitan Toronto Act. The first urban federation in North America came into being on January 1, 1954.

Metropolitan Council

The Metropolitan Council was composed of 24 members (exclusive of the Chairman), 12 from the city and 12 from the suburbs, with all committees being similarly balanced. Members of the Metropolitan Council were not elected directly but rather derived their seats by virtue of holding elective office in their own municipalities. The Council was to elect annually a Chairman who might or might not be an elected representative of a municipality. However, the province appointed the first Chairman, Frederick G. Gardiner.

Shared Powers and Responsibilities

The Metropolitan Corporation—established by the 1953 legislation—and its various departments, boards, and commissions were set up to provide those basic services which transcended the boundaries of the individual municipalities. The area municipalities, however, retained the responsibility for local services and facilities. The extent and quality of these services, within limits, were left to the discretion of the local councils.

Powers over certain functions were retained exclusively by the metropolitan government. These included assessment of property, construction and maintenance of expressways, and the development of regional parks. Other powers pertaining primarily to local matters, such as street lighting and community centers, were reserved entirely to the municipalities. The form of departmental organization, size of staff, and amount of expenditure per capita varied widely from one municipality to another, reflecting the basic autonomy of local government operations within the metropolitan framework. But for almost every metropolitan service, such as roads, water supply, sewage disposal, parks, and traffic control, the powers were shared, with the metropolitan government concentrating on the areawide needs and the individual municipalities on their own requirements. This interrelationship is best illustrated by examining the division of powers between the local municipalities and the metropolitan government with respect to specific functions.

Finance. The operation of the metropolitan government is based on the pooling of the financial resources of the area municipalities through a system of metropolitan assessment and taxation. The Metropolitan Corporation annually levies its requirements for funds on the basis of each municipality's share of the total assessment of the metropolitan area. However, the Metropolitan Corporation has no power to collect taxes directly and thus the metropolitan levy and those of the metropolitan and local school boards are included in the local tax bill collected by each municipality. Conversely, the local municipalities do not have the power to borrow money directly. As a result, their requirements for debenture financing are submitted to the

Metropolitan Council, which determines the total amount of money to be borrowed for local purposes each year and the proportion to be allocated to each municipality. Thus, all debentures are issued by the Metropolitan Corporation which borrows money on its own account and in behalf of the area municipalities. This means that the local municipalities by themselves no longer face the risks of the money market or shoulder the burden of major inter-municipal projects.

Water Supply. The construction and maintenance of pumping stations, filtration plants, trunk mains, and reservoirs for the wholesale distribution of water to the municipalities is a metropolitan responsibility. The Metropolitan Corporation sells water to the local municipalities on a wholesale basis, while the local distribution systems and the retail of water to consumers remain the responsibility of the local municipalities.

Transportation. The Metropolitan Corporation assumed jurisdiction over all major roads and established an arterial system of highways. The local municipalities continued to maintain minor collectors and local roads in their respective areas. With assumption of the arterial system, the metropolitan government has been able to institute an areawide traffic control system which is one of the most advanced in North America and which has yielded significant results in terms of greater safety and more efficient traffic flows. All public transit (except trains, planes, and taxis) in the metropolitan area is operated by the Toronto Transit Commission, whose members are appointed by the Metropolitan Council. The public transit system comprises an integrated network of subway, street car, and bus lines which carries over one million passengers on an average weekday.

Planning. The control of development of the area in and adjacent to Metropolitan Toronto was deemed of such importance that the province in the Metropolitan Toronto Act established the Metropolitan Toronto Planning Area, containing 720 square miles and comprising the 13 municipalities in Metropolitan Toronto and 13 surrounding municipalities. In this way it was felt that the Metropolitan Planning Board could guide development on a rational regional scale. The Planning Board was to study matters relating to the development of the area, to prepare an official plan, to advise the Metropolitan Council and other area councils, and to provide public information. Under the legislation, the preparation of official plans and subdivision control were shared responsibilities; zoning (except adjacent to metropolitan roads), redevelopment, land division, and building bylaws were reserved to the local municipalities. The Metropolitan Planning Board also has been concerned with the maintenance of basic planning standards and principles considered to be of areawide significance.

Additional Responsibilities

Since its formation, the metropolitan government has extended its jurisdiction into fields not covered in the original 1953 legislation.

Police. In 1957, the 13 area police forces were amalgamated into one metropolitan force. Earlier, the individual municipalities operated their own police forces, which varied greatly in terms of the number of officers, the area served, and the ratio of officers to residents. In addition, there was no central communications system to facilitate coordination among different police forces.

Today the Metropolitan Police Department is organized into five districts which cover the metropolitan area with no regard for local boundaries. This has eliminated artificial service areas and has aided in the integration of communications systems and the standardization of regulations and procedures.

Licensing. The Metropolitan Licensing Commission was created in 1957 to establish areawide standards and regulations for a variety of trades and services that had previously been licensed separately by the individual area municipalities. Earlier, licensing regulations had varied widely within the area, and not all the local municipalities had licensing boards. Fees also had varied widely across the metropolitan area. Today the Commission controls the licensing of some 90 different activities.

METROPOLITAN GOVERNMENT—PHASE II

During the first ten years of its existence the metropolitan government was the subject of both praise and criticism. One point of contention rested on the fact that although the 12 suburban municipalities varied greatly in terms of population—Weston had some 10,000 persons while North York had 360,000—they each had only one representative on the Metropolitan Council. The need for a complete appraisal of the metropolitan system appeared in order. Thus, in April 1963, Prime Minister Robarts of Ontario announced the appointment of a one-man Royal Commission, under the chairmanship of H. Carl Goldenberg, to provide an independent assessment and evaluation of all aspects of the metropolitan federation.

The Goldenberg Report

In June 1965, the Royal Commissioner issued the findings of his two-year inquiry. He had two basic recommendations: (1) that the metropolitan system of government be retained; and (2) that the 13 municipalities be consolidated into four cities. The Goldenberg Report and its recommendations were the subject of considerable discussion and debate. This is reflected in the statement of Prime Minister Robarts on the introduction of the Metropolitan Toronto Amendment Act of 1966:

While the position of the Government may not coincide with the recommendations of Dr. Goldenberg on all points, we accept and endorse the *main principles which he advocates: the continuation of the two-level federated system of Metropolitan Government; the consolidation of constituent municipalities rather than total amalgamation; an increase in the authority and responsibilities of the Government of Metropolitan Toronto; a Metro-wide uniform tax levy to provide a basic education program for the Metropolitan area; and a reform of the system of representation.*2

Although the provincial government accepted certain recommendations of the Goldenberg Report, it modified some and rejected others. Again, the provincial government exercised its prerogative.

The New Metropolitan Government

The final outcome was the Metropolitan Toronto Amendment Act of 1966 (Bill 81) which created, effective January 1, 1967, a new metropolitan government by consolidating the 13 municipalities into five boroughs and one city: the *Borough of East York*—East York, Leaside; the *Borough of North York*—North York; the *Borough of Etobicoke*—Etobicoke, New Toronto, Long Branch, Mimico; the *Borough of Scarborough*—Scarborough; the *Borough of York*—York, Weston; and the *City of Toronto*—Toronto, Forest Hill, Swansea.

Metropolitan Council

In addition, the composition of the Metropolitan Council was altered to provide for a 33-member body, including the Chairman, elected on a representative population basis. East York now has 2 members on the Council; York, 3; Etobicoke, 4; Scarborough, 5; North York, 6; and Toronto, 12. What was once a city-suburban split of 12-12 was altered to a 20-12 division in favor of the suburbs. The policy-recommending body of the Council, its Executive Committee, now consists of the Metropolitan Chairman, the six local municipal mayors, and the two senior controllers and two aldermen from the City of Toronto Council. Thus, in the Executive Committee the even (5-5) division remains. In case of a deadlock the Metropolitan Chairman has the deciding vote. The term of office for these elected officials was also extended from two to three years.

Responsibilities

The new metropolitan government was given several new responsibilities, and some of the functions for which it was already responsible were broadened by the new provincial legislation. Each of the new or expanded functions noted below exemplifies the sharing of power between the local municipalities and the metropolitan government.

Education. Despite an impressive record in providing school accommodation, there were continuing wide disparities in the burden of school costs. Therefore, the basic function of the Metropolitan School Board was altered from providing local boards of education with maintenance payments to providing them, through a metropolitan-wide levy, with funds necessary for a basic metropolitan-wide education program.

Under the new system, the Metropolitan School Board which previously had been equally divided between the city and suburban members, now comprises six representatives from the City School Board, nine from the suburban boards, and three from the Separate School Board. Each of the six local municipalities has retained its own elected board of education which is responsible for administering the local public school system. The Metropolitan School Board is responsible for receiving, altering, approving, or rejecting the operating budgets of the local boards of education; for receiving and distributing all provincial grants for school purposes; and for otherwise raising the money to finance the local school systems through taxation. A local board of education may levy a supplementary school tax on its own municipality to a maximum of 1.5 mills for public school purposes and 1 mill for secondary school purposes.

While the local boards retain autonomy in operating their individual school systems, the Metropolitan School Board exercises certain important functions in addition to its basic responsibility in financial matters. For example, it has the power to set attendance areas, and in this way, problems created by artificial municipal boundaries can be overcome. Moreover, the Metropolitan Board pays the full cost of classes for handicapped children and operates the Metropolitan School for the Deaf.

Welfare. Since a large proportion of the total metropolitan welfare load originated in the City of Toronto, a severe financial burden had been placed on the city. As a result, beginning in 1964, the Metropolitan Corporation voluntarily undertook to pay the local share (20 percent local, 80 percent provincial) of welfare assistance payments while the administration of the programs remained in local hands. This arrangement ensured that the burden of meeting the cost of mandatory welfare programs under provincial legislation would be spread across the metropolitan area, but it left the local municipalities responsible for a variety of optional services. In 1967, public welfare became solely the responsibility of the metropolitan government. This arrangement made it possible officially to provide a more uniform level of service in all parts of the area and helped to ensure that the needs of the inhabitants could be met regardless of their place of residence.

Refuse Collection and Disposal. In 1967, the responsibility for disposal of refuse and industrial wastes was assumed by the Metropolitan Corporation, while leaving collection as a local responsibility.

ACCOMPLISHMENTS
OF THE METROPOLITAN SYSTEM

Metropolitan government has achieved many things in its comparatively short period of operation. Specifically, it has solved the water and sewage problems by the construction of new sewage treatment plants, pumping stations, water filtration plants, and by the installation of many miles of large trunk sewers and trunk watermains. Transportation has also been vastly improved; today there is an integrated system of public and private, rapid and conventional modes of transport. There is now a centralized police force, and a 5,000 acre regional park system is under development. In addition, a metropolitan plan has been adopted to guide regional expansion on a rational basis.

The pooling of financial resources at the metropolitan level has provided a base from which projects, facilities, and programs beneficial to the entire area have been developed. Without this, it would have been impossible to provide for the expansion in services required by the region's growth. Not only has the metropolitan system supplied vast flows of capital funds, but it also has maintained the highest possible rating on Wall Street for foreign municipal bonds. It has been estimated that the resultant lower interest rates meant a saving between 1954 and 1967 of approximately $50 million.[3]

Finally, without doubt, the most important factor in Toronto's success has been the guidance and stimulus provided by the provincial government. Without this catalytic agent it is highly unlikely that the Toronto area would have metropolitan government today.

NOTES

1. The Ontario Municipal Board (O.M.B.) is a quasi-judicial board appointed by the Prime Minister of Ontario to review virtually all aspects of municipal government in the province.
2. *The Telegram*, Toronto, January 10, 1966, p. 9.
3. James Nathan Miller, "Metro: Toronto's Answer to Urban Sprawl," *The Reader's Digest*, August, 1967.

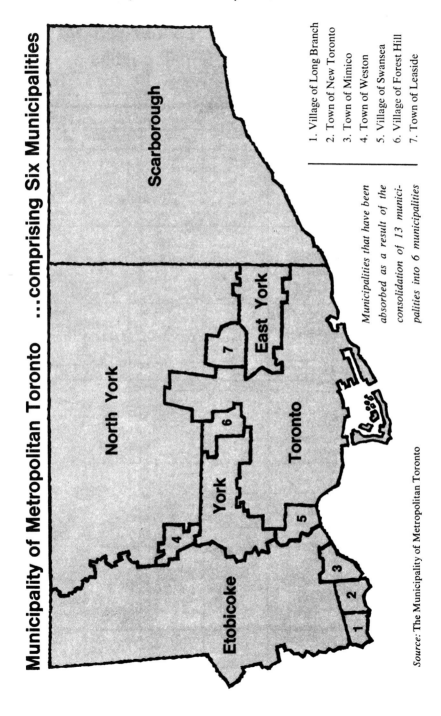

Municipality of Metropolitan Toronto   ...comprising Six Municipalities

Scarborough

North York

East York

Toronto

York

Etobicoke

1. Village of Long Branch
2. Town of New Toronto
3. Town of Mimico
4. Town of Weston
5. Village of Swansea
6. Village of Forest Hill
7. Town of Leaside

Municipalities that have been absorbed as a result of the consolidation of 13 munici- palities into 6 municipalities

Source: The Municipality of Metropolitan Toronto

MUNICIPALITY OF METROPOLITAN TORONTO
COMPRISING SIX MUNICIPALITIES

Municipality	Square Miles	Population		Members on Council
		Persons	Percent	
City of Toronto (City, Swansea, Forest Hill)	37.7	720,000	37	12
Borough of North York (North York)	68.1	475,000	21	6
Borough of Scarborough (Scarborough)	70.0	310,000	15	5
Borough of Etobicoke (Etobicoke, Long Branch, New Toronto, Mimico)	47.9	290,000	14	4
Borough of York (York, Weston)	9.0	150,000	8	3
Borough of East York (East York, Leaside)	8.3	105,000	5	2
Metropolitan Toronto	241.0	2,050,000	100	32

DISTRIBUTION OF RESPONSIBILITY

M—*Municipality of Metropolitan Toronto*
A—*Area Municipalities*

Finance and Taxation

Assessment of property	M
Courts of revision	MA
Taxation of property	A
Debenture borrowing	M
Local improvement charges	A

Planning

Official plans	MA
Subdivision approval	MA
Zoning	A

Recreation/Community Services

Regional parks	M
Local parks	A
Recreation programs	A
Community centres/arenas	A
Municipal golf courses	M
Municipal zoo	M
Regional libraries	M
Local libraries	MA
Grants to cultural societies	MA

Road Construction/Maintenance

Expressways	M
Arterial roads	M
Local roads	A
Bridges and grade separations	MA
Snow removal	MA
Street cleaning	MA
Sidewalks	A

Traffic Control

Traffic regulations	MA
Cross-walks	MA
Traffic lights	M
Street lighting	A
Pavement markings	MA

Public Transit

Toronto Transit Comm.	M

Water Supply

Purification, pumping and trunk distribution system	M
Local distribution	A
Collection of water bills	A

Sewage Disposal

Sanitary trunk system and disposal plants	M
Connecting systems	A
Storm drainage	MA

Garbage Collection and Disposal

Collection	A
Disposal sites	M

Air Pollution

Air pollution control	M

Public Education

Operation of school system	A
School sites, attendance areas, building programs	M
Operating and capital costs	M

Housing

Low rental family housing	M
Elderly person housing	M
Moderate rental family housing	A

Welfare

Welfare assistance	M
Hospitalization of indigents	M
Assistance to Children's Aid Societies	M
Homes for the aged	M

Health

Public health services	A
Chronic and convalescent hospital	M
Hospital grants	A
Ambulance services	M

Police and Fire Protection

Police	M
Fire	A

Administration of Justice

Magistrates' courts	M
Court house and jail	M
Juvenile and family court	M
Coroner's office	M
Registry and land titles offices	M

Licensing and Inspection

Business licensing	M
Dog licensing and pound	A
Marriage licenses	A
Buildings by-laws	A

Civil Defense

Emergency measures	M

Other Municipal Services

Collection of fines	MA
Collection of vital statistics	A
Distribution of hydro power	A
Harbor	A
Island airport	A
Municipal parking lots	A
Preparation of voters' lists and administration of civic elections	A
Redevelopment	MA

Introduction

In the article to follow, the author explores the roles of and interactions among those who are actively involved in the setting and carrying out of regional policy in the San Francisco Bay area. Consequently, the reader is treated to a bird's eye view of a complex yet functioning network of governmental fabric. As such, the San Francisco Bay area exemplifies an extraordinarily imaginative blend of regional experimentation in an area that encompasses four contiguous SMSA's. In short, there exists a uniquely fragmented and highly pluralistic political system.

*When reading **Bay Area Regionalism,** one should focus on the evolving role of the Association of Bay Area Governments (ABAG) toward functioning as a true multipurpose planning and service agency with very real policy-making powers over all local jurisdictions. The reader should then ask the following questions: (1) In either its present or some future form, could ABAG comprise a viable alternative to an actual METRO? (2) Could other Councils of Government follow this pattern of evolution in those SMSA's which remain fragmented?*

BAY AREA REGIONALISM: INSTITUTIONS, PROCESSES, AND PROGRAMS

Victor Jones
Department of Political Science
and
Institute of Governmental Studies
University of California, Berkeley

The Bay Area consists of nine counties touching San Francisco Bay, San Pablo Bay, and Suisun Bay; they are Alameda, Contra Costa, Marin, Sonoma, Napa, San Mateo, Santa Clara, Solano, and San Francisco. The regional population is estimated in 1972 as 4.75 million. The Bay Area is not a compact local community, but a region of four separate SMSA's and many distinct communities spread over 7,000 square miles. There is no single dominating city and the three largest cities—San Francisco, San Jose, and Oakland—are of medium size.[1]

In 1967, there were 562 local governments and 520 of them were authorized to levy property taxes. Among them are the consolidated City and County of San Francisco, eight counties, and 90 cities. Among the special districts are large and powerful regional and sub-regional agencies dealing with fields of highways and transit, liquid waste treatment and disposal, water supply, parks, air pollution, and the conservation and development of the Bay and its shoreline. Also, the State of California and the United States Government are active participants in formulating, and at times directly administering, public policies of regional and local impact. Neither is a single, integrated organization. Each, with a multitude of programs and agencies, is as "fragmented" as local government.

Home rule has been embodied in many constitutional and statutory provisions as well as in long-established practices and understandings. The latter are important as political constraints. There are no significant constitutional constraints to hinder the legislature in creating more special purpose agencies, in consolidating or abolishing existing ones, or in establishing a multi-purpose regional agency to exercise power over regional affairs.[2]

Home rule as an article of faith and practice is not held as tightly now by city and county officials as it was a decade ago. This is partly due to learning

From: *Regional Governance—Promise and Performance: Substate Regionalism and the Federal System,* Vol. II—Case Studies, May, 1973, p. 200.

from experience that many modern problems cannot be adequately managed by cities acting alone. It is also a pragmatic adjustment to the involvement of National and State governments in metropolitan affairs.

Local government, as it is now organized and as it now operates, is being challenged from many sides. Many critics see local government as unrepresentative in structure, parochial in orientation, overly concerned with petty matters, unable to make hard decisions where public interest is opposed to local interests, or where justice, equality, or ecology are opposed to private gain or prejudice.

Partly in response to this doubt, State and National governments are becoming heavily involved in metropolitan affairs. The most startling and far-reaching change in American federalism is the emergence of the National government as the focus for discussion of urban and metropolitan affairs. It is now the leader in formulating urban programs and in using the grant-in-aid to elicit intergovernmental cooperation among local governments in the San Francisco Bay Area.

THE INTERGOVERNMENTAL CHARACTER OF METROPOLITAN GOVERNANCE

The governance of the Bay Area is a mixture of public and private actions. Within the public sector, it is a mixture of Federal, State, and local governmental actions. Within the local governmental sector, it is a mixture of actions by a myriad of local agencies—large cities, small cities, large and small counties, regional special-purpose agencies, sub-regional districts and hundreds of small suburban "neighborhood" governments called fire districts, sewer districts, police districts, etc.

Efforts are being made by organized interests (including governments) in the Bay Area, the State, and the Nation to restructure the present mixture of relationships. Formal and informal understandings and regularized relations among "clients," influentials, and decision makers operating in and upon a metropolitan region constitute a system of metropolitan governance, but the balance of power within the diplomatic system of the region is not static. Changes in power and resources, as well as the emergence of new objectives and concerns, are constantly occurring. Many of these changes, as well as reaction to them, are small and incremental and are handled through the politics of accommodation.

Nevertheless, decisions must sometimes be made which are not incremental but involve major, high-risk public policies. The informal coordination which many consider satisfactory for normal decisions will not suffice for major changes involved in political and technological controversy. An example was the attempt of the council of governments in the Bay Area to develop through a joint powers agreement a policy for controlling bay fill and the over-riding of this effort by legislative creation of BCDC. In a similar manner, regulation of the development of the ocean coastline has now moved beyond the regional council. The voters of the State approved in November 1972, the creation of a State Coastal Zone Conservation Commission and six regional commissions to plan and regulate development of the Pacific Coast.

It is relatively easy to get a metropolitan system for planning, decision making, and administration, if a community is satisfied to have important decisions made by functional specialists with little or no relation to each other and without a means of establishing priorities. This can be done through the creation of special purpose authorities, which is the characteristic approach in the Bay Area. Or it can be achieved through State and National policies and regulatory agencies which administer such programs directly or through dependent regional special-purpose agencies. The major policy thrust in environmental protection—air and water quality, waste disposal, land-use controls, open space, etc.—seems to be shaping up in the latter direction.

Many city and county officials and civic leaders believe that regional government of some kind is inevitable, that in fact, it is already here in the form of special-purpose districts and agencies with more to come, and that it would be better if there were a limited, multi-purpose agency empowered to prepare regional plans and to require other agencies to conform to regional policies. The widespread support of a limited multi-purpose regional agency that has developed since 1960 is astonishing. In the Bay Area, agreement ends here, however, and disagreement over the composition and selection of a governing board has been bitter and intense.

In the Bay Area, the Association of Bay Area Governments (ABAG) considers comprehensive regional planning and multi-purpose regional coordination to be its primary responsibilities. Its principal sources of authority are its own definition of its role and its designation by the U.S. Office of Management and Budget and the U.S. Department of Housing and Urban Development as the areawide planning organization for the Bay Area. This recognition by the Federal government is not sufficient to explain the current role of ABAG as perceived by its members, officers, and staff, much less the role it aspires to play in the Bay Area. There are hundreds of areawide planning organizations in the country and several of them, as is ABAG, are evolving in scope, purpose, confidence, and capability toward an independent locally-based regional agency. Many, however, are, in the words of Melvin Mogulof, merely "insurance device[s] for the continued flow of federal funds to local governments."[3]

How congruent with its accomplishments are the perceived roles of ABAG as a *comprehensive* regional planning agency and as a coordinator of other regional planning done by other agencies in the Bay Area?

Most regional planning in the Bay Area is single-purpose functional planning. Only the Bay Conservation and Development Commission (BCDC) and ABAG have been engaged in relating functions to each other and to areal subdivisions within the region. In fact, much of ABAG's own planning has thus far been functional planning, e.g., planning to meet HUD requirements for open space, sewage, and water facilities grants.

> It should be observed that most of the new or increased [Federal] resources and requirements for planning have been "functional" as distinguished from "comprehensive" or policy and coordinative areas. Moreover, the number of directives and restrictions on the use of funds for comprehensive planning has increased, thus further limiting the resources available for policy development and coordination at a time when functional planning has grown tremendously and when the need for coordination has been increasing dramatically.

> These developments at the Federal level have created problems of coordination and policy development within regions that are very difficult to resolve. . . .[4]

PARTICIPANTS IN BAY AREA REGIONALISM

Before discussing regional planning, policy making, and administration in detail, it is desirable to take stock of the corporate actors in the governance of the Bay Area. The characteristics of the principal types of government need to be understood, and we should keep in mind the variety of interests of each type and the wide range of their resources. Not all interests are metropolitan and the play of State or National interest and regional interests is an essential ingredient in regional complexity. Furthermore, a knowledge of the interests and composition of private organizations and of the pressures and frictions of their contacts with public officials is essential to an understanding of how the Bay Area is governed.

The Association of Bay Area Governments
(ABAG)

Structure. The Association of Bay Area Governments is a central focus in this essay. Its objectives, origin and development, structure, finances, functions, and aspirations will be described and analyzed internally and in the political context of its relations with member cities and counties, regional special-purpose agencies, private organizations, State and Federal agencies, and the State legislature.

ABAG was organized in 1961 under the California Joint Exercise of Powers Act of 1921.[5] Its organizational structure includes the General Assembly, the Executive Committee, various standing and special committees, the president, the vice president, the executive director, and staff. Membership in ABAG is open to the City and County of San Francisco and eight counties in the Bay Area through execution of a joint powers agreement which provides for a ratification of the by-laws, payment of annual assessments, and other details.

Eighty-four of the 91 cities and eight of the nine counties in the Bay Area are members.[6] Although Solano County has never been a member, most cities in the county are members. All cities of over 20,000 population in the Bay Area are members. The Association also has 28 cooperating members with a voice but no vote at ABAG meetings. Any governmental agency in the Bay Area can apply for such membership.

The General Assembly regularly meets twice a year and consists of one representative from each member county and city. Voting in the General Assembly depends on the presence of a double quorum, i.e., a majority of the official city representatives, as well as a majority of official county representatives. Voting is on a bicameral basis. Each official county representative and each official city representative has one vote. Votes are tabulated separately for each set of officials. A majority of a quorum of county representatives *and* a majority of a quorum of city representatives is required for policy recommendations or actions. Voting within the Executive Committee is not on a bicameral basis but by a simple majority of a quorum of the total membership.

Until mid-1967, the Executive Committee consisted of a mayor or councilman from each county and a member of the board of supervisors in each county. These members could collectively elect no more than six other members at large from among the elected legislative officials of the counties and cities of the Bay Area. Members so chosen served one-year terms as full and equal members of the Executive Committee. At-large, membership was usually granted to Oakland and San Jose. San Francisco as a city and county would always have two members in the Executive Committee. Because the General Assembly follows a one government—one vote rule, this additional representation on the Executive Committee of the largest cities helped to overcome feelings of under-representation by the larger cities.

In 1967, after adoption of the Regional Home Rule Report of the Goals and Organization Committee, a new formula for representation on the Executive Committee was adopted. Known as the "modified population formula," it provided representation roughly on the basis of population, but the smallest county is entitled to both a county and a city representative. In the fall of 1969, another amendment was adopted which provides for direct election of the president and vice president by *all* supervisors, mayors, and city councilmen of member jurisdictions—an electoral college numbering 46 county supervisors and approximately 450 mayors and councilmen in 1972.

Financing. Funds for the support of ABAG programs and activities come from regular annual assessments of the members, special assessments levied by the General Assembly, and Federal grants. The amount assessed to individual cities and counties is based on population as determined by the State controller in making the most recent allocation to counties and cities pursuant to the Motor Vehicle License Fee Law.

Under this pattern, counties and cities are each collectively responsible for remitting one-half of the total assessment. Each county's assessment is the proportionate share of the county half of the budget total, determined by the ratio of the individual county's population to the total population of all member counties. Each city's assessment is a proportionate share of the city half of the budget total, determined by the ratio of the individual city's population to the total population of all member cities. In 1972, the by-laws were amended to require each member, irrespective of size, to pay a membership fee of $120.

Over 12 major regional planning activities between 1950 and 1970 cost approximately $22,700,000.7 It was estimated in 1970 that over $4 million was being spent annually in the Bay Area on regional planning.8 Less than 20 percent ($750,000) of estimated annual expenditures were under the direct control of ABAG. The association contributed or was otherwise involved in planning activities costing about $500,000 annually. Thus the total value of ABAG involvement in regional planning was less than 30 percent of the grand total for the year.

These estimates are probably too generous since ABAG's expenditures for A-95 review of applications for Federal grants make up a substantial part of regional expenditures for coordinative activities. The extent to which A-95 review results in coordination will be considered in a later section.

Functions. The association's by-laws, adopted in 1961, authorized the following functions:

a. Review of governmental proposals. This includes the making of appropriate policy or action recommendations.
b. Study of metropolitan area problems. This means the identification and study of problems, functions, and services in the San Francisco Bay metropolitan area, and the making of appropriate policy or action recommendations.
c. Other functions as the General Assembly should deem appropriate for the Association.

The concept of appropriate functions for ABAG changed drastically in its first five years. In the early years, ABAG was viewed as an advisory organization, which would study problems and recommend solutions but not institute programs. The first executive director stated in 1961 that ABAG was to serve as a "forum to discuss the study of metropolitan problems of the San Francisco Bay Area and to develop policy and action recommendations. It is merely a recommending agency." Although it was thus originally a narrowly-oriented discussion group, designed to meet once or twice a year to talk about regional problems, ABAG soon began to deal with regional problems more directly.

Immediately upon its creation, ABAG began to grow almost imperceptibly into an organization different from a regional forum of elected city and county officials. If its founders wanted it to remain a forum only, the first mistake they made was to create the office of full-time executive director and appoint to it a former city manager and staff member of the American Municipal Association.

The assumption by ABAG of responsibility for regional planning, four years before Congressional enactment in 1966 of the Demonstration Cities and Metropolitan Development Act, illustrates how an organization can develop over time in response to changing perceptions of needs among its members. It also suggests that, despite its potential and actual weaknesses, a voluntary association of governments, organized under a joint exercise of powers act, may evolve, in response to internal and external forces, into a viable and effective regional agency.9

ABAG is still alive and kicking eleven years after it was organized as a voluntary discussion forum. Both its friends and its enemies have repeatedly predicted its dissolution as it has faced and made tough decisions concerning regional planning, the acceptance of Federal aid and Federal program requirements, increased local contributions, the composition of the Executive Board, and approval of the regional plan. Other issues have included a request for legislation making membership mandatory and empowering ABAG to implement the plan and enforce compliance of local and special-agency plans with the regional plans. In 1971, ABAG also decided to support a mixed governing body of directly elected members and of city and county officials. Over each of these matters a significant minority of members became hurt, frightened, or angry. All but a few of them remained in the association to fight another day.

Undoubtedly, the Federal requirement that ABAG review and comment on applications for Federal grants was an important factor in keeping ABAG together. In fact, since 1966 the term "voluntary" may be inaccurate as a description of COG's, at least of ABAG. However, the preceeding analysis of the organizational development of ABAG shows that it has been strengthened by its own decisions and activities and by reaction to what its members perceive as threats from the outside.

Perhaps the acid test of its ability to survive was the Truax affair. In 1968, the diversion by the assistant to the executive director of nearly half a million dollars of Federal funds granted to ABAG was discovered. The widespread publicity given to the scandal made ABAG an unenviable household name and frightened many ABAG members and its State and Federal sponsors. Its enemies claimed that this demonstrated beyond doubt the inappropriateness of converting ABAG into a statutory regional agency. The scandal broke after ABAG had voted to request statutory status and authority and diverted the leaders' attention from legislative efforts.

However, very few cities resigned and most of them soon returned. The leaders of ABAG reorganized the administration, tightened fiscal procedures, and, in short, converted ABAG from the secretariat of a loose confederation into a tighter adminstrative organization. At the same time, they began the slow task of recovery of the stolen funds. Although done at a price one would never willingly pay, there is no doubt that the reorganization left ABAG stronger and more closely organized after than before the Truax affair.

Has ABAG made any difference in the attitudes toward regionalism of city and county officials? A before and after test of changes in attitudes cannot be made. However, both the behavior and public statements of local officials at the time ABAG was founded certainly lead one to conclude that they were more local than regional in their orientation to Bay Area problems and toward each other. Yet the ABAG General Assembly, consisting of representatives of each city and each county, voted in 1967 to ask the legislature to change ABAG from a voluntary association into a regional agency with mandatory membership and with power to implement the regional plan. This decision would have been inconceivable five years earlier.

Local governments are involved in regional governance in three ways. First, the manner in which they discharge some of their functions has consequences for people who live beyond their borders. Secondly, in any form of two-tier local government, the regional tier will have to depend on cities, counties, and special-purpose agencies to carry out important regional policies. In the third place, in the Bay Area at least, cities and counties and some special-purpose agencies later participate as distinct organizations in the selection of members of regional governing boards. One of their objections to the Knox bills of 1969 and 1970 to create a multi-purpose regional agency was that a directly elected regional body would exclude them from this kind of participation.

However, there is increasing concern among city and county officials, especially the former, over the heavy burden of active leadership and participation in one or more regional agencies. This is overtime work added to the time they must spend away from family and business on the civic and governmental affairs of their own municipality. This condition is the basis for allegations by proponents of a directly elected regional government that locally elected officials will be unable to give the time necessary to deal with important and increasingly complex regional problems. The result, they say, will be that regional business will go unattended except as administrators and functional specialists become *de facto* policy makers.

Mayors play an important role in the intergovernmental relations of the Bay Area. They constitute in each county a city selection committee to select from the mayors and councilmen of the county representatives to the Bay Area Air Pollution Control District, the Bay Area Rapid Transit District (BART), and the Executive Committee of ABAG. If the city is engaged in treating sewage, its mayor serves on a county selection committee to select representatives from the county to the newly created Bay Area Sewage Services Agency.[10]

Professional administrators play a major role in shaping and conducting intergovernmental relations in the Bay Area. Among the middle-sized and larger cities, an increasing proportion of the manager's time is given to negotiation, opposition, and cooperation with officials of counties, school districts and other special districts, other city governments in the county and in ABAG, as well as with many State and Federal agencies. City managers and county chief administrative officers have participated, along with mayors, councilmen, and county supervisors, in developing the consensus for special districts composed of elected city and county officials, such as the Bay Area Air Pollution Control Districts, BART, and ABAG itself.

Despite a few significant exceptions, little use has been made by ABAG of the expertise and policy leadership of the professional staffs of the Bay Area city and county governments.

Central city-suburban relationships are not only important at the present time, they are likely to become even more important as the suburbs continue to gain and the central cities continue to lose population. San Francisco's legislators in Sacramento are dwindling in numbers and are receiving into their constituencies many people from suburban San Mateo and Marin Counties.

Minorities are large enough and articulate enough to be a major political force in the Bay Area as well as in the cities where they are concentrated. Many of them are disadvantaged and their concentration creates the social disparities between central city and suburbs that is coming to be recognized as a regional problem.

The mayors and supervisors of San Francisco and the mayors and councilmen of Oakland, considering the high stakes of their residents and businessmen in regional developments, have played a relatively small role in ABAG. None of the three large central cities has attempted to develop a strategy for regional satisfaction of big-city interest, even though central city residents are more concerned with housing, income maintenance, and equality of opportunity than with such suburban concerns as environmental amenities. There is a magnificent opportunity for central city and suburb to trade off interests in the development of regional policies. On the face of it, it appears that the central city has the most to gain and the most to lose. With the shift of population and votes to the suburbs, likely to be accentuated in the coming decades, it seems appropriate, in fact, imperative, for the central cities to give up their traditional game of reacting to events, and take the initiative in developing regional policies and organizing the regional accommodations necessary to adopt and implement them.

The regional conflict is not a simple dichotomous one of suburb *vs* central city. In the first place, no central city is homogeneous. Elements within central cities and in some suburbs have mutual interest. Secondly, the three central cities themselves will often disagree. And, in the third place, suburbia is divided among itself on any issue that may arise. This is why it is needless to fear, as some environmentalists have, that city and county officials will present a monolithic front on regional issues.

Counties

The eight county governments of the Bay Area (excluding the City and County of San Francisco) have undergone more changes as a result of urbanization than any other type of local government. Not the least important of the new roles counties are playing in the Bay Area is that of participant in regional governance. County representatives to the ABAG General Assembly constitute in effect a second chamber since every motion requires a majority vote of both counties and cities. Counties are also represented on the Bay Conservation and Development Commission, Bay Area Air Pollution Control District, Golden Gate Bridge and Transportation District, Bay Area Rapid Transit District, and the Metropolitan Transportation District. County boards of supervisors select from nominees of special-selection committees representatives to the newly created Bay Area Sewage Service Agency (BASSA).

Finally, counties function as sub-regions in the fields of comprehensive health planning, criminal justice planning, solid waste disposal, and airport land use. Most metropolitan clearinghouses recognized by the Federal government are single-county agencies. The largest is the San Diego Comprehensive Planning Organization. There is some sentiment in other parts of the State for recognizing the county, rather than a multi-county region, as the areawide comprehensive planning agency. This feeling is much stronger in southern California than in the Bay Area. In part, as a response to pressure from southern California, the California Council on Criminal Justice has designated counties as regions.

The county is the only local government that can plan and regulate the use of land in the fast-growing unincorporated parts of the region. State law now requires cities and counties to include an open space element in their official plans by July 1, 1973. The reliance by ABAG on voluntary compliance by its member governments places a heavy responsibility on counties to implement the regional open space plan.

Conservationists and environmentalists have been especially critical of the actions of county planners and supervisors. They maintain that most local politicians (and county officials are in a critical position because of their control over the development of open land) are so imbued with the values of growth, development, and progress that they naturally favor the interests of builders and land speculators. Even if they were inclined toward the preservation of open land and the containment of urban growth, they are unable to withstand pressure from wealthy and influential interests. This is especially true when development is linked to enlargement of the tax base. Critics argue that a larger and more distinct government, such as a region or the State, would be able to resist such pressures.

Solano County has never joined ABAG, although five of its seven cities are members. For years, ABAG had noted in its review of Solano County applications for Federal aid, that the county did not cooperate in regional planning. The county refused to pay ABAG a processing fee of the amount requested in its applications for Federal aid. In 1970, however, an agreement was signed between ABAG and the county in which the latter agreed to pay the fee up to an annual total of 110 percent of what the county's dues would be if it were a member.

In 1970, while one of its supervisors was president of ABAG, Sonoma County voters approved 3 to 1 a proposition placed on the ballot by the board of supervisors to withdraw from ABAG and join an inactive northcoast regional planning district. The cities of the county are divided over this action and, along with the ABAG Executive Committee, are opposing confirmation of the action by the State Council on Intergovernmental Relations. This part of the dispute will be considered in the section on State agencies and Bay Area regionalism.

Special-Purpose Agencies

The third type of local governmental unit in the Bay Area is the special district, authority, or other form of special-purpose agency. Among those of regional significance covering all or extensive parts of the Bay Area are the East Bay Municipal Utility District (EBMUD), the East Bay Regional Park District (EBRPD), the Golden Gate Bridge and Transportation District, the Bay Area Air Pollution Control District, the Alameda-Contra Costa Transit District (A-C Transit), the San Francisco Bay Area Rapid Transit District (BART), the Bay Area Comprehensive Health Planning Council, the Metropolitan Transportation Commission (MTC), and the Bay Area Sewage Services Agency (BASSA). The Bay Area Social Planning Council is a private organization which is considered along with public special-purpose agencies.

Other special-purpose agencies, such as the Bay Conservation and Development Commission (BCDC), the San Francisco Bay Regional Water Quality Control Board, the Division of Bay Toll Crossings, and District IV of the State Division of Highways will be discussed in the section on State government.

Not all these agencies are special "districts," but they are special-purpose agencies.

Three of the large sub-regional special districts have directly elected governing boards: East Bay Municipal Utility District, East Bay Regional Park District, and the Alameda-Contra Costa Transit District. Most board members over the life of the districts have been first appointed to office and then reelected as incumbents.[11]

All or a good portion of the membership of the governing bodies of other regional special agencies consists of elective county and city officials or of members selected by cities and counties. In addition to city and county members, ABAG selects a member on MTC, the Bay Area Comprehensive Health Planning Council, and four members to represent cities on BCDC. It was unable to secure amendments allowing it to appoint four members to BASSA.

Some of these agencies are regulatory bodies (e.g., BCDC, Air Pollution Control District, Regional Water Quality Control Board); others are engaged in the construction and operation of facilities (BART, EBMUD, East Bay Regional Park District, A-C Transit, Golden Gate Bridge and Transportation District); and still others are primarily planning agencies (MTC, Bay Area Comprehensive Health Planning Council, BASSA). MTC will probably acquire regulatory powers and BASSA will undoubtedly exercise its residual power to construct and operate sewage treatment and disposal facilities.

All of them, however, are engaged in planning. Their policies may or may not be based upon such planning. There are many potential and actual interfaces among their plans and those of ABAG, cities, counties, and State and Federal agencies. There is as yet no unified regional planning program to bring such interrelationships into the open and develop consensus where desirable and possible. These intergovernmental relationships will be described and analyzed in a later section.

State Government

In 1970, almost 93 percent of the population of California lived in 16 standard metropolitan statistical areas. It is not surprising, therefore, that the State government, from the Governor and most legislators to influential members of various bureaucracies, is increasingly concerned with matters affecting urban dwellers.

The State is also responding to the policy leadership of the National government and the reaction of local governments to that leadership. Most State action to meet new Federal requirements or efforts by the State to assert its prerogatives in the Federal system have been sporadic and *ad hoc*. However, the Intergovernmental Council on Urban Growth, a predecessor of the Council on Intergovernmental Relations, has analyzed the emerging system of Federal-State-local relations and recommended a strengthening of the State's role in Federal urban programs and of the relationship of the State to local governments.[12]

A consultant to ABAG has divided State activities into three categories: (1) direct services to the public on a statewide basis; (2) statewide programs which "lean heavily on local government for their direct administration and constitute, in effect, joint ventures"; and (3) those activities "which respond to the needs of a particular area, as distinguished from a statewide need."[13]

Regional problems, it was said, arise only with respect to the third category of State programs, where in response to the needs of a particular area, the State usually established a special-purpose agency to meet each need: ". . . an area need arises, there is agitation for its being met, and an agency is created to meet it—this is the normal process."[14]

It is impossible to categorize State activities so neatly and to dismiss most of them because they raise "no regional problems." The extent to which this is so can be seen from the discussion in the section on regional planning and policy making.

Apart from the Governor's cabinet, which is more institutionalized than in previous administrations, there are two agencies attempting to develop intergovernmental policies and coordinate State-local and State-Federal relations.

The Council on Intergovernmental Relations and the Office of Planning and Research, both now located in the Governor's Office, are responsible for developing a wide range of policies affecting local governments. They are beginning to develop proposals that may lead to an active administrative role in Bay Area regional governance. In 1969, the Lieutenant Governor was designated by executive order as Chief Executive Officer for Intergovernmental Relations. As such, he heads an Office for Intergovernmental Management. This office is described as "the management and advice arm" of the Council on Intergovernmental Relations. However, the council was transferred from the Lieutenant Governor's office to that of the Governor in 1972 in response to the threat of budgetary sanctions by the chairman of the Assembly Committee on Ways and Means.

The Office of Planning and Research was created by statute in 1970. Although its primary purpose is to provide staff services to the Governor and the cabinet, the following specific objectives were listed in the 1972-73 budget:

1. to develop a comprehensive statewide land-use policy,
2. to coordinate all State departmental land-use planning activities,
3. to develop recommended statewide environmental goals and policies, and
4. to develop an environmental monitoring system.

The Council on Intergovernmental Relations was created in the wake of the ferment caused by the report of the Governor's Commission on Metropolitan Area Problems in 1960.[15] Its composition, patterned after the U.S. Advisory Commission on Intergovernmental Relations, gave representation to cities, counties, school districts, State officials, and the public. Since then, the membership has been broadened to include State legislators, areawide comprehensive planning agencies, and special districts.

In its first report, the council announced as a basic assumption on which its deliberations and recommendations would be based:

> That the local units of government in urban regions should be encouraged to solve common regional problems through voluntary associations of cities and counties, with decision-making responsibility vested in a general assembly composed of elected city councilmen and county supervisors representing their respective member units.[16]

Over the decade the council has adhered essentially to its position as first announced in 1965. However, after the ABAG Regional Home Rule Proposal in 1967, it modified its position to support mandatory membership of all cities and counties in the region, while continuing to insist on a regional governing board consisting only of elected city councilmen and county supervisors.

The first statutory provision for State designation of regional planning districts was enacted in 1963. Under this Act, the State Office of Planning proposed a division of the State into planning regions with boundary lines following topographical features rather than county lines. The proposal to divide counties was sharply protested by city and county officials. Responsibility for delineating regional districts was subsequently shifted to the Council on Intergovernmental Relations.

This year the council has been faced with two severe political crises over the boundaries of regional planning districts, one in the Bay Area and the other in southern California. After the Sonoma County electorate voted in 1970 to withdraw from ABAG, the council was requested to move Sonoma County from the Bay Area regional planning district to the North Coast regional planning district. When the council's budget came before the Senate Finance Committee, the committee chairman, representing Sonoma and the North Coast counties, made it clear that favorable action on the budget would have to be traded for a council vote to shift Sonoma County. On June 22, 1972, the council heard opposition from ABAG and from cities within Sonoma County to its transfer from the Bay Area, but voted 10 to 8 to approve the transfer. Several votes in favor of shifting were cast by telegram by members not present at the hearing. Following protests by the ABAG Executive Committee and the City Council of Santa Rosa, the Attorney General and the Legislative Council ruled that absentee votes were illegally cast, so Sonoma County remains in the Bay Area, but the county government itself is no longer a member of ABAG.

Other State agencies and programs will be discussed in a later section. The most important for this case study are the Business and Transportation Agency and two of its units, the Department of Public Works and the Office of Transportation Planning and Research; the State Transportation Board; the State Water Resources Control Board, along with its regional water quality control boards and its Bay-Delta water quality study; the Bay Conservation and Development Commission (BCDC); and the California Council on Criminal Justice (CCCJ).

The Federal Government

The Federal government was the most important actor in the upswelling of regionalism during the 1960s and early 1970s. Federal funds have largely supported both multi-purpose and single-purpose planning at the regional level. Federal requirements associated with grants-in-aid have raised many matters to the regional level for planning and debate, if not always for action. From the beginning of the decade the Federal thrust has been toward "comprehensive areawide planning" with little or no parallel thrust from the State government. In the absence of State legislation empowering regional agencies to require conformity to regional plans and to construct and operate regional facilities (except in Minneapolis-St. Paul, Atlanta, Indianapolis, Miami, and Jacksonville), all authority of regional agencies such as ABAG derives from Federal legislation as interpreted and administered by Federal agencies.

Joseph P. Bort, Alameda County supervisor and chairman of ABAG's Regional Home Rule Committee, testified before a congressional committee in 1971:

> There is no doubt that two federal policies—review and comment by regional planning agencies on applications for federal aid and the support, principally by 701 funds, of the development of comprehensive regional plans—have done more to encourage and to enable local governments to face up to regional problems than anything else during the past half century. Although ABAG was formed before the avalanche of regional planning agencies was started by federal action, and it formally began its regional planning program as early as 1962, it has certainly been helped by these two programs.[17]

During the same hearing, Assemblyman John Knox asserted that Federal support and the requirement of regional review and comment on applications for Federal aid has resulted in

1. The production of a great volume of so-called regional plans which

the COG formally adopts. "The result is that the COG is then able to represent that sundry regional plans do exist."

2. Misleading representation by COG's that they are determining regional priorities and are implementing regional plans.[18]

The U.S. Department of Housing and Urban Development (HUD) is the Federal agency with closest association with ABAG. In fact, one might ask whether HUD looks upon ABAG primarily as an agent to help implement at the regional level the special purpose of the department. One-half of the ABAG budget for comprehensive regional planning comes from HUD 701 funds. Most of its annual work program is designed to meet planning requirements for activities administered by HUD, such as open space, water and sewer facilities, and housing.

The comment and review function is authorized by rules and regulations issued by the Office of Management and Budget. Under its present by-laws as a joint powers agency and without additional authority from the State legislature, ABAG's primary authority derives from OMB Circular A-95. The extent to which Assemblyman Knox's charge that the exercise of this authority is a pretense will be examined later.

Other Federal agencies subject to A-95 review requirements or with regional planning or implementation requirements of their own are the Department of Health, Education and Welfare, Department of Commerce, Department of Transportation, Department of Justice, and the Environmental Protection Agency.

The Corps of Engineers is directly engaged in regional planning for the Bay Area. Two vast projects, estimated to cost ultimately $10 million, are now underway: The Bay Region In-Depth Study and the S-S-S (San Francisco—San Pablo Bay—Suisun Bay) Study.

Interest Groups

Formally organized groups are considered here only if they have an avowed regional objective and if they attempt to bring pressure upon government officials in an effort to realize that objective. Federal and State agencies, cities, counties, and special districts, as well as factions within such agencies or governmental units, frequently operate as pressure groups. In a system of intergovernmental relations, where power and authority are dispersed among many levels, units, and agencies, it is not surprising that each interested unit acts individually and in concert to secure from other governmental parties what it wants and to stop what it does not want.

Most important for the concern of this essay are the formal organizations of cities, counties, and special districts and of their officials and employees. The League of California Cities and the County Supervisors' Association of

California (CSAC) are well organized, well led, and well staffed. Once they bitterly fought each other, but in recent years they have presented a common front in defense of home rule.

The League of Cities has moved from an unmistakable support of particularistic handling of particular problems in 1962 to support of mandatory regional umbrella agencies consisting entirely of city and county elected officials by 1970. Furthermore, it maintains that regional organizations should be authorized to assume limited powers and functions with reference to the operation of regional services and that they should be granted necessary regulatory and taxing powers.[19]

The County Supervisors' Association of California (CSAC) staff jointly prepared with the league staff and with representatives of ABAG, SCAG, Sacramento Area Regional Planning District, and San Diego Comprehensive Planning Organization the draft document upon which league resolution No. 13 was based. CSAC adopted essentially the same resolution after modifying it to call for governing bodies consisting *primarily* of city and county officials.

In 1971, the league Board of Directors took another step—this time away from 100 percent membership of city- and county-elected officials on the governing body of a regional agency. It urged that the Regional Planning District Act, on the statute books since 1963 but never used, be amended to make it easier to activate a district by requiring favorable resolutions from a majority instead of two-thirds of the counties and cities within regional planning districts delineated by the Council on Intergovernmental Relations. Also, it urged that city, county, and special-district plans be required to conform to the mandatory elements of the regional plan. The big change, however, is with respect to the composition of the governing body. The league approves the provisions of existing law calling for a citizen to be appointed by the supervisors in each county to sit with elected city and county officials.[20]

Although the League of Cities and CSAC may not agree with regional councils of governments on particular legislation, they have been supportive of their local efforts to organize and operate. In fact, they played crucial roles in the creation of both ABAG and SCAG.

Yet public concern with water supply, air pollution, water pollution, transportation, recreation, filling and conserving the bay, parks and open spaces is ample evidence that most of the major problems are not being met in a way that satisfies many articulate groups in the Bay Area.

Pressure for governmental action develops at a different rate among various groups and is exerted with varying force at any given time on local, State, and Federal officials. If a locally arrived-at decision to create a special district or authority cannot be made, the "imposition" of a district by the State legislature is often sought. Frequently such efforts are defeated in the State legislature, but there are many instances of success.

Only a few of the multitude of formally organized groups in the Bay Area have a general and continuous interest in the government and politics of the region.

Between 1955 and 1961 the Bay Area Council shifted from sponsorship of special-purpose regional agencies to collaboration and support of ABAG to advocacy of a directly elected multi-purpose regional government.[21]

The most significant coalition of individuals and organizations in the Bay Area is AREA—Action for a Regional Environmental Agency. Its purpose in 1971 was to secure enactment of Assemblyman Knox's bill, AB 1057, to create the Bay Area Conservation and Development Agency. Leaders of AREA and the Regional Home Rule Committee of ABAG were able to compromise their positions on the composition of the governing board for the proposed regional agency. As a result, the bill almost passed in 1971. More important for the future, contacts established between ABAG and AREA have continued and chances are good that a mutually acceptable bill can be drafted for 1973.

Out of the Bay Area Congress of Citizens' Organizations came the campaign, in the Bay Area and in Sacramento, to enact a strong act to "save the Bay." This movement, joined by the Sierra Club, Friends of the Earth, and People for Open Space, supported the Knox bills to create a directly elected regional planning agency, bills to regulate development of the Pacific coast, and other environmental protection bills.

The 22 local Leagues of Women Voters in the nine Bay Area counties have organized on a regional basis "to increase the knowledge and effectiveness of the local Leagues in the field of areawide government, and to coordinate League work on the metropolitan level." The leagues began in 1959 with a study of Bay Area problems and possible governmental solutions. They are still strongly committed to a directly elected regional agency, even after the 1971 compromise over representation.

Although most organized groups are locally oriented and concerned with advancing or protecting a single interest, they frequently see their interests threatened by proposed regional policies. Organized labor is now alert to secure representation on regional bodies. They successfully amended the Act creating the Bay Area Comprehensive Transportation Study Commission to require the governor to appoint four labor representatives. The San Francisco Central Labor Council has come out for direct election of all regional agencies, whether special or multi-purpose. At the same time, they are increasingly active in opposing environmentalist groups on the ground that their efforts result in fewer opportunities for jobs.

These examples of non-official interest groups remind us that there are powerful political forces other than local governments operating in the Bay Area. Such forces can be brought to bear upon State and Federal governments to assume the direct administration of certain urban affairs or the indirect administration of others through grant-in-aid programs, or to secure the creation of new units of local government to be responsible for the discharge of urban functions on a metropolitan scale.

Much so-called imposition by the State is actually policy developed by local groups and interests, and implemented through the machinery of State government. Frequently, local officials join with other local groups to seek legislation of this kind. Certainly this makes questionable the characterization of such State and Federal action as "an imposition from above." Even if the local pressures are entirely unofficial, they are still *local*, and it is incorrect to call such State and Federal legislative responses "impositions."

Cronin finds that only 37 percent of city councilmen of the Bay Area in 1966-67 were localists who perceived public problems only in terms of their effect on one's own city and who never considered a regional approach to them or, if they did, considered such approach to be inappropriate. Of the remaining 61 percent, a little over 36 percent were decidedly regionalist in perspective and 64 percent had a mixed metropolitan perspective. Similar findings about the attitudes of leaders other than public officials were found by Scott and Hawley.[22]

A 1971 survey of blacks holding elective and appointive public office showed clearly that they were aware of the metropolitan dimensions of their problems, that they believed that metropolitan government was already here in the form of special districts, and that blacks were likely to be more influential in a multi-purpose elective regional government than in a system of single-purpose districts.[23]

REGIONAL PLANNING, POLICY MAKING
AND ADMINISTRATION

ABAG's principal means of implementing the regional plan are its review and comment authority derived from the Federal government and management of a unified planning program in which affected governmental agencies at all levels will participate. It seems desirable, therefore, to use certain elements in ABAG's unified regional planning management program as an outline for this discussion of current Bay Area activities that make up regional planning, policy making, and administration.

Operational Support Systems

Basic Research and Development. Much of the time and costs of all planning efforts is consumed by data gathering and analysis. Each project is usually designed and carried out independently, without utilization of data gathered in previous inquiries. Functional planning, organized by projects and agencies, is necessary but coordination, collaboration, or participation should begin at the design stage. This would require at least a review and comment by other regional agencies and might lead to joint work programs, such as those between ABAG and MTC, and ABAG and the State Water Quality Control Board. Collaboration in designing projects, gathering and analyzing data may lead to collaboration in policy making.

ABAG looks upon itself as responsible for establishing population and land-use bases for all other regional planning. However, it cannot do this alone and expect other regional agencies to accept its analyses and projections.

ABAG has prepared a regional base map and proposes to keep it up to date through a continuation of the aerial photographing begun jointly with the U.S. Geological Survey (USGS). ABAG has been participating in the USGS-HUD Environmental Resources Study since 1970. It proposes to continue this work after the USGS-HUD program is finished in 1974. But a continuing program of updated base maps and aerial photographs "can be provided more efficiently and inexpensively through a coordinated regional program."[24]

An indispensable element in ABAG's influence is the quality of the data it collects about the Bay Area, the quality of its analysis of those data, and the public policies it adopts and supports. ABAG is the only regional agency in the Bay Area to plan a unified regional information system.

Almost simultaneously with the assumption by ABAG of responsibility for regional planning, it organized a forum where public and private agencies collecting and using quantitative data could exchange information and discuss technical developments. The Bay Area Automated Information System Coordinating Committee (BAAISCC) met regularly at times and intermittently at other times between 1964 and 1969. The need for a systematized regional information center to service both regional and local public and private agencies was frequently discussed by BAAISCC. However, not until 1972-73 were funds included in the budget to undertake development of a Bay Region Planning Information Support Center (BRISC). ABAG is now recruiting a director for BRISC (funds are available for one-half man-year) to set up the center, develop a work program for 1973-74, and execute agreements with public and private agencies operating within the region.

In the meantime, the void was partially filled by the establishment of the Census Service Facility in the Institute of Governmental Studies, University of California, Berkeley. The relationship of the Census Service Facility to BRISC will have to be negotiated.

ABAG and MTC are faced with the necessity of bringing up to date the transportation data collected and analyzed by the ABAG-BATSC program between 1965 and 1969. MTC will be a principal user of BRISC and will provide about 43 percent of its funding. The principal source of MTC funds will be the State Department of Public Works, which will in turn utilize Federal highway planning research funds. MTC is not likely to play the role of minor partner since it will contribute twice as much to the support of BRISC as ABAG.25

Information Exchange and Citizen Participation. A small community relations staff is responsible for contacts with the press, answering public inquiries, and keeping the staff, the Regional Home Rule Goals Committee, the Executive Committee, and the General Assembly informed of legislative developments. The community relations officer also handled the initial phase of organizing a citizens task force to develop proposals for a permanent Regional Citizens Forum. The public information program needs to be expanded to inform many more special groups, as well as the general public, of ABAG activities. The need will be much greater when the Regional Citizens Forum is operating.

It is proper for ABAG to include activities to support citizen participation under the rubric of information exchange. The process of exchange should be two-way, with information going out from ABAG and information coming into ABAG from people and organizations who are concerned about ABAG's action or inaction. It would be a mistake to channel all such contacts through a single point in the organization, but the Office of Community Relations will play a major role in preparing and distributing information in a form that can be understood critically by laymen and in analyzing feedback information.

ABAG did not solicit citizen input into its deliberations and decisions during the first decade of its existence. In 1970, the General Assembly authorized a large committee on the environment to be broken down into subcommittees on open space, solid waste disposal, and water quality control. Although the immediate past president of ABAG was appointed chairman of the overall committee and subcommittee chairmen were appointed, the process never got underway. One reason offered for the tardiness was the lack of staff. This hesitancy was confirmed when a lay member of the Open Space Subcommittee took a position on pending legislation without clearing it through the association.

In spite of HUD's requirement of "citizen participation" in some grant projects, ABAG began sustained efforts to formalize a Regional Citizens Forum only after the National Committee Against Discrimination in Housing and La Confederacion de la Raza Unida objected to the development of a regional housing element in the Regional Plan by the staff. The two groups insisted that they be designated by ABAG as the agency to prepare the regional housing plan. This pressure and a HUD deadline led the Regional Planning Committee to propose to the Executive Committee that a citizens' task force be established to prepare a plan for organizing a permanent citizens forum.

The Citizens' Task Force consists of three delegates from each of the nine counties selected by open citizens' meetings in each county, a representative appointed by each of 17 regional interest groups, and members at-large appointed by the ABAG Executive Committee.

Conservation and Development

Conservation and development planning elements are a re-naming of what used to be called physical planning. In a 1967 survey of 156 leaders in Bay Area governments and civic groups, mass transportation led the list of problems, followed by air pollution, bay conservation and development, solid waste disposal, airports, water quality control, regional planning, regional parks and recreation, and conservation of open space—all traditional physical planning elements.[26]

Similar priorities would be found in most metropolitan areas. It is not surprising that ABAG has devoted most of its attention to these problems and still considers "comprehensive regional land-use planning . . . [to be] its central area of responsibility."[27] In fact, almost all Federal requirements for regional plans have been directed at physical development and control. Furthermore, all special-purpose regional agencies except the Bay Area Comprehensive Health Planning Council have been similarly oriented.

The ABAG General Assembly approved the *Regional Plan: 1970-1990* in 1970.[28] This event was the culmination of ABAG planning activities begun in 1962 and the start of other activities to refine the plan and make it more specific by developing special element plans for water resources, housing, airports, open space and regional parks and promoting special element planning for transportation and environmental health.

The refinement and specification of the Regional Plan is necessary in order to develop usable guidelines, standards, and criteria to resolve such policy conflicts as arise from "actions by appropriate agencies that will initiate, direct and promote regional growth and development as well as conservation of the environment."[29] This conflict is likely to be sharpened in the debate now developing in ABAG and in the Bay Area over proposals to restrain the growth of population.

In the *Regional Plan: 1970-1990* an effort was made to "present policies and objectives as comprehensively as possible. . . . Differences in interpretation are therefore minimized, leading to a greater agreement among those concerned with planning the region's future. The development of such a consensus has been one of the association's major goals in its continuing regional planning efforts."[30]

Undoubtedly the Regional Plan document approved by the General Assembly in 1970 is a major symbol of regionalism in the Bay Area. Also of undoubted value in achieving consensus among representatives of eight counties and 84 cities was the frequent ambiguity of goals and policy recommendations in the document. The need for specification of the goals and policy guidelines was soon demonstrated when the Regional Airport System Study Committee had to agree on regional airport goals in the context of overall regional goals.[31] The same problem must be faced in using the Regional Plan as a context for developing regional plans and policies for transportation, air pollution control, water pollution control, regional parks and open space, and conservation and development of the ocean coastline. ABAG is moving on its own or jointly under agreements with other governmental agencies to revise and make more specific each of these special elements.

Population Growth. The first major question about the Regional Plan came within a year of its approval from planners, politicians, and environmentalists. They questioned whether "present population growth trends" would or should remain constant. ABAG planners have since reestimated population growth and revised their original figure of 6.2 million people by 1980 downward to 5.5 million.

Following the February 1972 meeting of the General Assembly, the Executive Committee and policy committees of ABAG were instructed to report recommendations to the Fall General Assembly "which would focus upon a specific regional policy with respect to population growth rates in different areas of the region and provide a basis for sound short- and long-range planning."[32]

Although local and regional governments have little authority to control growth, there are alternative policies that would discourage or encourage growth.[33] Land-use controls and the extension of such facilities as water, sewage, and transportation are especially significant. Many agencies are involved in these activities and have an immediate need for an agreed population projection for 1980 upon which to base their functional planning. The ABAG staff paper proposes a coordinated effort of ABAG and other interested parties "to come together to design a comprehensive regional growth plan that is responsive to the major planning issues facing the region."

The staff paper does not specify how such cooperative effort is to be structured, but it does refer to bilateral agreements executed separately with MTC, the Bay Area Comprehensive Health Planning Council, the State Water Resources Control Board, and one under discussion with the Bay Area Air Pollution Control Board.

Land Use. The use of land is controlled by several agencies in the Bay Area: cities and counties through zoning, subdivision, and building regulations; the Bay Conservation and Development Commission through permits over salt ponds and managed wetlands, the bay itself, and a 100-foot strip around the shore of the bay; the Regional Water Quality Control Board through its authority to halt additional sewer connections in jurisdictions not in compliance with water quality control standards; and now the Air Pollution Control District which requires that a permit be obtained prior to construction and operation of certain facilities which may pollute the air in excess of Federal and State standards.

Land-use controls are presumably based on plans designed to protect the people of a given jurisdiction from undesirable consequences of certain types of land use. Even more significant are governmental actions that encourage or facilitate certain uses of land that are considered desirable, e.g., increase of uses leading to population growth, expansion of economic base, or improved tax base. Frequently, land-use policies desired by different segments of the public are incompatible, as with open space vs. housing. Both the impact of different uses of land and of programs designed to affect those uses differ from one part of a locality or region to another. At the same time these effects are seldom restrained to the immediate zone, district, or locality where the use is located or policies are applied.[34]

Thus, in a complex metropolitan region such as the Bay Area there are many more agencies engaged in land-use planning than in land-use control.[35] ABAG has no authority to control the use of land nor can it implement plans to locate or restrict the location of transportation, water, and sewage facilities. It may influence other decision makers through the development of regional plans and its review and comment upon applications for Federal assistance.

Yet it maintains that its central function is regional land-use planning. *The Regional Plan: 1970-1990* is primarily concerned with sketching the location, in relation to a regional transportation network, of residential and basic employment areas and open space. Within the open space, pockets for controlled development beyond 1990 were designated.[36]

The generalized land-use scheme of the Regional Plan was not presented in sufficient detail in 1970 to enable either ABAG or cities and counties to identify and begin to reconcile differences between regional and local plans. It was intended, however, that more specific plan elements be amended into the Regional Plan and that ABAG involve other regional agencies in coordinated planning, decision making, and implementation. Land use is the common base for ABAG's interest in functional planning.

Even though regional action in these functional fields is an important influence on the form and performance of the region, land uses change or persist on a particular parcel of land located in a particular area. Several members of the Executive Committee and of the General Assembly expressed concern during discussions of the proposed Regional Plan in 1970 over inconsistencies between local plans and the regional plan and over means of reconciling such differences. At the Executive Committee meeting of April 16, 1970, the following motion by Councilman Dillon, now president of ABAG, was unanimously passed:

General Plan Revision. —When the region's municipal and county plans are aggregated on a regional composite basis, the result is an unsatisfactory program for future regional development. The association should develop a continuing program of reviewing municipal, county, and regional plans. Where inconsistencies occur in areas of regional concern in these plans, such inconsistencies will be resolved by changing the Regional Plan, modifying the local plan, or the developing of a mutually acceptable compromise to be embodied in both the regional and local plans.

This statement was not explicitly included in the published *Regional Plan: 1970-1990,* although it was suggested that "municipalities and counties within the region should be encouraged to submit their present land-use ordinances to the association for review and comment based upon criteria drawn from the Regional Plan."[37] In the two years since the Regional Plan was approved, ABAG has not undertaken either a systematic analysis of the consistency of local and regional plans nor has it requested local agencies to make such an analysis.

Most staff attention has been devoted to work on plan elements required by HUD and to establishing working relations with special-purpose agencies. Furthermore, HUD is losing interest in supporting comprehensive regional planning as such and shifting its 701 general planning assistance funds to support functional planning of special interest to HUD.

Transportation.[38] There are more regional special districts dealing with transportation than with any other regional problem. There are three operating districts—Bay Area Rapid Transit District (BART), Golden Gate Bridge Highway and Transportation District (GGBHTD), and Alameda-Contra Costa Transit District (A-C Transit). A fourth transportation district was created by referendum in 1972—the Santa Clara County Transit District.[39] These are not the only regionally important transportation agencies in the Bay Area. San Francisco Municipal Railway (MUNI) is an important feeder and distributor line to BART and to all other transit lines entering the city. There are at least two important private transit agencies operating in the region—Greyhound buses into Contra Costa County and Southern Pacific commuter trains through San Mateo County to San Jose.

Planning, construction, and maintenance of highways are State and local responsibilities. All bay bridges, except the Golden Gate Bridge, are constructed and maintained by a State agency (the Division of Bay Toll Crossings in the Department of Public Works).

The capstone of the regional transportation system is the Metropolitan Transportation Commission (MTC). Created by the legislature in 1970, the commission is the culmination of over a decade of effort to develop regional comprehensive transportation planning and coordination.

Prior to MTC, the Bay Area Transportation Study Commission (BATS) was created by statute in 1963 to meet Federal highway planning requirements; it continued until 1969. BATS had 41 members, 19 of whom were representatives of cities and counties and of ABAG. Through overlapping membership, the Executive Committee in effect sat on BATS, thus affording a basis at the policy level for close liaison. BATS recommended the creation of a directly elected multi-purpose regional agency which would be responsible for planning and implementation, including transportation. In the event that a multi-purpose regional agency was not established, BATS recommended the creation of a special-purpose regional transportation agency. In 1970 the Metropolitan Transportation Commission was established.

In the interim between BATS and MTC, a Regional Transportation Planning Committee of ABAG acted as a "regional transportation planning agency" to comply with the requirements of the Federal Highway Act. Strenuous though unsuccessful efforts were made during this period by ABAG to secure recognition by DOT as a class-A planning area. Such recognition would have enabled local and regional transportation agencies to secure Federal grants covering two-thirds instead of one-half of project costs. Soon after MTC was created, but before it was operational, DOT recognized the region as class-A.

The commission consists of one member each appointed by ABAG and BCDC, two members each from San Francisco, Alameda, Contra Costa, San Mateo and Santa Clara Counties (one representing cities and one representing the county), and one member each from Marin, Solano Sonoma, and Napa Counties. In the four smaller counties, a mayor's selection committee nominates three persons and the county board of supervisors appoints one of them to the commission. The State Secretary for Business and Transportation appoints one non-voting member.[40]

By June 30, 1973, the commission must adopt a regional transportation plan. Thereafter "the operation, construction and modification of those transportation systems under the purview of the Commission" must be in accord with the regional plan. Even before 1973 all new transbay bridges and multi-county transit systems using an exclusive right-of-way must receive commission approval before construction. The California Highway Commission is required to allocate funds for construction of the State highway system in accordance with the regional transportation plan, except when deviation serves "an overriding State interest." MTC is authorized to plan only for the "role of airports and harbors as they relate to ground transportation."

The Act states that MTC "shall merge with or otherwise join any multifunctional regional government organization, if it has transportation responsibilities."

The commission is also responsible for allocating funds within the region for the support and development of public transit which come from a 1/4 of a cent sales tax.[41] A spirited contest for major allocations from the funds available in San Francisco, Alameda, and Contra Costa Counties is being waged by BART, AC-Transit, and MUNI.

MTC is already presiding over efforts to resolve disputes among transportation agencies, for example, proposals to extend the BART system. An East Bay-San Francisco split, which has developed occasionally on the BART Board, is likely to deepen as the board has to deal with proposals to connect BART to the San Francisco Airport, located in non-member San Mateo County, and to extend the system. Another problem of coordination and accommodation among separate transit systems involves the rearrangement of bus routes by A-C Transit to feed BART stations, the determination of joint fares, and competition of A-C Transit buses to San Francisco.

The most ambitious program of cooperation among governmental agencies in the Bay Area is being organized by ABAG, MTC, and District 4 of the State Division of Highways. In many ways this is a continuation of a relationship first established in 1964 among ABAG, the Bay Area Transportation Study Commission (BATS), and the State Department of Public Works. Close relationships are easier to establish and maintain with MTC (as was BATS before it) and ABAG located in the same office building.

ABAG's land-use plan is still very general and judgemental in character. This is desirable as one moves toward policy making and away from analysis. It is not, however, an instrument that can be used without further refinement to direct such specialized activities as transportation and air pollution control.

During 1973 the joint ABAG-MTC land-use transportation team will make the goals in the regional plan more precise and develop a quantified regional land-use and transportation data base to serve the urban forecasting modelling system. The basic objective of the ABAG-MTC joint program is to determine "whether the impact of transport policies upon land use, the environment, housing, densities, etc., would help to accomplish the goals of the Regional Plan."

The ABAG-MTC agreement also provides that MTC will review all transportation-related applications for Federal funding before they are reviewed by ABAG. MTC's comments will be forwarded with the application, regardless of whether ABAG agrees with the comments.

Airport Planning. Regional airport system needs were among the eight "district problem areas" identified by ABAG in 1966 as "regional in nature and significantly interrelated which are so urgent and serious as to require immediate attention and priority."[42] Earlier in the same year, the executive director recommended that ABAG create a special regional airport committee consisting of representatives of airport agencies along with others "to insure balance and perspective."

ABAG did not create such a committee, but the San Francisco Public Utilities Commission, the Port of Oakland, and the San Jose Municipal Airport executed in 1967 a joint powers agreement creating a joint agency called the Bay Area Study of Aviation Requirements (BASAR). ABAG's continuing interest in airport planning and the need on the part of BASAR for HUD 701 planning assistance, led to the establishment in 1969 of a joint ABAG-BASAR regional airport systems study. The study has been carried out under an ABAG committee (RASSC) consisting of either a county supervisor, mayor, or city councilman from each county and representatives of the three major airports. Several regional agencies such as BCDC and BATSC (later MTC) served as non-voting members.

All local contributions towards the cost of Phase 1—a study of aviation requirements—were contributed by the three airport agencies in BASAR. Major contributions were continued in subsequent phases by BASAR although some local matching funds came from the ABAG budget. In 1971-72, for instance, ABAG and BASAR each contributed $10,000. The total cost of the study was $587,500. Two-thirds of the funds came from the Federal government: most of them from HUD and the rest from FAA.

Largely on the basis of reduced estimates of regional population growth and increased estimates of aircraft seat occupancy, the Regional Airport Systems Study Commission recommended that a ceiling on passenger capacity be placed on San Francisco International Airport, that San Jose Municipal Airport be allowed to grow only "within the limits of its environmental constraints," that one or perhaps two military airports in the northern counties be jointly used by military and civilian planes, and that most of the growth be centered at Oakland Airport. The committee maintained that using existing airports instead of constructing new ones will contribute to the realization of the city-centered concept underlying ABAG's Regional Plan.

The proposed plan was favorably received by most people and organizations. However, an additional runway to be built on bay fill would be required at the Oakland airport by 1985. This will require a permit from the Bay Conservation and Development Commission, which has already made it clear that if and when an application to fill is filed BCDC will make its own decision as to whether "no feasible alternative is available."[43] Both the Sierra Club and the Save the Bay Association oppose any plans requiring bay fill. Some individuals and groups, anxious to keep both the bay from being filled and open space despoiled, are urging that the growth of the region be slowed, that as a matter of public policy potential demand not be met, and that means of travel alternative to airplanes be developed.

During public hearings before the ABAG Executive Committee, an inter-regional complication arose when Sacramento County and the Sacramento Regional Planning Commission requested that the portion of the plan calling for development of joint civilian-military use of Travis Air Force Base be deleted from the Bay Area plan until a joint study could be made of the impact of a major airport halfway between Sacramento and San Francisco.

In November 1972 ABAG adopted the proposed regional airport plan as a special element in its comprehensive regional plan. Sole reliance for implementing the airport plan is placed upon the weight that ABAG review and comment on applications for Federal assistance can carry with State and Federal agencies. The committee explored the possibility that State and Federal regulatory agencies might assist in implementation through allocations of routes and scheduling.

For airports, as for other regional problems in the Bay Area, there is some talk about the desirability of creating a special regional airport agency.[44] One possibility is to give regulatory authority over the location and expansion of airports to the Metropolitan Transportation Commission. It is now confined by statute to deal with only the interface between air transportation and ground transportation. In its work program for 1973, MTC speaks of assuming "the responsibility for continuing airport planning functions" and of making an in-depth survey of airport needs and a major review of airport development plans in 1977 and thereafter at five-year intervals.

The State Department of Aeronautics is required by statute to prepare a Statewide Master Plan of Aviation, which is being funded in part by HUD. A joint coordinating committee has been created consisting of the project directors of the ABAG study, the SCAG study, and the State study.

Water Management and Water Quality Control. There are 32 water districts and 44 sanitation districts in the Bay Area. Six water districts and ten sanitation districts had expenditures in 1966-67 above the median of all units of local government in the region. In addition to the East Bay Municipal Utility District (EBMUD), four water districts and two sanitary districts had expenditures in excess of a million dollars each.

EBMUD is the oldest multi-county special district in the Bay Area. It was organized by referendum in 1923 under the Municipal Utility District Act of 1921, which authorized a municipal utility district to provide many services other than water supply, such as electricity, transportation, communication, waste disposal, and recreation. EBMUD has extended its functions only to the treatment and disposal of sewage within a special service district in northern Alameda County. It is now developing recreation facilities on its reservoir lands, but its refusal in the early 1930s to develop its surplus lands into regional parks led to the creation in 1934 of the East Bay Regional Park

District. The park district subsequently purchased EBMUD land in the Berkeley hills. EBMUD has recently indicated its willingness to consider assumption of responsibility for sub-regional solid waste disposal.

The Water Department of the San Francisco Public Utilities Commission has to be considered a regional agency even though it is a division of the City and County of San Francisco. The Water Department is a major wholesaler of water to a large portion of the region outside the city—San Mateo County and portions of Santa Clara and Alameda Counties. It serves more people indirectly outside the city than are served inside—a total of over two million people in a 500-square-mile area. San Francisco pays about $1 million annually in property taxes on its watershed lands in other counties. [45]

The State Water Resources Control Board and its regional water quality control boards not only furnish an example of statewide regulation but also of a system of regional administration of its regulatory process. The regional boards exercise jurisdiction over delineated geographical areas, but they are State agencies with respect to authority, financing, responsibility, and method of appointment. The system of a parent State agency with statewide coverage by subsidiary regional boards may well be the pattern adopted in California to regulate pollutants of air and land, as well as water. A bill representing a compromise between the Governor and environmentalists which would apply this policy-making and administrative pattern to air and water quality, solid waste management, noise abatement, pesticide usage, and nuclear radiation (AB 2376, Z'berg-Way) was killed this year on the Assembly floor.

The formulation of State and regional water quality control policies, the establishment of waste discharge requirements, and the enforcement of such requirements put the State and regional boards in the center of regional governance. There is a clear interface between their activities and those of ABAG in water management planning. The State Water Resources Control Board is responsible for developing 16 comprehensive basin plans and 15 regional area plans required for eligibility to receive Federal grants for construction of treatment facilities. At the same time ABAG has been required by HUD to prepare water and sewage elements in its regional plan. The State seems effectively to have preempted the field of regional water quality planning.

The State Water Resources Control Board has contracted with ABAG to provide data and analyses of land uses, population changes, etc., for incorporation into the "Fully developed Water Quality Management Plan" for the San Francisco Bay Area Basin. ABAG is also supplying a staff consultant as a member of the planning team under a grant to ABAG from the State board, but there is no liaison at the policy level. [46]

The State Water Resources Control Board has been involved in planning for wastewater treatment and disposal in the Bay Area since 1965 when the legislature authorized it to make a comprehensive study and develop a water quality management program for San Francisco Bay and the Sacramento-San Joaquin delta. The study cost approximately $3 million of State and Federal Funds.

The following recommendation is of special interest to this study:

A regional agency, either single- or multi-purpose be formed as soon as possible to plan, design, construct and operate a comprehensive water pollution and water quality control system throughout the 12 counties comprising the Bay-Delta area.

Most criticisms were over the projected costs of the proposals, both overall and to particular jurisdictions; over the location of proposed regional treatment plants; the use of the ocean as the final receiver of discharges; and the allegedly insufficient attention paid to alternative methods, such as reclamation and reuse of wastewaters.

As of 1972 we find that the Bay-Delta Plan is being reviewed and revised as part of the Basin Plan now being conducted by the State and regional boards; that a multiple-purpose regional agency has not been created in the Bay Area but that a special district—BASSA—has been established; and that the State board, fortified by a $1.5 million bond issue voted in 1970 and by Federal matching funds and regulations, is dominant within the Bay Area with respect to the treatment and disposal of liquid wastes.

Both EBMUD and the State Water Resources Control Board played important roles in the creation of BASSA. ABAG was effectively shut out of playing any role.[47] The new agency is formally organized with the mayor of San Jose as chairman and a former president of ABAG as vice-chairman. It remains to be seen, however, whether effective working relations can be established. BASSA's regional water quality control plan must be submitted to ABAG for review and comment. Amendments in 1972 provide that the agency will merge with any regional comprehensive planning agency created by the legislature, provided it has substantially the same powers. San Francisco had succeeded a year earlier in having such a provision deleted.

Air Pollution Control. The San Francisco Bay Area Air Pollution Control District (BAAPCD), after years of low-key policy-making and enforcement of air quality standards, has suddenly become more active in response to the Federal Clean Air Act of 1970.[48] In May 1972 the district board adopted amendments to District Regulation 2, which requires after July 1, 1972, a permit from the District to "construct any facility or building, or erect, alter or replace any article, machine, equipment or other contrivance, the use of which may cause the emission of air contaminants." Nonindustrial construction is exempted from the permit requirement for four years, at which time the district board will review exemptions from the regulation.

Los Angeles has long used the permit system without any of the horrendous consequences predicted in the Bay Area. It seems likely, however, that its use now under authority of the Federal Clean Air Act of 1970 and air quality standards of the California Act will lead the district into the regulation of land use. The Attorney General of California has ruled that

> pursuant to the existing statute the Bay Area Air Pollution Control District has authority to adopt general regulations [as required by the Clean Air Act as amended in 1970] setting up standards to control the release of air contamination in order to reduce air pollution within the District and to couple such regulations with a regulation or regulations setting up a permit system requiring authority from the Board prior to constructing a possible source of air pollution to assure that anticipated discharges will be in compliance with the general standards.[49]

The board also is authorized by statute to divide the district into zones for this purpose. "This authority is of the same nature as that now exercised by cities and counties in the form of zoning regulations.[50] Within the district as a whole or in particular zones, the board may "set up . . . general performance standards and a permit system."[51]

The Air Pollution Control District is now part of a Federal-State-regional air pollution control operation. The district has authority to regulate stationary pollution sources, but authority over mobile sources, principally automotive vehicles, is vested in the State Air Resources Board. The State legislative analyst has commented on this dual assignment of responsibility for controlling two elements which together constitute the ambient air quality of an air basin:

> Both the board and the local agencies are attempting to control the emissions for which each has responsibility with the best methods available to each. There is a natural tendency for each agency to attribute any lack of improvement in air quality to the other agency while emphasizing its own accomplishments.[52]

The relationship of the Federal government to the State and its subdivisions under the Clean Air Act does "not fully resolve this problem of responsibility but instead tend[s] to lift the problem to higher levels of government."[53] Although control over new car emissions is preempted by the Federal government, the Act does require the State to assume responsibility for developing plans to enforce the national ambient air quality standards in each air basin.

The Federal Environmental Protection Agency, according to the Bay Area Council, has also established direct contacts with the Bay Area Air Pollution Control District. The recent amendments to Regulation 2 requiring permits for construction was said to have provided originally for a denial of permits beginning in 1976 when "air quality standards are or would be exceeded. . . . A representative of the federal Environmental Protection Agency told the District that would not be good enough, so the Board—rather than exploring other alternatives—simply withdrew the four year provision, making it effective as of the first of next month."[54]

ABAG's Regional Home Rule Proposal of 1969, noting that both ABAG and the Air Pollution Control District consisted of elected city and county officials, recommended that negotiations be immediately undertaken to establish a working relationship between the two agencies. There is no evidence, however, that it is easier to coordinate the activities of two agencies if both are governed by city and county officials. A purposive corporate body, regardless of how its board of directors is constituted, develops a distinctive coloration as it adjusts to its habitat, its clients, specialized professional staff, and its financiers.

It was not until April 1971 that ABAG sent a draft proposal for a joint working agreement to the Air Pollution Control District. On March 1, 1972, the air pollution board instructed "the District Staff to meet with the ABAG staff and prepare a proposal of understanding between ABAG and the District."[55] On August 10, 1972, ABAG received a draft of an agreement prepared by the district staff and dated July 19, 1972. The joint agreement was approved in December 1972.

Regional Open Space. ABAG's first planning report, issued in 1962, was an *Inventory of parks and Open Spaces* prepared by a Technical Advisory Committee on Recreation. Throughout the past decade, the preservation of open space has been a major concern of the ABAG regional planning program, as well as of articulate individuals and many Bay Area organizations.

The many regional, county, and local groups interested in the preservation of open space and the development of parks and recreation were affiliated in 1958 into The Citizens for Regional Recreation and Parks. The new organization prepared an inventory of publicly owned, relatively permanent, open space areas in the region, which was incorporated into the California Outdoor Recreation Plan of 1960. Citizens for Regional Recreation and Parks (CRRP) has been credited with persuading ABAG to undertake regional land-use planning.[56] In 1964, it collected and analyzed for presentation to ABAG the views of its constituent organizations, other interested groups, and many individuals on which areas should be preserved as open space or used for recreation.

To many people, the outstanding feature of ABAG's Preliminary Regional Plan (1966) was the open space element. Under the Preliminary Plan, 2.0 million acres would be designated as permanent open space and 1.7 million acres would be temporarily reserved for future urban expansion.

In 1968, CRRP became a non-profit corporation under the name of People for Open Space in order to receive a Ford Foundation Grant to study the economic impact of open space preservation in the Bay Area. According to the study report, the proposal for permanent open space in the ABAG Preliminary Regional Plan is economically sound and financially practicable.[57]

People for Open Space (POS) recommended that a regional open space agency be established as part of a regional government. If a regional government were not created, then POS urged that an independent commission similar to BCDC be established. At the very least, it urged legislative creation of a special land-use study commission.[58]

Two bills to create a limited but multiple-purpose regional government were introduced in 1969—one (AB 711) by Assemblyman Knox, chairman of the Assembly Committee on Local Government and of the Joint Committee on Bay Area Regional Organization (BARO), and the other (AB 1846) by Assemblyman Bagley on behalf of ABAG. Neither bill was passed out of committee. In 1970, although another Knox bill to create a regional conservation and development agency was introduced, People for Open Space decided to pursue its second alternative and seek legislation creating an independent Bay Area Open Space Commission (SB 1400—Marks). The Marks bill was killed in the Senate Finance Committee.[59]

ABAG has continued to keep open space high on its agenda of regional issues. The *Regional Plan: 1970-1990,* a refinement of the preliminary regional plan of 1966, increased the target of permanent open space from 2 million to 3.4 million acres and reduced the temporary reserve for urban expansion from 1.7 million to 0.6 million acres.

The ABAG Executive Committee has approved for transmission to the General Assembly, on November 10, 1972, the Phase II Open Space Element, which accepts the target in the 1970 Regional Plan, develops it in more detail, and recommends an action program for the next five years. City and county plans are required by statute to have an adopted open space element by July 1, 1973. ABAG will coordinate regional open space planning (Phase II) with county and municipal planning during the coming year. At the same time, it has already engaged in developing a Phase III Open Space Plan in collaboration with the East Bay Regional Park District. In the meantime, Phase II will satisfy HUD requirements and keep local agencies eligible to apply for Federal assistance.

In 1970, only 14.2 percent of the 3.4 million acres targeted for the regional open space system were in the status of permanent preservation. The Phase II plan presents two alternative five-year acquisition programs that would raise the level of open space reservation to 20.8 or 21.6 percent. "Neither of these two programs can be described as making great progress toward meeting the open space deficit."[60]

Since ABAG is a voluntary council of governments, it can only establish priorities and then use its persuasion with local, State, and Federal governments to act in accordance with the regional plan. The program will be used by ABAG as standards against which it reviews application for Federal assistance. If ABAG is able to develop a "capital improvements programming process," of which open space preservation would be an element, its capacity to use the A-95 review and comment as means of implementation would be greatly enhanced.

ABAG is already developing a Phase III program in collaboration with the East Bay Regional Park District. This should be ready for review and adoption in two years. In the meantime, ABAG will consult with county and municipal governments as they prepare the open space elements of their own plans and with other governments that own or manage public lands. It proposes to create an open space preservation information system which will collect up-to-date data on all applications for rezoning, variances from zoning regulations, subdivision of land, and building permits. "Participation in the information system is considered as a requirement for any local government in the Bay Region to be in conformity with the Regional Plan."[61]

An immediate step has been taken by the ABAG Executive Committee in its recommendation to the General Assembly that the State and Federal governments be requested to finance and assist in collecting and analyzing more precise environmental data[62] and to commit all relevant State and Federal agencies to implement the open space element of the ABAG Regional Plan.

The resolution also repeats a plea first made by ABAG in 1967 that

The State of California recognize the urgent need to authorize an ongoing multi-functional planning and implementation agency for the San Francisco Bay Region, one of whose highest priorities must be to continue planning and coordination and to begin to implement aggressively a definitive system of open space for the region as well as to assist local governments in meeting their responsibilities in managing the open space resources of the region.

Regional Parks and Recreation. After long negotiations with HUD, funding approval was secured in November 1971 for a parks and open space program to be jointly conducted by ABAG and the East Bay Regional Park District.[63] The joint program is now underway by consultants who will prepare simultaneously a report on a regional parks program for the nine-county Bay Area and a two-county master plan for the East Bay Regional Park District. Part of the regional plan report for ABAG will contain analyses and recommendations on organizational structures, functions, powers, finance, and other legislative recommendations.

The East Bay Regional Park District is the only multi-county park agency in the region. Voters in Marin County and Northern Santa Clara County approved in November the creation of two additional regional park districts.

The joint ABAG-East Bay Regional Park District program may be a prototype of bilateral or even multilateral collaboration between ABAG and other special-purpose agencies. It could also be used as the vehicle for joint sub-regional planning and implementation agreements between ABAG and one or more counties, one or more cities, or a combination of cities and counties.

Bay Conservation and Development. The San Francisco Bay Conservation and Development Commission (BCDC), backed up by the U.S. Army Corps of Engineers, controls the filling and dredging of the bay. In 1969, the legislature made BCDC a permanent agency and adopted its Bay Plan. In exercising control of a 100-foot-strip around the bay, BCDC is directed by statute to require maximum public access to the bay and to see that land on the shore suitable for high-priority water-related purposes be reserved for these purposes.

The following list of purposes for which filling may be allowed under the Bay Plan illustrates both the pressures upon the bay and the intergovernmental context in which BCDC must operate:

Developing *modern port terminals,* on a regional basis, to keep San Francisco Bay a major world harbor during a period of rapid change in shipping technology.

Developing sites for *industries that require access to the Bay* for transportation of raw materials or manufactured products.

Developing *new recreational opportunities*—shoreline parks, marinas, fishing piers, beaches, hiking and bicycling paths, and scenic drives.

Developing expanded *airport terminals and runways, if* regional studies demonstrate that the growth in air transportation cannot be accommodated in any other way.

Developing new *transportation routes* (with construction on pilings, not solid fill), *if* thorough study determines that no feasible alternatives are available.

Developing new *public access to the Bay and enhancing shoreline* appearance through filling limited to Bay-related commercial recreation and public assembly.[64]

The U.S. Army Corps of Engineers plays a vital role in regulating the uses of the bay. The Corps, the U.S. Environmental Agency, and the San Francisco Bay Area Regional Water Quality Control Board are cooperating with BCDC to develop new rules for bay dredging. The Corps has recently required that dredge spoils be dumped 25 miles at sea instead of at previously used sites within the Bay. The Corps is also enforcing provisions of the Rivers and Harbors Act of 1891 by requiring a permit for any "new work" within the tidal margins of the bay.

Ocean Coastline. After the successful fight to establish BCDC, the attention of conservationists and of many public officials was turned toward the enactment of legislation to conserve and develop the coastline of the Pacific Ocean. No coastline bill was enacted during the 1970, 1971, and 1972 sessions. During the summer of 1972, however, sufficient signatures were secured to place an initiative proposal on the November ballot and the electorate affirmed the creation of a State Coastal Commission and six regional commissions.

Members of the ABAG Executive Committee and General Assembly are divided over supporting the initiative proposal. This division reflects a division among city and county officials—a division further exemplified by the decision (11-8) of the Board of Directors of the League of California Cities to support the initiative proposal. However, an ocean coastline plan is considered by ABAG to be an important element in its regional plan.

The first phase was completed almost concurrently with approval of the *Regional Plan: 1970-1990* by publication of a report entitled *Ocean Coastline Study*. The report contained descriptive data on the natural features of the coastline, changes in those features resulting from human use of the coastline, issues involved in conserving and protecting the coast, and the public and private interests in the coastal conservation and development.

Phase II is now being completed by an Ocean Coastline Committee consisting of representatives of cities and counties bordering on the ocean. Santa Cruz County, outside the Bay Area but included in the 1970 study area, is not involved in Phase II. Financial support came from contributions by the ocean counties of San Mateo, San Francisco, Marin, and Sonoma, which were matched by HUD 701 funds through the California Council on Intergovernmental Relations.

The Phase II report will delineate the coastal area; project economic and demographic developments; specify alternative land-use patterns; evaluate the economic, environmental, and ecological impacts of these alternatives; and identify Federal, State, regional, and local governmental policies for coastal management.

It is proposed to move this year into Phase III, again to be supported by contributions from the coastal counties and the California Council of Intergovernmental Relations. The objectives of this phase will be "to develop planning and regulatory approaches which reconcile coastal growth and non-growth policies. . . [and to] produce an enforceable management program for the Bay Area's coastal lands and resources."[65]

Solid Waste Disposal. Again, as in open space and parks regional planning for the disposal of solid waste was one of the earliest of ABAG concerns. However, ABAG has not been directly active in developing a regional plan for solid waste disposal. In 1965, ABAG requested the State Department of Public Health to make an inventory study of refuse disposal needs for the Bay Area.[66] Refuse disposal was singled out as a special element in the *Preliminary Regional Plan* of 1966 and the Goals and Organization Committee in the same year listed it as one of three regional problems for which "there is no well-organized effort at the present time to find regional solutions." In 1969, ABAG requested the legislature to give it authority to plan and implement a regional refuse disposal system. But in 1970 the *Regional Plan: 1970-1990* only recommended that

> The Association should undertake studies to identify the functions of solid waste management as well as the operating, coordinating and planning responsibilities.[67]

In the same year, a Subcommittee on Solid Waste Disposal jointly sponsored with the San Francisco Planning and Urban Renewal Association (SUR) a feasibility study of the disposal of solid waste in the Delta as a means of building up the surface of subsiding peat bog islands. Despite the value of the study, ABAG did not undertake to develop a regional program for managing the disposal of solid waste.

The vacuum has been filled by unilateral action by several of the Bay Area counties, the State Department of Public Health, and the State legislature. In the 1971 session a bill was introduced by Senator Nedjedly of Contra Costa County, which designated the State Department of Public Health as the State solid waste management agency. The bill requiring counties to prepare a "coordinated, comprehensive solid waste management plan," passed the Legislature but was vetoed by the Governor. However, a 1972 Nedjedly bill creating a State Solid Waste Management Board and requiring county solid waste plans was signed into law.

ABAG opposed both bills because they did not provide for regional solid waste planning. However, there was division of opinion among local officials. Many supported the Nedjedly bill because they did not consider solid waste disposal to be a regional affair. Some maintained that only San Francisco stood to gain by a regional approach and that it was attempting to dump its garbage in other counties and make them help to pay the costs. Others asserted that their own county planning was too far advanced to be replaced by a time-consuming transfer to regional planning.

Under the Nedjedly Act, county plans must be approved by a majority of the cities within the county containing a majority of the incorporated population of the county. The Act does provide that a county may, "with the agreement of a majority of the cities of the county which contains a majority of the incorporated population of the county," transfer responsibility for preparing the plan to a regional planning agency recognized by the State Council on Intergovernmental Relations.

There is no provision for regional review and comment on county plans. But the Act as enacted does not require, as did the 1971 Nedjedly bill, that the county plans be submitted to the "appropriate areawide environmental health planning agency for review and comment."

Current activity in ABAG involves efforts to persuade the counties to discuss the desirability and feasibility of a joint ABAG-county planning effort and to assist in organizing a group of cities and counties, some in the Bay area, some in Sacramento, Yolo and San Joaquin Counties, to develop a proposal and to secure financing of a demonstration disposal-land reclamation project on a Delta island.

Social Policy Development

It is a truism, almost a cliché by now, to observe that metropolitan governments and even metropolitan planning agencies—the few we have—will emphasize construction projects and physical planning and avoid social problems and policies as long as possible. Most regional planning and operating agencies arise out of a delicate balance of trust and distrust among existing power centers. Any such organization will seek to avoid disruptive conflict where possible and this is wholly functional in the formative years. Only after the organization has jelled and supportive relationships have been established is it safe to leave the hard issues of physical planning and policy for the soft shoulders of social policy.

ABAG was pushed out of areawide criminal justice planning before it could successfully face the conflicts between functional and comprehensive planning. It waited too long before asserting an interest in comprehensive health planning, but it may still arrange a working truce with the health planners. Regional housing policy is currently the only active element of regional social planning in which staff, politicians, and citizen activists are engaged.

Comprehensive Health Planning. The Bay Area Comprehensive Health Planning Council (BACHP), organized under a State statute enacted in 1969, is responsible for comprehensive health planning. The scope of activities of the areawide and local CHP councils is determined by the State Health Planning Council. The State Department of Health is required to submit for review by local and areawide comprehensive health councils all applications for license to construct and operate health facilities. Under this law the local and areawide CHP council (not a board of supervisors or city council) must make the findings of fact as to desirability of the proposed health facility. Appeals from findings and recommendations of the areawide CHP council may be made by a dissatisfied applicant—first to another CHP council. The appellate body designated to hear appeals from the Bay Area is the San Diego and Imperial County Comprehensive Health Planning Council.

State law also empowers areawide CHP councils to review all applications for grants of public funds if they relate to health and if they are administered either directly or indirectly by State agencies. Such programs include hospital construction (Hill-Harris), mental retardation, community mental health centers, sewage treatment plant construction, and solid waste disposal facilities.

The Bay Area Comprehensive Health Planning Council is headed by a 40-member Board of Directors. The board is composed of representatives of the nine county comprehensive health planning councils, and such other agencies as the Regional Medical Program, Bay Area Health Association, Bay Area Social Planning Council, and the Hospital Council of Northern California. ABAG has one member on the board, a position filled until recently by the executive director or his designee. There has been little participation in comprehensive health planning by elected city and county officials.

Each Bay Area county has a county comprehensive health planning council. Six of them have their own staff and the three northern counties have a joint staff. During the developmental period, (1968-70), the program was financed with a grant from HEW matched by contributions from county health departments and private organizations. The budget for first-year "operational" planning called for total expenditures of $776,764 to support the regional and county planning programs. Again, the Federal share was almost 50 percent, although local funds made up 56 percent of the total in the North Bay Counties and 63 percent in Santa Clara County.

ABAG did not play a strong role in the activities of the council during the developmental period. It was not represented at the board meetings by elected city or county officials. Strong feelings were expressed at times by other members of the council that ABAG was meddling in other people's business by occupying the single chair assigned to it. During this period, the professional health and hospital members consolidated their position through a merger of the Health Facilities Planning Association with the council.

The role of ABAG might have been much stronger if the State legislature had not enacted several bills in 1969 giving the comprehensive health planning councils statutory powers. As the ABAG staff viewed the developments:

In the Bay Area the initial formula for the development of an organization was discussed by a broad range of interests including the county medical societies, county health officers, and other voluntary health agencies, ABAG, the Health Facilities Planning Association and the Bay

Area Social Planning Council. The final outcome of these discussions was the formation of county CHP councils who formed into a "confederation in order to meet the Federal requirements for an areawide agency. The emphasis of the program was primarily planning and coordinative. However, in 1969, the California Legislature passed several bills which gave the Comprehensive Health Planning Program additional review and regulatory responsibilities. This action substantially broadened the powers and responsibilities of the program. It should be noted that this was done during the *organizational* period prior to the final designation of a permanent comprehensive health planning agency.68

The ABAG Executive Committee approved the CHP application for first-year operations with the condition that an agreement be signed by the two agencies to develop a joint work program on those elements of mutual interest. The application was granted by HEW without any reference to ABAG's recommendations. Nevertheless, an agreement was signed, with reluctance on the part of many members of the BACHPC Board.

After a year of joint inactivity, a new agreement was signed in 1972. Under a new executive director of BACHP, there has been a sharp increase in collaboration with the staff of ABAG. The new agreement provides for:

1. Written comments "prior to formalization" by each agency on the language and annual work programs of the other;
2. A bi-monthly review of "the on-going health-system related activities" of the two programs;
3. ABAG becomes responsible for processing and storing health-system related information as part of its BRISC program;
4. BACHP will review health related applications filed under A-95, and ABAG will have the opportunity to review Federal grant applications filed with CHP under State statute; and
5. Both agencies pledge to integrate and coordinate current and projected plans and programs, especially in "the area of environmental quality and control."

A draft of stage I of the comprehensive health plan for the Bay Area was released for public hearing and board consideration in May 1972. Its findings and recommendations were developed by a general planning committee of 28 members and five planning task forces: Environmental Health, Health Facilities, Health Manpower, Organization of Personal Health Services, and Social Issues Related to Health. A representative of the State Office of Comprehensive Health Planning served on each task force.

Four problems were designated for immediate attention: (1) cost of heath care, (2) transportation to health facilities, (3) effect of laws against sexual practices and the health of homosexuals, and (4) health manpower. Special attention was given to groups which are "underserved" and "excluded" from the process of health services delivery.[69]

This report has made no mention of other local and regional agencies that are also concerned with social issues related to health, including schools, the criminal justice system, and the social welfare agencies.

The section on delivery of health care services was concerned with the training and distribution of manpower, health care facilities (including transportation), and the means of paying for care, but the discussion of health care facilities is of more immediate concern to ABAG, the Metropolitan Transportation Commission, and the Air Pollution Control District than other parts of the section. The only specific reference to ABAG was the recommendation that it and the Bay Area Health Association, consisting of county public health directors, investigate the provision of "air transported emergency service on a regional basis to . . . areas difficult to reach by ground travel."[70] Cities and counties were urged to "improve public transportation service connecting low-income areas with health facilities and other health care providers," but there were no references to MTC, BART, Alameda-Contra Costa Transit District or the Golden Gate Bridge, Highway and Transportation District.

The location of facilities, especially those serving all or large parts of the Bay Area, is intimately related to regional as well as local land-use planning. BACHP has also prepared a separate *Regional Health Facilities and Services Plan, 1972.* Because of ABAG's responsibility for regional land-use planning and for A-95 review of applications for Federal grants, it should have participated in the development of this document. *Post hoc* review and comment is not enough to assure inter-agency coordination.

The overlay between the interests of ABAG and BACHP is complete with respect to environmental planning. Also, many other regional agencies can claim the right to be involved: BCDC, the Bay Area Regional Water Quality Control Board, East Bay Municipal Utility District, Bay Area Sewage Services Agency, San Francisco Bay Area Pollution Control District, and the East Bay Regional Park District.

Environmental planning was discussed in the BACHP draft report in two phases.[71] The primary purpose of Phase I was "to involve the citizen in the protection of his environment."

It was also planned to establish "working relationships" with all environmental agencies and "to bring environmental protection agencies and community groups to review and comment on all grants and other documents which will have an impact on the environment. ABAG as the A-95 agency was specifically mentioned, but there was no reference to the agreement between ABAG and BACHP which calls for such joint participation in review and comment. There may also be some overlap and at times jurisdictional friction between the ABAG Regional Citizens Forum and citizen forums planned by BACHP.

Phase II, entitled Community Oriented Planning, was more action-oriented than the process plans of Phase I, but it is still only a plan for a plan. Four goals are specified:

1. Establish an adequate and effective land-use policy for the Bay Area;
2. Make mass transportation systems more responsive to enhancing the quality of life of the people in the Bay Area;
3. Prepare special projects about issues salient in the county forums; and
4. Develop a clearing house of information on environmental grant funds.

The draft report maintained that land-use planning is not a function of comprehensive health planning. But it was recognized that environmental health planning is inseparable from land-use planning. The problem is that "the Bay Area has no unified regional land-use policy." Therefore, it was recommended that BACHP:

1. Work with existing agencies to assist in the adoption of a regional land-use policy for the Bay Area;
2. Review and comment on existing plans and assist in the synthesis of comments into a unified plan for the Bay Area;
3. Support the establishment of a regional land-use agency to coordinate planning, implementation and control of a regional land-use policy; and
4. Be cognizant of the interrelationship of land use and transportation, air pollutants, water quality and waste disposal.

With respect to mass transportation, BACHP should

1. Provide MTC with information about the needs for public transportation to health care facilities and related services in the Bay Area; and
2. Develop reports on the fragmentation of services to communities in the Bay Area.

The draft report also recommended that BACHP and MTC develop a working relationship "to undertake joint ventures in improving the region's mass transportation system."

The county CHPC's reacted strongly to the draft plan, interpreting it as a threat to their perceived role in comprehensive health planning. The draft was also criticized for the low level of professional input and for an unbalanced emphasis upon the interests and needs of a miscellany of minorities.

ABAG was especially critical of the sections on environmental health and the failure to recognize the involvement of other public and private agencies in environmental protection. The BACHP board of directors accepted the plan but refused to adopt it.

In May 1972, under a new executive director, BACHP was reorganized to emphasize the federative character of its relationship to the county CHPC's. The regional staff was cut by two-thirds and the funds thus saved were used to increase the staffs of the county CHPC's.

The issues raised in the earlier draft plan have been restated along with goals and policies necessary to meet them. The regional work program for 1973-74 calls for the development of alternative action recommendations from which specific proposals will be selected and implementation policies approved, put into effect, and evaluated before 1975.

Criminal Justice Planning. After two years (1969-1971) of effort, frequently indecisive and contradictory, to develop a State-regional partnership in spending monies appropriated under the Omnibus Crime Control and Safe Streets Act of 1968, the ABAG Criminal Justice Planning Program was reduced to the level of a consolation prize when counties were recognized as "regions." In early 1971, the California Council on Criminal Justice (CCCJ) recognized six distinct regions within the Bay Area: Alameda County, Contra Costa County, City and County of San Francisco, San Mateo County, Santa Clara County, and the counties of Marin, Napa, Solano, and Sonoma. The council also voted to allocate $390,000 in Part B planning grant funds to these regions and the three major cities, reducing the ABAG allocation from $225,556 to $40,000.

Undoubtedly, 1970 amendments to the Safe Streets Act requiring States to assure that major cities and counties receive planning funds "to develop comprehensive plans and coordinate functions at the local level" affected the decision of the CCCJ, but it was already seeking relief from irritating situations within ABAG and in the Southern California Association of Governments (SCAG). Strong efforts were made by criminal justice groups in California to get CCCJ approval of county autonomy from SCAG. There was some effort along the same lines, but not so intense, in the Bay Area. On January 7, 1971, for instance, Mayor Alioto of San Francisco proposed the creation by the Board of Supervisors of the San Francisco Criminal Justice Council.[72] He did not mention the ABAG criminal justice program. The city manager of Berkeley, among others, testified before CCCJ in favor of designating counties as regions.

However, the principal regional irritation from the Bay Area was an internal fight within ABAG over the administrative relationships among the executive director of ABAG, the regional coordinator of Criminal Justice Planning, and the executive director of CCCJ. A correlative question, over which most of the debate took place, was the relationship among the Executive Committee of ABAG, the Regional Advisory Criminal Justice Planning Board, and CCCJ.

In the early days of the Safe Streets program, when both State and local agencies undertook a crash program to prepare a State plan in time to qualify the State for a block grant, CCCJ turned to ABAG, SCAG, the Sacramento Regional Area Planning Commission, and the San Diego Comprehensive Planning Organization for help. CCCJ adopted in December 1968, the regional planning area boundaries established by the California Council on Intergovernmental Relations and took steps to establish a regional advisory board in each except where there was an existing regional planning organization.

ABAG agreed in January 1969 to act as the regional criminal justice planning agency, requested a planning grant from CCCJ, and appointed a coordinator who was to be responsible, under the direction of the ABAG executive director, "for all aspects of the program." A Regional Advisory Board and eight task forces were established by the Executive Committee. In July 1969, the Executive Committee authorized the enlargement of the advisory board to not more than 40 members "to increase participation and achieve a desirable balance between public, private, and community members." However, the president did not make appointments to the reconstituted advisory board.

Two months later, the Executive Committee voted again to reconstitute the advisory board, this time to include some elected officials, a county manager, a city manager, and the public members who had served on the initial advisory board. These members were considered as the core group of an expanded advisory board. However, before the expansion, the core group was designated as a Special Study Committee to

1. Review various applicable guidelines concerning Regional Advisory Boards.
2. Review the Criminal Justice planning project and action programs conducted thus far.
3. Prepare recommendations to the Executive Committee on the composition and membership of an advisory body.
4. Prepare recommendations to the Executive Committee as to the proposed Advisory Board's functions, duties and responsibilities.
5. Any other pertinent factor which the reconstituted Board will wish to submit to the Executive Committee.

During the deliberations of the Special Study Committee, the regional coordinator of Criminal Justice Planning argued that the difficulties of the regional program were not only due to the vastness, complexity, and newness of the program but were principally caused by organizational ambiguities and administrative indecision.[73] The criminal justice program is pulled toward two parents at the same time: the CCCJ and ABAG. While it is necessary for CCCJ to clean up the ambiguities in its relationship with regional programs, the crucial difficulty is fitting a highly specialized program into the concerns of a voluntary council of governments. The regional coordinator told the Special Study Committee:

> It might be assumed, as was mentioned at the meeting, that when people work cooperatively together toward common objectives, problems of this nature do not reach significant proportions. Yet, examples of delay and indecision have been too numerous and these have not been the result of a lack of cooperation and common objectives. There simply have been and there continue to exist, priorities and concerns with the ABAG spectrum of programs that interfere with and prevent the natural but rapid growth of any new program. The more obvious examples are ABAG's restricted financial resources to guarantee a 10 percent match; inability to provide sufficient office space, and financial services, thus restricting a rate of program growth commensurate with resources available. There are less obvious examples that include very limited actual involvement in the CJP program on the part of the Executive Committee, and a consequent lack of precise knowledge about it; the policy that one program should not grow more rapidly if such growth would disturb other existing programs. To these may be added a perceived lack of confidence in the future of ABAG, as reflected in the actions and statements of many persons.[74]

On the other hand, the ABAG executive director insisted that all that was necessary was for the Regional Advisory Board to present a work program containing a list of priorities. This is expected of all program divisions of ABAG and there is no reason to make an exception for criminal justice planning.

> There has never been a set of clear-cut priorities in CJP, therefore, why should it purchase more typewriters? ABAG has the internal financial structure and the possibilities of space but CJP does not have any clear-cut priorities. If the Region's role were determined, there would be no question of CJP getting the things they are requesting.[75]

The conflict between the executive director of ABAG and the regional coordinator of criminal justice planning underlaid most of the committee's deliberations. In fact, the regional coordinator had discussed his problems with the executive director of the State agency and the latter had written the executive director of ABAG, with a copy to the Regional Coordinator:

> [the Regional CJP Coordinator] and I have had some discussion over the

past few weeks which cause me some concern, which I, in turn, would like to share with you.

Let me preface this by making clear that my concerns are specifically directed to the status of criminal justice planning. You, as Executive Director of ABAG, have a number of other planning activities and programs, many very sensitive politically and of far-reaching impact on the region you serve. I appreciate your broader planning responsibilities and the attendant problems you have establishing priorities internally.

Nevertheless, in view of the national interest in criminal justice planning and system strengthening, I am sympathetic to the problems expressed by [the Regional CJP Coordinator].

I am disturbed when I hear that the Region V staff members may be leaving because of what they regard as insufficient support by ABAG. I am disturbed that despite more than adequate funding made available by the Council, [the Regional CJP Coordinator] believes that he does not have sufficient space, cars, and other physical support. Most importantly, I am disturbed at mounting evidence that the structure is not adequately involving both local governments and criminal justice agencies throughout Region V in a coherent effort to address well-defined needs with broad-scale projects.[76]

Direct reporting between the ABAG regional coordinator and the staff of CCCJ was not limited to this occasion. Budgets and work programs were cleared and preliminary approval secured from the State agency before they were introduced into the ABAG decision-making process. The executive director got news of State action from his department head and not by direct communication from CCCJ.

It was natural under these circumstances for the regional CJP component to seek autonomy—within ABAG if possible, but outside ABAG if necessary. The regional coordinator asserted to the Special Study Committee that "the most effective relationship between CCCJ, ABAG and the regional board is one in which *ABAG* designates the present Regional Advisory Board to act on its behalf as the regional criminal justice planning agency." He recommended that the Regional Advisory Board be "a formal arm of ABAG" but "constituted as an 'Institute of Criminal Justice Planning and Research,' incorporated under the non-profit corporation laws of California."

The principle objective appears to have been the removal of the executive director of ABAG from any control of the criminal justice planning operation. He would be expected to maintain liaison between CJP and other ABAG programs, provide auxiliary services under "written agreement and at the CJP Board's request" and attend regional board meetings. The Executive Committee of ABAG would appoint members and the chairman of the Regional CJP Board, "review" the annual budget, "while delegating to the

Board the authority to award contracts approved under the budget, and to fill positions included within the budget." All other authority would be vested in the regional board and the regional CJP director.

The recommendations of the Special Study Committee paralleled the recommendations to it by the regional CJP coordinator, except that it did not recommend that the board be reconstituted as a non-profit corporation. Instead it recommended that "Criminal Justice Planning and administration of the grant program should continue as a joint State-local function with the Association serving as the regional umbrella agency."

No one knows how the debate, if any, would have shaped up at the Executive Committee nor what its decision would have been, because the whole matter became moot when word arrived from Sacramento just before the meeting that the Bay Area would be carved up into five countywide "regions" and a sixth region made of the four smaller counties.

Among other consequences, this action by CCCJ was another refusal by a State agency to sue the sub-State planning region designated by the Council on Intergovernmental Relations. But the CCCJ maintained that its job is to administer criminal justice planning and action programs, not to improve intergovernmental relations.

Regional Housing. ABAG did not seriously undertake to develop a housing component for its regional plan until 1971. In response to pressure from the National Committee Against Discrimination in Housing and to threatened budgetary constraints by the area director of HUD, regional housing policies have been given a much higher priority rating in ABAG's current and three-year work programs.

Prior to 1970-71, ABAG realized that some day it would have to face the division among its members over the proper regional distribution of low- and moderate-cost housing, but was not willing to do so before it had to. In 1969, the Executive Committee appeared ready to omit any reference to regional housing planning in its bill to create a regional home rule agency (AB 1846 Bagley). At the insistence of San Francisco, it agreed that the regional planning function included housing, although it refused to specify housing as a separate function of the proposed agency. In the same year, ABAG published a substantial analysis of housing needs in the Bay Area, including some recommendations of the consultant who made the study.[77]

The *Regional Plan: 1970-1990,* approved in 1970, contained positive statements about the need for a regional housing policy and referred especially to the problem of housing low- and middle-income families. Among the six primary regional goals was one

> To provide the opportunity for all persons in the Bay Area to obtain adequate shelter convenient to other activities and facilities, in neighborhoods that are satisfying to them.[78]

Two other statements about the content of a needed regional housing plan went unchallenged in the General Assembly debate over approval of the regional plan:

> Population growth, shifts and separations are matters of regional concern. To the extent that issues such as racial segregation affect population changes and shifts, they also become matters of regional concern and policy. The Regional Plan necessarily addresses these problems as it proposes residential-employment relationships, and space, location, and forms of residential growth to 1990. Regional residential growth policy must involve social, economic and political questions such as zoning, taxes, price of land, development costs, density, relation to intra-urban recreation, transportation facilities, etc.[79]

The Regional Plan also referred to the desirability of developing completely new communities which, among other advantages, would "broaden and diversify employment opportunities" and "foster social integration and balance."

It was anticipated that a detailed housing plan element would be prepared and a housing planner was added to the ABAG staff. Then a new phenomenon appeared in ABAG deliberations—an active organization dedicated to influencing ABAG policy. For a decade the meetings of ABAG policy committees, the Executive Committee, and the General Assembly had been attended by a few observers, such as representatives of the League of Women Voters, and by representatives of parties interested in the A-95 review of grant applications. However, on April 7, 1971, an outside group, the National Committee Against Discrimination in Housing (NCDH) announced to the ABAG Regional Planning Committee that, as part of an urban renewal demonstration project in the Bay Area funded by HUD, it was "not here to criticize ABAG for its past mistakes" but "to insure that ABAG performs in such a manner, now and in the future, that each citizen in the San Francisco Bay Area can be proud of its accomplishments."[80]

It recommended the adoption by ABAG of a "scatteration or distribution plan for the entire region for the production of low- and moderate-income housing units."[81] Before such planning, however, ABAG should develop and implement an affirmative action program, create a citizens participation component, and establish a citizens and technical advisory committee on housing. NCHD would advise ABAG in these activities. It also requested that it be allowed to participate with ABAG staff in reviewing housing and redevelopment applications.

Following the NCDH presentation, a representative of La Confederación de la Raza Unida stated that NCDH did not represent Chicanos and demanded that a form of citizen participation be established to permit them to participate.

On May 13, 1971, a meeting was held to discuss the formation of a citizens' housing committee. Minutes of the meeting report:

Some citizens stood up and expressed their concern at the formal structure of the meeting. . . .

[Another participant] objected to the procedures of the meeting and refused to follow them.

People expressed their dislike of the seating arrangement and the formal speaking procedure. There was a ten minute break to rearrange the seats.

Nevertheless, there was agreement by the end of the meeting that an ad hoc citizen's committee of groups represented at the meeting be formed and that it concern itself with *all* aspects of the ABAG regional planning program. A steering committee was formed to recommend a process for forming the citizens committee.[82]

On July 6, 1971, La Confederación de la Raza Unida filed suit in U.S. District Court against ABAG and HUD to force HUD to cut off Federal funds to ABAG on the grounds that the latter had not implemented an affirmative action program or allowed citizen participation in its planning and decision making.[83] The suit has not been set for hearing.

Affected at least in part by the actions of NCDH[84] and La Confederación de la Raza Unida, but also reacting to what he considered to be dilatory action by ABAG in assuming responsibility for regional housing planning and implementation, the area director of HUD held up approval of ABAG's application for 701 planning assistance funds for three months after the beginning of fiscal year 1971-72.

This waiting experience is in part the basis of the statement by the ABAG regional planning director that "At a time when the need for regional land-use planning is increasing so we can maintain the quality of life in our metropolitan area, we are finding that HUD's priorities and funding support to ABAG for land-use planning has decreased dramatically."[85]

The controversy also illustrates the dependence of a regional planning agency upon the program interests and priorities of its principal source of funds. An independent and steady source of regional funds, or even a broad mix of State and Federal grants, would allow the regional planning agency to maintain the integrity of the regionally originated elements in its work program. In this instance, by withholding all 701 planning funds, HUD threatened ABAG's ability to pursue a joint regional parks and open space planning program in conjunction with the East Bay Regional Park District. ABAG has been developing on an *ad hoc* basis as many agreements as possible with special-purpose agencies in the Bay Area. The HUD conditions for a major shift to housing planning, if accepted by ABAG, would have undermined almost two years of negotiations between ABAG and the park district.

On the other hand, HUD has specific program responsibilities apart from its general commitment to encouraging comprehensive regional planning. It is proper for HUD to insist that regional housing planning be pursued energetically.

Perhaps the dilemma could be resolved by enactment of a separately funded Intergovernmental Planning Act as suggested by Supervisor Bort of Alameda County,[86] with mandatory elements (e.g., housing) to take care of the interests of functional agencies. To recommend this Federal action, however, is not to suggest that the State of California should not help to support regional planning or that a statutory regional planning agency should not be created with an independent basis of regional financial support.

In the second half of 1972, regional housing is high on the ABAG agenda, as are joint regional parks and open space planning. A regional housing task force has been created along with a technical advisory committee. The task force has been given the following assignments:

1. Design of the regional housing planning process (completion by July 1974, at which time it is recommended that the Task Force disband);
2. Initiation of development of the Regional Housing Plan (completion date is indeterminate; finished by the adopted regional planning process);
3. Development of guidelines for HUD use in allocating its housing funds in the region (completion by December 1972); and
4. Develop recommendations for specific programs or actions that could be undertaken immediately to increase the supply of low- and moderate-income housing in the entire nine-county area and housing opportunity for low- and moderate-income persons in the nine-county area.[87]

The task force has already responded to the last assignment by presenting a resolution to the Executive Committee (adopted October 19, 1972) supporting the reintroduction of a bill vetoed by the Governor. The bill would reorganize the State Department of Housing and Community Development and authorize interest-free loans and grants for development and other costs to make housing available at low and moderate rentals. The Executive Committee also is to "express its concern by letter to the Governor of the State of California concerning his veto of said bill."

At the same meeting of the Executive Committee, the task force entered into the discussion of the Issue Paper on Regional Growth Policy and requested that

no policy on this subject be adopted by any governmental unit in the region until the issue of equity in housing access, economic balance in the housing supply, improved job market and economic growth, equity in access to economic opportunity, and prohibitions against exclusionary zoning are assured throughout the region.

HUD has recently expressed its pleasure at the approach of ABAG to regional housing planning:

> At such time as the required housing planning process which is now beginning is developed, adopted and considered to be an operating instrument we offer to engage in a series of periodic negotiations with ABAG regarding the allocation of HUD resources in the Bay Area. We expect this to include guidance for HUD-FHA insurance decisions and for allocation of subsidized housing based upon a fair share distribution model. We would expect these negotiations to be related to revenue sharing community development programs of the various Bay Area cities and counties. Given lack of such a plan HUD is already making decisions affecting regional growth.[88]

REGIONAL REVIEW AND COMMENT

Most local officials in the Bay Area look upon membership in ABAG as a necessary condition for their city or county to be eligible for Federal aid. Even officials from cities and counties that seldom or never apply for Federal aid are concerned about continued eligibility.

The increased importance of Federal grants in Bay Area community affairs and of ABAG review and comment on applications for Federal assistance is shown by a comparison of ABAG activity in 1971-72 and in the five-year period 1962-67. There were Federal requirements before 1966 for regional review of applications to the Housing and Home Finance Agency (succeeded by HUD) for Federal assistance for open space, water, and sewer facilities. Between 1962 and 1967 ABAG reviewed 296 applications with total project costs of $290 million and requests for grants or loans of $118 million. In 1971-72, ABAG processed 260 applications with total project costs of $310 million and requests for Federal grants of $194 million. The number of applications in one year (1971-72) equals 89 percent of the number filed in the first *five* years of ABAG's existence; project costs are 94 percent of the total costs of the earlier period. The amount Federal aid requested in 1971-72 exceeded the requests of 1962-67 by $76 million, an increase of 64 percent. Some of the difference between these two periods is due to the expanding coverage of A-95 review.

ABAG, unlike most COG's in the United States, was not created to meet the requirement in the Demonstration Cities and Metropolitan Development Act of 1966 that applications for certain Federal grants-in-aid be reviewed by a regional planning agency for consistency with regional plans. Established five years earlier, by 1966, ABAG was considering on its own initiative whether it should continue as a voluntary organization or request the legislature to reconstitute it as a limited but multi-purpose regional agency.[89]

Nevertheless, the Federal requirement of regional review and comment is the principal source of the authority which ABAG exercises within the Bay Area. This is another instance of a local agency's receiving authority from the Federal government in the absence of a grant of authority from the State. Melvin B. Mogulof says that COG's have only an "aura of authority" from the Federal government since their legitimacy comes from their member governments, who "do not seem to want the COG to emerge as a force different and distinct from the sum of its governmental parts." COG's, then, are little more than "an insurance device for the continued flow of federal funds to local governments."[90]

The requirement that there be regional review and comment is Federal law. Presumably it is based on congressional conviction that it will enable Federal agencies to make more rational decisions and, at the same time, enable local governments in metropolitan areas to act jointly in regional planning and the implementation of regional plans. As Mogulof points out, these two objectives may be inconsistent. Regional policies regionally arrived at may be contrary to the redistributive housing policies of HUD.[91]

Federal agencies are not required to accept the recommendations of ABAG or any other areawide planning agency. In fact, no one knowns how Federal grant agencies use regional comments or whether, in fact, they are at all influential. It would not be surprising to find that different Federal agencies, or different segments of any given Federal agency, differ in their use of regional comments. But no one in the San Francisco Bay Area knows or is sure that anyone in the Federal government knows.

Uncertainty about what happens to the review document after it leaves the COG, accompanied by a suspicion that most of the time, applications are only checked to see if the comment is present, affects the behavior of the COG staff in preparing the review and the policy body in considering staff recommendations. There is no premium on considering an application as more than an isolated project.

It is difficult to imagine that review documents as now prepared are useful to the granting agency in distinguishing between projects or between applicants as claimants for limited funds designed to achieve specified objectives. However, there is no feedback from federal agencies and no rewards or deprivations for useful or perfunctory regional reviews.

Many people maintain that city and county officials acting together in a COG would never act to hurt a fellow member. Senator Petris from Alameda County has called ABAG a "mutual back scratching society." Assemblyman Knox has said

> the A-95 review process tends to become one which simply weeds out projects which are obviously "inconsistent" with regional plans. It virtually never becomes a process which assigns grant priorities to projects which implement and goals and objectives of the regional plans.[92]

Both Assemblymen Knox and Mogulof assert that COG's (ABAG) will never act to injure the interests of a member government, although they do oppose projects of non-member governments and especially of special-purpose agencies, which may be considered as competing for the legitimate role of regional planner.

Part of the difficulty is that most applications are for support of particular projects initiated by local governments, not by ABAG. When viewed separately, they are not inconsistent with regional plans. On the other hand, no one should expect a voluntary association of local governments to take the initiative in blackballing a member government's application for Federal funds. But the behavior of an areawide planning organization would change if there were qualitative standards for regional review and if no applications were granted until those standards were met. At the least a Federal grant agency could require that the consistency between the application and the regional plan be spelled out in detail with references by chapter and verse to both application and plan.[93]

The content of a review and comment will necessarily be skimpy as long as there is no regional plan. Even the first accepted version of a regional plan may well be judgmental and rhetorical—ambiguous in order to secure acceptance and also for lack of experience and feedback among regional planners and policy makers. There is, for example, a marked increase in detailed comparison between applications and plans in ABAG comments now that Phase II of the regional water, sewerage and drainage element of the Regional Plan has been completed and adopted. As other elements are refined one would expect the usefulness of review and comment to increase across the board.

Review and comment is also viewed by ABAG staff and members of the Regional Planning and Executive Committees as the major means of implementing regional plans and policies. They admit, however, that it is a weak instrument. We have seen in discussing regional open space planning by ABAG that major reliance is placed upon the hope that the Federal and State governments will make extensive funds available for the purchase of open space lands. Even the limited Federal funds now available are expended on a project-by-project basis. Most requests, and therefore most grants are for relatively small amounts to finance the acquisition and/or development of small acreages. Many are for proposed neighborhood parts—worthy enterprises to meet undoubted needs—but not even through aggregation can they be considered as regional open space.

ABAG is fully aware that A-95 review and comment is a frail reed to lean on in the midst of the rough political maneuvering in the region, State, and Nation. At the General Assembly meeting of November 10, 1972, a two-part resolution was adopted on the implementation of the regional open space plan. The first part urged the Federal and State governments to increase and channel their funds to acquire priority open space designated in the regional plan. This is fully in accord with the tactic of using grants-in-aid to other units of government to implement a regional plan. However, in the second part of the resolution ABAG again urged, for the sixth time since 1966, that the State legislature give it statutory power to make regional plans and to require cities, counties, and special-purpose agencies to act in conformity with the plan.

Observation of the behavior of city and county officials in regional organizations with statutory authority and operating under statutory standards supports Mogulof's assertion that the voluntary structure of councils of governments such as ABAG is inherently conducive to "a log rolling style of decision making."[94] However, the same city and county officials who sit on ABAG have not hesitated to act contrary to the interests of individual cities and counties when they sit on statutory regional bodies such as BCDC.

Unsuccessful efforts to secure legislative enactment of a bill establishing a multi-purpose regional agency in the Bay Area suggests that a backup effort should be made by the Federal government to encourage and direct COG's to develop as a regional force, although one sensitive to the variations of local interests within the region.

Mogulof, after observing ABAG and other COG's, has recommended a Federal strategy of "sustain and strain." Among other specific recommendations, he urges that the review process be improved at both the Federal and regional levels and that COG's be required to set regional priorities and relate review of project applications to regional policy.[95]

Alameda County Supervisor, Joseph P. Bort—Chairman of ABAG's Regional Home Rule Committee, Chairman of the Metropolitan Transportation Commission, and a member of the board of the Bay Area Air Pollution Control District—has testified before a congressional committee that steps should be taken to prevent regional review and comment from levelling "off into a *pro forma* ritual among local, regional and federal officials." His first recommendation to prevent this is the enactment of State legislation to establish a limited, multi-purpose regional agency with authority to plan and to require cities, counties, and special-purpose agencies to conform to the plan.[96]

He also urged that review and comment should be extended to cover applications for State financial assistance and that it be applied to State plans affecting metropolitan areas.

> More specifically, I believe that there should be a State review and comment process [similar but more extensive than the OMB A-95 process.] It should operate on a two-way street with State review and comment on local and regional plans and regional review and comment on State plans and projects. It should not be confined, therefore, to review and comment on applications for financial assistance. In fact, the structure of such an

intergovernmental review and comment process was beautifully laid out in Assemblyman Knox's 1967 regional government bill [AB 711] but there it would only have applied to highways. All State agencies and all local and regional agencies should be subject to mutual review and comment on all plans, regulations, capital improvement programs, and applications for financial assistance if they have regional or Statewide impact.[97]

However, it has not yet been possible to secure State action to "sustain and strain" multiple-purpose regional planning and action. Supervisor Bort therefore recommended seven specific steps that the Federal government should take to keep A-95 from becoming perfunctory and useless.

1. Sufficient funds should be appropriated to enable a comprehensive regional plan to be completed within a reasonable time.
2. Congress should enact an Intergovernmental Planning Act to replace the scores of planning requirements in the many categorical grant programs.
3. The Intergovernmental Planning Act should provide for multi-year funding.
4. Regional COG's should be required to set priorities for projects of areawide significance.
5. An evaluation should be made of the usefulness to Federal agencies of the A-95 review and comment by regional planning agencies of applications for Federal assistance.
6. The impact on other aspects of community life of the implementation of particular functional plans should be studied and the results reported to planners and decision makers.
7. All Federal, State and regional programs should have an independent scheme of evaluation worked into the program design.[98]

At the same congressional committee hearing, Assemblyman Knox urged the subcommittee:

acting through the Congress, to direct both the Office of Management and Budget and The Department of Housing and Urban Development to establish a policy and put it into immediate operation . . . which insures that individual grants will be used to implement the regional plans which the Federal Government has previously insisted upon and, in large part, funded.[99]

Assemblyman Knox's objectives, when associated with the recommendations of Supervisor Bort, are desirable directions of Federal policy. In fact, if COG's ever move from the present plateau of development to which they have been brought by A-95, a renewed tactic of "support and strain" along these lines is necessary. However, the State legislature can establish as State policy the exact policy Assemblyman Knox urged upon the Congress. ABAG has repeatedly invited the State legislature to do exactly that.

CONCLUSIONS AND RECOMMENDATIONS

The San Francisco Bay Area, large in area and population, is politically as well as socially and economically complex. Part of its complexity comes from the many governments and quasi-autonomous governmental agencies operating within the region. It is not impossible to reduce the number of governmental entities but significant action along these lines appears unlikely. Even if such action were feasible, any imaginable reduction would still leave many governmental units, including State and Federal agencies. Complete consolidation of all units of local government would be undesirable for a region of 7,000 square miles and 4.5 million people.

It is also possible to retain all existing units of local government and insert an independent regional government between them and the State government. This has been done in the Minneapolis-St. Paul region. But this action would not eliminate or substantially reduce the system of intergovernmental relations now governing the Bay Area. It would only add another government, powerful and influential that it may be, to the existing mix of influential private and governmental actors.

The present mixture of intergovernmental relations can be restructured. In fact, this happens constantly as new governments or agencies are created or the jurisdiction and authority of existing governments and agencies expand or contract. The Association of Bay Area Governments is attempting to coordinate governmental action with regional significance through comprehensive regional planning, review and comment of applications for Federal aid, and the negotiation of bilateral agreements with State and regional special-purpose agencies.

This case study is a description of ABAG's efforts and of the reaction to them of other actors within and outside the region. The major regional planning thrust, organizationally, financially, and programmatically, is toward functional planning. In order to relate these functional planning efforts to each other and to ABAG's Regional Plan, ABAG negotiated agreements for joint planning with MTC, the Bay Area Comprehensive Planning Council, the East Bay Regional Park District, and the State Water Resources Control Board. Except for the Council on Intergovernmental Relations and the State Division of Highways, there is no State recognition of ABAG as a comprehensive regional planning agency. Current efforts by the council to develop a statewide policy for regional planning in substate districts may rectify this condition. Its success, however, depends upon strong gubernatorial support and legislative acceptance of the policy. The legislature has refused thus far to strengthen ABAG's authority or to create any other general regional planning agency. Instead, it continues to create new special-purpose regional agencies.

Federal agencies, other than HUD, pay only lip service to comprehensive regional planning while supporting and encouraging functional planning with respect to air and water pollution control, health, transportation, solid waste disposal, and criminal justice. HUD has functional programs of its own, such as the spread of low- and moderate-income housing throughout the metropolitan region. If the COG is used by HUD as a primary agent for furthering its own functional interests, then the COG will not be acceptable to other local, State, and Federal agencies as the comprehensive regional planning agency and regional coordinator.

Despite its name, the Association of Bay Area Governments is not an association of all the regionally significant governmental units operating in the Bay Area. Excluded are school districts and a score of major regional and sub-regional special-purpose agencies—each with ties to a powerful constituency and to a State and/or Federal agency. The Metropolitan Transportation Commission and the Bay Area Sewage Services Agency would merge with a regional planning agency whenever the legislature establishes it. However, the older special-purpose agencies need to be involved in the process of regional planning, decision making, and administration at the same time that they, along with cities and counties, are required to conform to regional policies.

While waiting for legislation, ABAG could initiate the process of formalizing the entry of other regional governments into an inclusive council of governments. It has already moved in this direction through negotiating active joint agreements with the State Water Resources Control Board in water quality planning,[100] with the Metropolitan Transportation Commission in the interface between transportation and land-use planning, and with the East Bay Regional Park District in regional recreation and open space planning. It has an agreement with the Bay Area Comprehensive Health Planning Council which has not been implemented. Efforts have been underway for more than a year to sign an agreement for joint planning with the Bay Area Air Pollution Control District.

Reliance thus far has been exclusively on bilateral agreements as instruments of coordination. These have been excellent means of inserting ABAG staff input into a limited amount of functional planning. There is, however, no concomitant input from, or feedback to, the governing bodies of ABAG and other regional agencies.

In September 1970, ABAG published a consultant's report entitled *Toward a Unified Planning Program for the San Francisco Bay Area.*[101] Since then the ABAG planning staff has used the concept of the management of a unified regional planning program to guide it in developing its annual work programs and to relate the elements of its work programs to the interests of other regional agencies. However, the concept has not become an organizing principle outside the staff—neither at the Executive Committee level of ABAG nor in the policy making and work programming of other regional agencies.

Even within the staff implementation of the concept is somewhat fuzzy. Can ABAG develop unified planning through unilateral action to establish regional priorities and flesh out the *Regional Plan: 1970-1990?* Can it do this by a series of bilateral agreements with each (or as many as possible) of the other regional agencies? Can bilateral agreements, each different in scope, method, and content from the others, be aggregated into regional policies and regional priorities? Even if such an aggregation might be managed at the staff level, how can staff decisions and recommendations be subjected to unified regional political scrutiny, review, and revision culminating in unified regional policies? In short, can unified planning management be developed regionally without some form of statutory regional government?

ABAG recognized in 1966 that a voluntary association of cities and counties was unable to make and implement comprehensive regional plans. Seven years later it is still seeking legislative action to empower it to make regional plans and require cities, counties, and special-purpose agencies to conform to the plan.

The principal recommendation of this study is that ABAG move now to explore jointly with all significant governments operating in the Bay Area the use of the Joint Exercise of Powers Act to create a Bay Area Regional Agency. These explorations should be carried on at both political and staff levels. They should include Federal and State agencies operating in the Bay Area. Fortunately, the Joint Exercise of Powers Act authorizes agreements with State and Federal agencies as well as local agencies. Also fortunately, there are now a regional organization of the Federal government (the Federal Regional Council) and an organization in the Governor's Office (the Council on Intergovernmental Relations) that could participate in explorations and negotiations leading to the formation of a Bay Area Regional Agency.

Recent sessions of the legislature have demonstrated that proposals to create a regional home rule agency which are not supported by the special interest constituencies may be in mortal political danger. However, the case for broadening the membership of the council of governments rests on more than tactical grounds. The principle underlying ABAG's Regional Home Rule Proposal is that the governance of the Bay Area must be based on a system of intergovernmental relations. This principle loses its credibility and much of its utility if governmental units which are not going to fade away are excluded from intergovernmental collaboration.

Except for moral support from the Council on Intergovernmental Relations, there has been little support and use of ABAG by State Agencies. At least the council, now located in the Governor's Office, is strengthening its policy of support for regional COG's and developing an active policy of sub-State districting. How far it will go and whether the Governor will embrace the policy is uncertain. The whole issue of regional organization will arise in another but related inquiry by the Governor into the structure and functions of local government. On the legislative side, ABAG has not been able to secure enactment of legislation to make membership in ABAG mandatory, to give it an independent source of financial support, and to require compliance with the regional plan. Nor have other regional interests been able to secure legislation to supplant ABAG, with another form of regional agency. In the same period, however, several new special-purpose agencies have been created.

Without a State policy on regional planning, decision making, and administration, Federal and local action is likely to be tenuous. Nevertheless, I have recommended that ABAG take the initiative to form a more inclusive voluntary regional agency of all governmental units with regional impact. Such an agency would undoubtedly suffer from the infirmities of a voluntary council of cities and counties. However, it is more likely than ABAG alone to move the region along to the next step of regional development.

The great danger is that ABAG and other COG's, having been brought by Federal-local collaboration to the present level of development, will be unable to develop further without State legislation. There are actions that the Federal government can take to avoid loss of momentum and to encourage, if not require, State policies on substate regionalism.

The most immediate needs for Federal action can be met without additional legislation:

1. require COG's to prepare specific comments on the relationship between applications for Federal aid and the regional plan;
2. require that regional plans meet the statutory definition in the Demonstration Cities and Metropolitan Development Act of 1966, including
   a. programming of capital improvements *based on a determination of relative urgency;*
   b. long-range fiscal plans for implementing such plans and programs; and
   c. proposed regulation and administrative measures which aid in achieving coordination of all related plans of the departments or subdivisions of the governments concerned and intergovernmental coordination of related planning activities among State and local governmental agencies concerned; and

3. require Federal grant agencies to report to the respective COG's on the usefulness of the review and comment in deciding whether specific applications should be granted.

Congress decided during the 1960s that the quality of local programs supported in part by Federal grants would be improved if individual projects were related to regional objectives as determined by a regional agency. Statutory requirements of regional review and comment, as implemented in OMB Circular A-95 have resulted in a restructuring of horizontal as well as many vertical intergovernmental relationships in metropolitan areas. What is needed now is a Federal-State-regional-local strategy for the 1970s built upon the accomplishments of the 1960s.

The experience of the 1960s has demonstrated that a Federal strategy of "sustain and strain," however hesitantly and tentatively it may have been executed, can have a profound effect on the behavior and attitudes of local officials in metropolitan areas. Now the Federal government should take the initiative in calling for an intergovernmental strategy to replace, or to supplement, an exclusively Federal strategy. The new strategy should be based on three premises:

1. The Federal government has an obligation to see not only that it itself is operating effectively but that other governmental units receiving Federal funds are organized to plan, make decisions, and administer public policies. It is more, not less important now that mandated programs are to be loosened under general and special revenue sharing that State and local governments meet performance standards with respect to planning, budgeting, and personnel management. The Intergovernmental Personnel Act should be supplemented by enactment of an Intergovernmental Planning Act to replace the scores of planning requirements in existing legislation.

2. State governments should act to provide a statutory base for substate planning and the Federal government should require that they do so as a condition for the continued receipt of Federal funds. Although proposed Federal land-use planning acts might be used as the vehicle for this requirement, it would be better to make it part of an intergovernmental Planning Act.

3. The strategy should be jointly developed and operated by all three levels of government. Such an intergovernmental approach should be taken as sub-components are developed at Federal, State, and regional levels.

This strategy, if executed, would meet ABAG's expressed needs for conversion from a voluntary COG to a statutory multi-purpose agency in which local governments would play an important but not exclusive role. It would also provide the context in which the multi-purpose regional agency could function as an effective partner in the governance of the Bay Area and in the development of urban policies for the State and Nation.

NOTES

1. This essay is undoubtedly colored, I hope faintly, from my close association with ABAG. I have been consultant to the Goals and Organization Committee and to the Regional Home Rule Committee since 1965. Although I assume full responsibility for my objective subjectivity, I have asked people associated with all other regional organizations and movements to criticize the first draft of this essay. I am grateful to them for helping to keep me honest if not wholly objective. The intergovernmental relations of metropolitan governance have been examined from a more political point of view in my essay "Bay Area Regionalism: The Politics of Intergovernmental Relations," in *The Regionalist Papers* (Detroit: The Metropolitan Fund, 1973).

2. See *Younger v. County of El Dorado,* 5 Cal. 3d 480 (1971).

3. Melvin Mogulof, *Governing Metropolitan Areas: A Critical Review of Councils of Governments and the Federal Role* (Washington, D.C., The Urban Institute, 1971), p. 15.

4. Barton-Aschman Associates Inc., *Toward a Unified Planning Program for the San Francisco Bay Area* (ABAG, 1970), p. 6.

5. California, *Government Code,* Secs. 6500-6513.

6. For voting and assessment of dues, San Francisco is counted both as a city and as a county.

7. Barton-Aschman Associates, Inc., *Toward a Unified Planning Program . . . .* pp. 3-5.

8. In 1967-68 regional planning by ABAG, Bay Conservation and Development Commission, Bay Area Transportation Study Commission, and the Bay-Delta Water Quality Study cost over $6 million. Stanley Scott and Harriet Nathan (eds.), *Adapting Government to Regional Needs* (Institute of Governmental Studies, University of California, Berkeley, 1971), pp. 275-277.

9. For details see Victor Jones, "Bay Area Regionalism," in *The Regionalist Papers.*

10. In two counties, Alameda and Contra Costa, the mayors' conferences have moved toward a more formal organization with part-time executive officers and offices located in the same building as ABAG and the Metropolitan Transportation Commission.

11. See Institute of Local Self Government, *Special Districts or Special Dynasties* (Berkeley, The Institute, 1970), pp. 24-25. For the State it was reported that over 50% of incumbents on district boards originally were appointed. For 86 cities in the Bay Area, almost a fourth initially gained office in this manner. See Kenneth Prewitt, *The Recruitment of Political Leaders: A Study of Citizen-Politicians* (1970), p. 131.

12. California. Intergovernmental Council on Urban Growth, *Recommended Roles for California State Government in Federal Urban Programs* (1968). See also the survey on "Alternative Roles for California State Government in Federal Urban Programs," prepared for the Council by Baxter, McDonald & Co., March 24, 1967.

13. Public Administration Service, *Regional Government Agencies and Programs in the San Francisco Bay Area* (1966), pp. 7-8.

14. Public Administration Service, *Regional Government Agencies and Programs in the San Francisco Bay Area,* p. 9.
15. The council was first organized in 1964 as the Coordinating Council on Urban Policy. In 1965 its name was changed to Intergovernmental Council on Urban Growth and in 1968 it assumed its present title.
16. California. Coordinating Council on Urban Policy, *California Urban Policy for Intergovernmental Action* (January, 1965), p. 10.
17. U.S. Congress, *Regional Planning Issues,* Hearings before the Subcommittee on Urban Affairs of the Joint Economic Committee (92d Cong., 1st sess.), May 20, 1971, Part 4, p. 606.
18. U.S. Congress, *Regional Planning Issues,* p. 623.
19. League of California Cities, Annual Conference, October 28, 1970. Resolution No. 13.
20. ABAG has its own proposed amendments to the Regional Planning District Act (1972 session. AB220 Knox). These will be discussed later.
21. The council had provided the central leadership in the movement between 1957 and 1961 to create a Golden Gate Authority or Transportation Commission. The council was also active in urging regional planning and in securing legislative creation of the Bay Area Air Pollution Control District and the Bay Area Rapid Transit District.
22. Stanley Scott and Willis D. Hawley, "Leadership Views of the Bay Area and Its Regional Problems: A Preliminary View," *Public Affairs Report.* Vol. 9, No. 1, February, 1968 (Institute of Governmental Studies, University of California, Berkeley).
23. William J. Middleton and Michael Preston, "Black Power and Metropolitan Politics" (unpublished paper, 1973).
24. ABAG, *Overall Program Design. 1972-75,* pp. 14, 18.
25. ABAG, *Bay Region Planning and Information Support Center Review and Recommended Work Program* (June, 1972), tables 1-3.
26. Stanley Scott and Willis D. Hawley, "Leadership Views of the Bay Area and Its Regional Problems: A Preliminary Report," *Public Affairs Report* (University of California, Institute of Governmental Studies, Berkeley), February, 1968.
27. ABAG, *Overall Program Design.* p. 31.
28. The General Assembly *approved* the Regional Plan instead of *adopting* it, in order to quiet the fears of those who considered it a step toward a binding plan under a regional government.
29. ABAG, *Regional Plan! 1970-1990* (1970), p. 15.
30. ABAG, *Regional Plan: 1970-1990,* p. 1.
31. See Paul D. Spiegel, "Looking into the *Regional Plan: 1970-1990* as it Relates to Goals and Policy Formulations for the Regional Airport Systems Study Committee of ABAG," A Report to the ABAG Regional Airport Systems Study Committee, February, 1971.
32. ABAG—General Assembly Resolution 1-72.
33. The State Assembly Committee on Environmental Quality has held a public hearing in San Francisco on whether there should be a State policy on population growth and distribution. *San Francisco Chronicle.* September 19, 1972.
34. See Paul Fullerton, *Land-Use Patterns in the Bay Area* (a position paper prepared for ABAG's Regional Housing Task Force, June, 1972).
35. The State Office of Planning and Research, created by statute in 1970 and placed in the Governor's office, is assigned the task of developing a "comprehensive statewide land-use policy" and coordinating all State depart-

mental land-use planning. If the Jackson bill to provide Federal assistance in State land-use planning is enacted, the Office of Planning and Research plans to move rapidly toward statewide land-use planning. In the meantime, the Office of Planning and Research and the Council on Intergovernmental Relations are developing for cabinet consideration a system of regionalization of State activities that will interface with regional planning activities.

36. See ABAG, Preliminary Regional Plan (1966) for a discussion of concepts of regional form for the Bay Area composite plan concept, the urban corridor concept, the city centered concept, and the suburban dispersion concept. In 1968, the ABAG General Assembly endorsed the city centered concept and instructed that the Regional Plan be based on the assumption that regional population would increase from 4.6 million to approximately 7.5 million in 1990.

37. All bills introduced in the legislature since 1969 to create a multi-purpose regional agency, provide for either "review and comment" or empower the agency to order cities, counties, and special districts to comply with the regional plan.

38. Airports will be considered in a later section.

39. Following secession from BART, transit districts were set up in San Mateo and Marin Counties.

40. The act invites HUD and DOT each to appoint a non-voting member.

41. In the same act (SB 325-1971) the legislature subjected gasoline to the sales tax. The total sales tax is 5 cents except in San Francisco, Alameda, and Contra Costa Counties where an additional 1/2 cent is collected to help finance the construction of BART.

42. ABAG, *Regional Home Rule and Government of the Bay Area*, report to the General Assembly of ABAG from the Goals and Organization Committee, September 26, 1966.

43. BCDC, *San Francisco Bay Plan* (1969), p. 5c; see also *San Francisco Bay Plan Supplement* (1969), pp. 227-240, for a digest of the consultants' report on airports on the bay.

44. The chairman of ABAG's Regional Airport Systems Study Committee, long associated with aviation in Contra Costa County and the Bay Area, is running for election to the State legislature. If elected, he may be expected to continue his interest in a regional airport system.

45. Alameda County Comprehensive Health Planning Council, *Solid Waste Management Workshop Proceedings*, February 26, 1972, pp. 7-8. The study by a EBMUD staff committee was made at the request of the League of Women Voters.

46. Memorandum to Executive Committee of ABAG, November 10, 1971.

47. See Jones, "Bay Area Regionalism," for the politics of drafting a BASSA bill and getting it enacted.

48. See Stanford University Workshop on Air Pollution, *Air Pollution in the San Francisco Bay Area* (Stanford, 1970). California's legislative analyst reports that "the Los Angeles County Air Pollution Control District has developed an Evaluation and Planning Division which is the only known staff in California having any significant capability to study, evaluate and plan comprehensive air control actions, even though the district is only countywide and does not cover all the coastal air basin in which it lies.

"On the other hand, the San Francisco Bay Area Regional Air Pollution Control District is the only regional agency in the state, but it has not yet developed a staff equivalent to the Evaluation and Planning Division. The Air Resources Board similarly does not have such a staff. As a result, California does not now have fully in existence anywhere the capability to manage an air basin on a comprehensive basis." Legislative Analyst, *Air Pollution Control in California* (January, 1971—a report pursuant to ACR131-1970 Session), p. 40.

49. Evelle J. Younger, State Attorney General, to John A. Maga, Executive Officer, State Air Resources Board, October 6, 1971, p. 4.

50. Evelle J. Younger to John A. Maza, p. 4.

51. Evelle J. Younger to John A. Maga, p. 6. The board is prohibited by statute from specifying the "design or equipment type of construction or particular method to be used in producing the reduction of air contaminants. . . . [But the board may set up] maximum pollution standards of general application and the person constructing or operating a structure or other source of pollution is free to do whatever he sees fit so long as he does not violate the standard," pp. 5-6.

52. California Legislative Analyst, *Air Pollution Control in California*, p. 36.

53. California Legislative Analyst, *Air Pollution Control in California*, p. 37.

54. Bay Area Council, *Regional Report* (June, 1972), p. 3.

55. BAAPCD, *Minutes*, March 1, 1972. The motion was made and seconded by county supervisors who are also members of the ABAG Executive Committee.

56. "Recognizing the importance of establishing a continuing long-range planning program for a permanent regional open-space system, CRPP asked . . . ABAG to develop a long-range, comprehensive regional land-use plan for the nine-county Bay Area. Parks and open space would be one element of that plan. With the assistance of CRPP President Mel Scott, ABAG applied for and received a federal planning grant to undertake such a study." Kenneth C. Frank, "A Brief History of People for Open Space," Appendix III in T.J. Kent, Jr., *Open Space for the San Francisco Bay Area: Organizing to Guide Metropolitan Growth* (University of California, Institute of Governmental Studies, Berkeley, 1970), p. 71.

57. People for Open Space, Inc., *Economic Impact of a Regional Open Space Program* (1968).

58. People for Open Space, Inc., *Economic Impact of a Regional Open Space Program*, p. 43. See statement by John H. Sutter, President of POS, to BARO, March, 1968.

59. See Jones, "Bay Area Regionalism," for further discussion of efforts to enact regional legislation.

60. ABAG, *Regional Open Space Plan*, Phase II (1972), p. 12. The percentage of the target already preserved varies greatly among the nine counties. ". . . less than 4 percent of the target has been preserved in Sonoma County and less than 6 percent in Santa Clara County, areas clearly under the pressure of urbanization." p. 44.

61. ABAG, *Regional Open Space Plan*, p. 81.

62. This would be an extension of work begun by the USGS-HUD-ABAG San Francisco Bay Region Environment and Resources Study.

63. The HUD-ABAG budgetary and program impasse of 1971 will be discussed in the section on housing.

64. BCDC, *The Bay Commission: What It Is and What It Does* (April, 1970).

65. Statement of Supervisor Michael Warnum, Marin County, and chairman, ABAG Ocean Coastline Committee before Senate Committee on Local Government, April 10, 1972.

66. ABAG, *Refuse Disposal Needs Study* (July, 1965).

67. In October 1970, after the Regional Plan had been approved, the Alameda County Planning Commission adopted a resolution urging ABAG "to give the highest priorities to concentrate manpower and fiscal resources to prepare the plans and programs necessary to solve the problems of solid waste management in the Bay Area."

68. ABAG—Staff Paper on Bay Area Comprehensive Health Planning Council, 1970, p. 3.

69. Bay Area Comprehensive Health Planning Council, *The Public's Health—Bay Area, 1972: Stage One, Comprehensive Health Planning* (draft version, May, 1972), pp. 31-57. For supporting background documents, see pp. 163-179.

70. BACHP, *The Public's Health . . . .*, p. 90.

71. BACHP, *The Public's Health . . . .*, pp. 116-128.

72. *San Francisco Chronicle*, January 8, 1971: "The council would present 'a united front' to federal and state agencies, said the mayor, and would spare individual departments from 'diverting their limited resources away from the urgent day-to-day justice system needs of the city to play complicated games with proposals, grants, evaluations, design and all other attendant paraphernalias of this federal grant program.' "

73. *Caveat emptor!* I prepared for the Special Study Committee a memorandum entitled "Items for Consideration in Preparing Report of Special Study Committee (November 30, 1970) and a memorandum to the executive director commenting on the draft report of the Committee (December 29, 1970).

74. Memorandum from Regional CJP Coordinator to Special Study Committee to Review Criminal Justice Planning, December 10, 1970, pp. 5-6.

75. Regional Criminal Justice Advisory Board—Special Study Committee, *Minutes*, November 6, 1970, p. 6.

76. Robert H. Lawson, Executive Director, CCCJ, to J. Julien Baget, Executive Director, ABAG, October 2, 1970.

77. ABAG, *Regional Housing Study* (1969).

78. ABAG, *Regional Plan: 1970-1990*, p. 13.

79. ABAG, *Regional Plan: 1970-1990*, pp. 16-17.

80. National Committee Against Discrimination in Housing, "Presentation to ABAG's Regional Planning Committee Meeting," April 7, 1971, p. 4. "We may be called upon to assist you in the matters of housing and pledge our total staff support both national and local to support you in this effort. However, we may have to say at any time that ABAG is 'A-BAG' and cannot assist in providing a decent home for every San Francisco Bay Area family and state why. We hope this will not be the case," (p. 5).

81. "The need is to develop, ultimately, an intergovernmental instrument, such as a metropolitan or regional authority or commission, that can deal systematically with the problems of race, residence, economics and related opportunities, set goals for the region and local areas and require their implementation; and further, that this new type of governmental authority have built-in safeguards to assure that it reflects the interests and concerns of the poor, the black, the Mexican-Americans, and other racial and ethnic minorities." National Committee Against Discrimination in Housing, "Highlights and Excerpts from Report on NCDH Demonstration Project, San Francisco Bay Area," n.d., p. 1.

82. The creation of the Regional Citizens Forum is discussed above under "Information Exchange."

83. *San Jose Mercury*, July 7, 1971.

84. Letter from James Price, HUD Area Office Director to J. Julien Baget, Executive Director, ABAG, May 19, 1971. It indicated that NCBA concerns about the housing element and equal opportunity would be considered in reviewing the application for 1971-72 funds.

85. Statement of Rudolph Platzek before California Senate Committee on Local Government, San Francisco, April 10, 1972.

86. U.S. Congress, Joint Economic Committee, Subcommittee on Urban Affairs. *Hearings: Regional Planning Issues*, Part 4. (May 19, 1971), p. 606.

87. ABAG, *Framework for Establishing a Regional Role in Housing* (adopted by Executive Committee, March 16, 1972), p. ii.

88. James H. Price, Director, San Francisco Area Office, HUD, "Perspectives on a Regional Housing Plan: Federal Programs, Policies and Problems" (July, 1972), pp. 10-11.

89. Even this self-examination was supported by a $16,000 Federal grant under Section 701g of the Housing Act of 1965.

90. Mogulof, *Governing Metropolitan Areas . . . .*, p. 15. His criticism will be considered in this essay as specifically referring to ABAG unless he explicitly excludes it from his observation. His study is based upon an intensive examination of ABAG and the COG's in the Sacramento area and the Puget Sound Area, along with less extensive observations in the Minneapolis-St. Paul, Chicago, Jacksonville-Duval, and Dallas-Fort Worth areas (pp. 6-7, 24-26).

91. Mogulof, *Governing Metropolitan Areas . . . .* pp. 28-32. This possibility is increased, of course, if there is any suggestion that agency policies are not supported by the President or other important members of the Administration.

92. U.S. Congress. Joint Economic Committee. Subcommittee on Urban Affairs. *Regional Planning Issues.* Part IV (May 20, 1971), p. 623.

93. The statutory definition of comprehensive regional planning in the Demonstration Cities and Metropolitan Development Act of 1966 seems to give full scope to the Federal government to require that regional plans (policies) be finer grained than for example, ABAG *Regional Plan: 1970-1990.* In addition to "general physical plans," the statutory definition includes:
    B. programming of capital improvements *based on a determination of relative urgency* [emphasis added];
    C. long-range fiscal plans for implementing such plans and programs; and
    D. proposed regulation and administrative measures which aid in achieving coordination of all related plans of the departments or subdivisions of the governments concerned and intergovernmental coordination of related planning activities among State and local governmental agencies concerned.

94. Mogulof, *Governing Metropolitan Areas . . . .*, p. 67.

95. Mogulof, *Governing Metropolitan Areas . . . .* pp. 112-121. See my testimony in 1967 before the Senate Subcommittee on Intergovernmental Relations: "A good case can be made for . . . some form of block grants either to replace or to supplement program grants . . . provided that the recipient governments are capable of planning, of responsible decision making, and of effective administration.

"Block grants are not more desirable than categorical grants just because they are nonconditional grants. In fact, it is even more desirable that such grants be made conditional upon the existence of an adequate planning process, a political decision making process, a budgetary process, and a process of personnel management." U.S. Senate Committee on Government Operations. Subcommittee on Intergovernmental Relations. *Hearings: Intergovernmental Personnel Act of 1967 and Intergovernmental Manpower Act of 1967,* April 27, 1967, p. 146.

It is even more important that such performance standards should be established as conditions of Federal revenue sharing. See my testimony before U.S. Congress. Joint Economic Committee. Subcommittee on Urban Affairs. *Hearings: Regional Planning Issues,* Part I (October 13, 1970), p. 44.

96. U.S. Congress. Joint Economic Committee. Subcommittee on Urban Affairs, *Regional Planning Issues,* Part IV (May 20, 1971), pp. 601-605.
97. U.S. Congress. Joint Economic Committee. Subcommittee on Urban Affairs. *Regional Planning Issues,* pp. 604-605.
98. U.S. Congress. Joint Economic Committee. Subcommittee Urban Affairs. *Regional Planning Issues,* pp. 606-611. Further details of his proposals will be found in his prepared statement for the subcommittee. I was associated with Supervisor Bort as a consultant to ABAG's Regional Home Rule Committee and therefore the above recommendations can be viewed as ones which I would make.
99. U.S. Congress. Joint Economic Committee. Subcommittee on Urban Affairs. *Regional Planning Issues,* p. 624.
100. Actually, the State board has contracted with ABAG to perform certain planning functions in the preparation of basin plans. However, the effect of the arrangement is that ABAG participates at the staff level in water quality planning for the basin.
101. Prepared by Barton-Aschman Associates, Inc.

Introduction

*While some metropolitan reformers have recommended that many local functions and even regional functions be transferred to state government, the case study to follow illustrates a kind of **indirect** state control via statuatory creation (by the Minnesota state legislature) of the **Twin Cities Metro Council**—a regional policy-making organization whose decisions are implemented by the more than 300 state, local, and regional jurisdictions located within the Twin Cities metropolitan area.*

In reading the study, one should attempt to differentiate between this kind of a state created and state represented policy-making body, as opposed to the similar, but locally created and locally dominated organization such as San Francisco's Association of Bay Area Governments. It might, therefore, be beneficial to contrast the relative costs and benefits of regional policy-making as a state function versus regional policy-making as an evolutionary function of COG's.

GOVERNANCE
IN THE TWIN CITIES AREA
OF MINNESOTA

Ted Kolderie
Executive Director
Citizens League
Minneapolis

In 1970, the 3,000-square-mile Twin Cities region included 1,865,000 people in seven counties—Hennepin, Ramsey, Anoka, Dakota, Washington, Scott, and Carver. The corporate cities of Minneapolis and St. Paul are joined in a residential area near the University of Minnesota campus, and both are surrounded by a quilt-like pattern of suburbs. On the Minneapolis side, which has experienced two-thirds of the growth since 1945, the third tier of suburban municipalities is complete and a fourth is beginning to form. Within the region, there are approximately 300 units of local government, including seven counties, 60 townships, 136 municipalities.

Until about 1945, when the two central cities accounted for almost 90 percent of the area population, the story of the Twin Cities was a story of the difference between Minneapolis and St. Paul. Postwar suburbanization has produced geographical polarization. As average homes were located in north Minneapolis and the east side of St. Paul, higher valued homes were built to the west and south. The northern suburbs came to have low valuations, high tax burdens, and relatively poor services; while those to the south had high valuations and relatively low tax burdens despite somewhat better services. The central cities are in the middle; their own relatively high valuations resemble the southern suburbs, and their high-cost populations produce fiscal problems which resemble those in the northern suburbs.

Prior to the mid-1950s, suburban expansion was almost entirely residential. However in 1956, the first enclosed shopping center opened in Edina to the southwest. Subsequently, the headquarters of several major national corporations relocated into first-tier suburbs. The circumferential freeways, finished ahead of the radials into the cores, further stimulated the decentralization of warehousing, manufacturing, and office employment. As a result, by the mid-1960s, large, wealthy suburbs were created, psychologically and financially independent of the central cities.

From: *Regional Governance—Promise and Performance: Substate Regionalism and the Federal System,* Vol. II—Case Studies, May, 1973, p. 200.

This suburbanization was almost totally unaffected by the racial issue. In 1970, non-whites represented only about 2.8 percent of the population of the seven-county area. Some dispersal has occurred from the old concentrations of blacks and Indians, but it has been confined largely to central-city neighborhoods. Black migration to the suburbs has consisted almost exclusively of relatively higher-income and professional families who have created no new racial enclaves.

PURPOSE AND EVOLUTION

Basic Institutional Factors

A number of special factors help explain both the emergence of a strong regional governance arrangement and the particular form it took.

The State of Minnesota is involved with the Twin Cities area to an exceptional degree. The metropolitan area represents one-half of the State's population and more than one-half of its wealth. The Capital is located in St. Paul, as is the University of Minnesota (itself a combined State and land grant institution). The major newspapers, the headquarters of most statewide trade and professional organizations, and the State Fair are in the Twin Cities area.

With two central cities, metropolitan unification presented itself first not as a demand for city/suburban cooperation but for cooperation between Minneapolis and St. Paul. Suburbanites were, therefore, ambivalent. A Minneapolis citizen might feel suburbanite in relation to Minneapolis, yet a Minneapolitan *vis-a-vis* St. Paul.

The governmental system tended to be dominated by legislative bodies, and the State government was dominated in many respects by the strong State legislature, which maintained close control over local government. A municipal home rule amendment was not passed until 1958, and no concept of county home rule ever effectively emerged. However, the legislature was an essentially passive institution with regard to initiating local policy and waited for issues and proposals to be brought to it.

The Twin Cities area has a strong tradition of citizen involvement in government. In recent decades, both the political parties and the government have had youthful leadership. With little patronage, political and governmental activity has tended to focus on the identification and resolution of problems. This issue orientation is reinforced by the close division between the two major parties, and by the competing newspapers and major television stations which are locally owned and competently staffed.

Emergence of Regional Problems

Because of the recessive policies followed by the two central cities through the 1940s and 1950s, regional issues were created. St. Paul used its water and sewer systems to restrict the rate of suburban expansion; Minneapolis was fiscally conservative. Neither city moved aggressively to provide services to the new suburban community. By the time regional issues emerged, in the mid-1960s, an almost even balance existed between the total central cities area and the suburban area, in population and in property valuation. Neither could clearly dominate the other.

An awareness of the growth of the area, and of increased complications in its governmental pattern, led the executive secretary of the League of Minnesota Municipalities, C.C. Ludwig, to propose creation of the Metropolitan Planning Commission (MPC). The bill was killed by Minneapolis legislators in the 1955 legislative session, but it was enacted in 1957 with the help of Senator Elmer L. Anderson. After 1957, MPC began adding regional dimension to the continuing urban problems discussion with its reports and discussion programs.

In the 1955 session a legislative interim study on municipal laws also was commissioned. It was directed by a lawyer, Joseph Robbie, who quietly rewrote the entire statute on municipal incorporation and annexation. The statute passed the legislature in 1959 without receiving a great deal of attention, and transferred the responsibility for the creation of new village government from the legislature to a State commission.

A major crisis surfaced in 1959, with the discovery that nearly one-half of the individual home wells in the suburban residential subdivisions were contaminated by nitrates recirculating from backyard septic tanks. An intense effort to get central sewer and water to about 300,000 persons in the suburbs began immediately. Municipal water was finally provided by the drilling of wells into the deep strata, but sewers were another problem. Several sharp divisions of interest appeared almost immediately. One was between the central cities and their nearby suburbs, regarding the rates to be charged for service through their interceptors and for treatment at their jointly owned plant downstream on the Mississippi. The second was between those unsewered suburban communities fortunately located on a major river and thus able to solve their own problems and those not-so-fortunate communities located inland, who were faced with building their own way to the river.

The inter-community implications were apparent. A proposal for a metropolitan sanitary district was defeated in the 1961 and 1963 legislative sessions. However, the second time the concept of sub-regional groupings of municipalities joining together to build interceptors to jointly owned treatment plants was beginning to emerge.

In 1964, the area's major electric power utility announced its intention to build a 500,000-kilowatt plant and an 800-foot smokestack near Stillwater on the St. Croix River. Two important conclusions emerged from the intense and frustrating struggle with this major development. First, municipal tax base considerations could defeat any effort to plan land uses in an orderly manner. Second, the Metropolitan Planning Commission, composed basically of representatives from various governmental units, could not effectively grapple with an issue where serious interests conflicted.

Efforts were being made to cope with these issues. The Metropolitan Planning Commission reports made an important contribution. The newspapers were becoming more aware of these developments. The League of Minnesota Municipalities' committees, at both the State and county levels, were engaged in intense discussions. Private organizations, such as the Citizens League and the League of Women Voters, were growing toward their own understanding of the problems. So was the legislature, which in 1963 took an important step with the creation of a Metropolitan Affairs Committee in the lower house.

The Governance Proposal and Its Purposes

The 1965 legislative session took little action with regard to the sewerage problem. Toward its close, the discussion of regional issues and organizations began to emerge.

This was the third legislative session to struggle unsuccessfully with the metropolitan sewerage problem. Although no action was taken, the idea of a sub-regional solution continued to gather strength. Since it was clear that sewerage service could be provided, it was increasingly a debate between those who preferred to see it provided through the emerging sub-regional districts, and those who preferred to work for the creation of a fully metropolitan sanitary district. The latter did not attempt to argue on engineering grounds that an areawide or single downstream plant system was in all respects preferable. Instead they argued that the decision on the location of treatment plants, whether there was to be one plant or several, ought to be made consciously by a regional body reviewing all the engineering and fiscal considerations. More and more, the critical need appeared to be the creation of a regional policy body capable of reaching a consensus on what kind of legislation the region wanted from the State.

The failure of proposals to begin the planning of a metropolitan transit system, in the same session, added further to the community's disappointment.

In the fall of 1965 and into 1966, the question of a regional policy body was discussed by many community organizations. Some of these were the League of Minnesota Municipalities, Metropolitan Section; Hennepin and Ramsey County leagues; the issues task forces of the two political parties; the Minneapolis, St. Paul, and suburban chambers of commerce through an Urban Study and Action Committee; and the League of Women Voters. In June 1966, the Citizens League formed a Metropolitan Affairs Committee to

begin developing a specific proposal. The issue also entered the gubernatorial and legislative campaigns in the fall, with the candidates broadly
concurring on the need for major action in the 1967 session. Key legislators,
feeling the changing climate, visited Washington for communication with
Federal officials and the staff of the Advisory Commission on Intergovernmental Relations.

By late fall, the broad outlines of the consensus were fairly clear. With a
few exceptions it was agreed that planning for major sewerage works, major
open space, transit, metropolitan airports, and the zoo were appropriate
topics for the new areawide body. This judgment was in no sense scientific,
and came not as a result of the application of rigorous criteria to the problem
of areawide functions, but from a kind of impressionistic judgment on the
part of knowledgeable citizens and local officials. Perhaps the distinguishing
feature of this decision was the fact that the functions which they identified
had never been handled (and were not then sought) by municipalities individually.

Rough agreement on the nature of a policy body was also achieved when
Mayor Milton Honsey of New Hope and Mayor Kenneth Wolfe of St. Louis
Park helped persuade the Hennepin County League of Municipalities to endorse the idea that members of the proposed Metropolitan Council ought to
be elected directly by the people on a "one man, one vote" basis.

The 1967 Legislative Battle

The arrival of metropolitan issues in the 1960s coincided with a transfer
of power within the Minnesota legislature. The legislature had been non-
partisan for many years. Prior to 1960, it had not been reapportioned for 43
years. The 1963 session brought new members, suburban representation, individuals more closely allied with the party organizations, and a challenge to
the traditional outstate domination. Through 1971, the legislature met in
session for 120 days, confined within the first five months of each biennium
for which it was elected.[1]

The symbol of the traditional legislature was State Senator Gordon
Rosenmeier of Little Falls, who dominated the entire institution with
parliamentary skill and control of key committees. In resisting the home rule
amendment in 1957, he understood the need for legislative authority in the
reconstruction of local government. However, he tended to focus the opposition of both local officials and the younger, party-oriented legislators on
himself. This common interest in their contest with the established power in
the legislature had a considerable effect in drawing together local officials
and legislators of both parties from within the Twin Cities area.

The Legislators moved first with a bill proposing the creation of a 30-
member, elected metropolitan council responsible for planning and
operating the agreed-on regional functions. As this idea began to attract

growing support, particularly from influential sectors of the business community, Rosenmeier encouraged several conservative members of the metropolitan legislative delegation to introduce the "state solution." This legislation called for a smaller council, whose members would be appointed at-large by the governor, and responsible for planning and coordinating the operation of such regional State-created agencies as existed at the moment or might be created in the future. The state solution did not provide the council with the power to operate metropolitan functions. As a result of Rosenmeier's efforts, the question with respect to a regional council was no longer whether it should exist, but how it should be constituted.

Those opposed to any metropolitan council proposal were intellectually confused and politically disorganized. Outstate legislators were vaguely concerned about the creation of what might become a "second legislature." Although some suburbanites, legislators, local officials, and weekly newspaper editors were opposed generally to bigger government, there was really very little ideological opposition. Counties were not enthusiastic, but in 1967 they played such a minor role in the discussion that they had no leverage. The opposition was ineffective because of the urgent need for a mechanism which could find a solution to the pressing problems of the Twin Cities area. In short, the opponents were obliged, in the prevailing climate of opinion, to come up with a better solution, and none did.

The two bills were deadlocked in committee for most of the session while pressures built up. A group of metropolitan mayors spoke out strongly in favor of the elected, operating council. Mayor Al Illes of Minnetonka told the Senate committee that "we look on metropolitan government as local government."

At the end of the session, it was the Rosenmeier concept that prevailed. The bill was amended on the floor by metropolitan representatives to provide for representation by districts. In a final climactic move, amendments were offered for direct election of members. This lost in the House 66 to 62, and four days later in the Senate 33 to 33. A move to break the tie failed, after Rosenmeier rose to argue with his outstate colleagues regarding the dangers of creating an elected body for the emerging dominant community in Minnesota.

The bill, which created a coordinating council, was signed by the Governor, along with a separate bill establishing a Metropolitan Transit Commission. For the fourth time, a bill proposing a metropolitan sanitary district failed to pass.

NATURE OF THE METROPOLITAN COUNCIL

The arrangement evolving in Minnesota for the governance of the Twin Cities metropolitan area is so different from what is occurring elsewhere that some discussion of its central principles is required. Its structure was designed for the special situation existing in the Twin Cities area, and was little influenced by other urban models or political science prescriptions. As a consequence, it does not fit the standard typology of metropolitan government.

The fundamental fact about the regional arrangements in the Twin Cities area is that they are, in the main, *statutory*.[2] As a result, this is a case study in the response by the State legislature to problems in the governance of this major urban region. The Metropolitan Council itself is only one, albeit the principal, piece of a continuing legislative reorganization of the systems of local government and finance in the Twin Cities area. The sweeping reorganization of the local fiscal system in 1971, the reorganization of county government, and the transfer of functions between municipal and county governments are all interrelated parts of this ongoing review. None of these is significantly the result of the work of the Metropolitan Council; they are the work and the responsibility of the legislature.

The keystone of the legislature's work is the general policy council created in the Metropolitan Council in 1967. Regional functions had existed in the Twin Cities area prior to that time, and there had been regional structures through which these programs were administered. There had also been regional planning for ten years prior to the Council's creation. The really innovative and significant development was the creation by the legislature of a truly representative and politically responsive general-purpose, policy-making body at the areawide level.

Yet the whole effort does not really represent the transfer of functions to State government if by that is meant the vesting of responsibility in the standing departments of the State government. The legislature did not assign the new operating responsibilities to State administrative departments or the State Office of Local and Urban Affairs. Rather, it assigned these responsibilities—both for policy and for program operations—to regional agencies of less than statewide jurisdiction. The Attorney General determined the Metropolitan Council to be neither an agency of State government nor an agency of local government, but a new unique agency lying somewhere between, possessing some of the powers and characteristics of each.

In this reorganization the legislature had not been consolidationist, with respect either to local government units or to existing areawide special districts. The legislature's determination in 1967 and in 1969 to establish a "coordinating" Metropolitan Council reflects a fairly conscious conclusion that existing agencies were doing their assigned tasks with considerable competence. The central purpose of the Metropolitan Council is to provide the general framework of regional policy for these other "implementing" agencies.

Further, by providing representation directly from the citizenry and by structuring the Council explicitly on an equal-population-district basis, the legislature was making a conscious effort to design into the Council a system of representation and voting genuinely able to resolve conflict and to produce a consensus with political validity.

In the Act creating the Metropolitan Council in 1967, therefore, a pre-existing statutory program of regional planning was essentially transformed into a statutory program of regional decision making when as the legislature abolished the Metropolitan Planning Commission, and replaced it with a politically responsible board which took over both the law and the staff of its predecessor. What resulted was a new blending of planning and decision making which has produced not plans, but guidelines, proposals, and policy directives to State, local, and regional agencies. A new kind of authority has appeared for implementation which rests largely on the unmatched credibility of the Metropolitan Council as the designated policy body, the only entity with responsibility both for the entire seven-county region and for the broad range of public functions.

Far from attempting to tidy up the regional structure by making im-plementation or program operations directly a function of the Council, the legislature has so far continued to establish the major regional programs in separate, though subordinate, agencies. Thus, it has maintained the concept of a coordinating council required to focus its energies on policy considera-tions, and forced to give direction to implementing agencies at all levels.

The Metropolitan Council's own best effort to depict responsibilities and relationships is shown in Figure IV.1. The Council districts established in 1967 and in use until 1973 (when a reapportionment is required) are shown in Figure IV.2.

CHRONOLOGY OF LEGISLATIVE
AND REGIONAL ACTION

1967 to 1969: The Start-Up

Governor LeVander moved quickly to implement the law. For council chairman, he chose James L. Hetland, Jr., a 43-year-old law professor at the University of Minnesota. It was arranged that Hetland would work half-time on Metropolitan Council affairs. In selecting the Council, the Governor followed to a reasonable degree the political character of the legislative districts from which the members were to be appointed. The notable excep-tions were the two districts in central and eastern St. Paul, which were strong Democrat-Farmer-Labor (DFL) and labor areas. Here Governor LeVander appointed a black woman social worker and a Lutheran minister. The initial members included two former presidents of the Minneapolis City Council, the then mayor of White Bear Lake, and an attorney who was a former presi-dent of the League of Minnesota Municipalities. Beyond this, he drew rather heavily from the business community.

Hetland retained the acting director of the Metropolitan Planning Com-

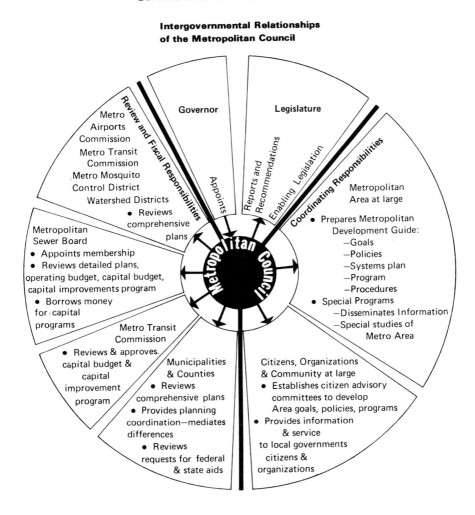

Intergovernmental Relationships of the Metropolitan Council

Governor

Legislature

Metro Airports Commission
Metro Transit Commission
Metro Mosquito Control District
Watershed Districts
● Reviews comprehensive plans

Review and Fiscal Responsibilities

Appoints

Reports and Recommendations

Enabling Legislation

Coordinating Responsibilities

Metropolitan Area at large
● Prepares Metropolitan Development Guide:
—Goals
—Policies
—Systems plan
—Program
—Procedures
● Special Programs
—Disseminates Information
—Special studies of Metro Area

Metropolitan Sewer Board
● Appoints membership
● Reviews detailed plans, operating budget, capital budget, capital improvements program
● Borrows money for capital programs

Metro Transit Commission
● Reviews & approves capital budget & capital improvement program

Municipalities & Counties
● Reviews comprehensive plans
● Provides planning coordination—mediates differences
● Reviews requests for federal & state aids

Citizens, Organizations & Community at large
● Establishes citizen advisory committees to develop Area goals, policies, programs
● Provides information & service to local governments citizens & organizations

mission to be the Council's director of planning, and for the new post of executive director secured the services of Robert T. Jorvig. Jorvig was viewed as the area's leading urban professional, due to his service as Housing and Redevelopment Authority director both in St. Paul and in Minneapolis and, just previously, as city coordinator of Minneapolis.

As a result of the Attorney General's ruling that the Council was neither a State nor local agency, the Council was permitted to have its own counsel, its own depositories, and its own personnel system separate from the State civil service. After a brief struggle, the Council was located in St. Paul.

The First Legislative Proposal

The real test of the viability of the new Council was the issue of metropolitan sewerage. It was not clear, however, in the fall of 1967, that the issue could be delayed until the 1969 session. The sub-regional districts, particularly in the northern suburbs, were pressing hard on the State Water Pollution Control Commission to grant a permit for a major treatment plant

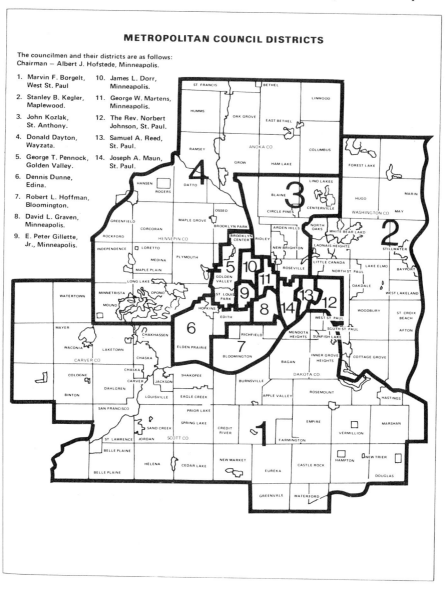

METROPOLITAN COUNCIL DISTRICTS

The councilmen and their districts are as follows:
Chairman — Albert J. Hofstede, Minneapolis.

1. Marvin F. Borgelt, West St. Paul.
2. Stanley B. Kegler, Maplewood.
3. John Kozlak, St. Anthony.
4. Donald Dayton, Wayzata.
5. George T. Pennock, Golden Valley.
6. Dennis Dunne, Edina.
7. Robert L. Hoffman, Bloomington.
8. David L. Graven, Minneapolis.
9. E. Peter Gillette, Jr., Minneapolis.
10. James L. Dorr, Minneapolis.
11. George W. Martens, Minneapolis.
12. The Rev. Norbert Johnson, St. Paul.
13. Samuel A. Reed, St. Paul.
14. Joseph A. Maun, St. Paul.

upstream on the Mississippi at Fridley, arguing both that an outlet for that area's waste could not, in good conscience, be denied; and that the plant proposed would meet State standards. The Council opened with a major seminar (a practice it was to follow repeatedly late in 1967 and pushed its consultants hard through early 1968). The Water Pollution Control Commission indicated it would wait on the Fridley plant no longer than June, to see if an adequate metropolitan solution was forthcoming from the Council. The Council just made the deadline with its proposed plan. Its ideas were translated into bill form during the fall, and widely discussed with local officials and legislators. A plan for sewer service areas was developed late in the year, and a financing policy in December.

Basically, the sewer program was hammered out by Council members themselves. Other major projects were delegated to a set of advisory committees, composed of citizens and local officials, charged with the task of recommending legislation in the areas of parks, open space, refuse disposal, a zoo, and modification of the State law providing for municipal veto of highway routes. This decision to spread out across a broad front, with fairly detailed policy studies conducted by specialized committees under the Council, proved a rewarding one. The advisory committees reported in the fall of 1968 with their recommendations, which were rapidly drafted into bill form for presentation to the legislature.

Some uncertainty was evident with regard to progalley 8-hs . . . for a coordinating council, some key members of the Council staff were reluctant to propose the creation of one or more separate agencies. Also, some county representatives on the advisory committees were beginning to press, in the case of the solid waste and open space programs, for *no* regional operating bodies.

Coincident to the preparation of the legislature program were the activities occurring in other areawide functional areas. One was the announcement, in April, by the Metropolitan Airports Commission (MAC) that it would propose a new metropolitan airport, to be located in a boggy area next to a game refuge in the northern township of Ham Lake. Another, at the end of 1968, was the disagreement over the re-formation of the transportation planning program, required by the Federal Highway Act of 1962, which had expired a year earlier. A third was the Council's publication of the first effort at an overall department guide, prepared by the former Metropolitan Planning Commission. Issued by the Council without endorsement, it was regarded generally as a disappointment as an effort to come to grips with overall metropolitan development.

A few new fields were also opening up during this period. In August 1968, the Council moved to end the confusion created by the 1967 Federal Partnership for Health Act by undertaking the job of setting up the comprehensive health planning agency for the Twin Cities area. And in the spring of 1969, already looking toward the 1971 legislative session, it made its first move into housing with the appointment of a 26-member housing advisory committee.

The 1969 Legislative Session

The 1969 legislative session was a triumph for the Council. Rosenmeier and others made one fundamental change in early hearings on the Council sewage bill to preserve the concept of a coordinating council, making it clear that the Metropolitan Sewer Board would be separately established by the legislature, and would hold title to the major sewerage works, with the Council's control coming through its authority to appoint board members, to set its plans, and to provide its finances. With this done, however, the bill moved through both houses with no setbacks, the Council's proposal providing, as hoped, the consensus which made legislative action possible. Toward the end, the central cities became visibly concerned about the role provided for them as "bankers" for the financing of sewers into the urban fringe. But with significant help from the Governor's office, the bill passed with substantial majorities.

An act providing for the first public program in solid waste disposal was adopted, which directed the Council to prepare a plan and assigned implementation to the county governments. A board was established to begin planning for a zoo though the legislature's decision was to develop it as a State, rather than a metropolitan program. Early involvement was substituted for municipal veto of State highway locations. The bill establishing a program of major parks and open space in the metropolitan area was also approved. However, this was done on what had traditionally been regarded as the last day of the session, when passage of bills was forbidden, as a part of the legislature's effort to test the limits on the length of its session. Late in the session the Council prepared and passed a bill assigning the Council the responsibility for land use and zoning in a three-to-five-mile belt around any major new airport.

Implementation of the 1969 Legislation

The actions of the 1969 Legislature established a lengthy agenda for the Council in implementing the new legislation. Top priority was reserved for the new Sewer Board. The Metropolitan Council appointed the Sewer Board in July, chaired by Honsey, former mayor of New Hope. A chief administrator was appointed by late summer, and instructions for the take-over of municipal and sub-regional facilities were issued in the fall. The Council's development guide on sewers was completed in November and hearings held in January 1970. Once the Metropolitan Council plan was adopted, the Sewer Board began acquisition of local treatment plants and the interceptors which were to become part of the metropolitan system. All facilities were in metropolitan ownership by January 1971. Guidelines were then issued to municipalities for the preparation of their comprehensive sewer plans. In April 1971, the Council sold its first bond issue for the expansion of new regional plants and the modernization of the old metropolitan plant downstream on the Mississippi.

Solid Waste. A plan for solid waste disposal was adopted in March 1970. Guidelines and procedures for the development of county landfill programs were approved in July. In December 1970, plans from four counties were approved, with the remaining three returned for modification.

Parks. The new Metropolitan Park Reserve District Board was appointed in August 1969, and the development guide for parks and open space was approved in June 1970. However, in July the Supreme Court ruled against the legislature on its test of the legislative day, thereby invalidating the statutory existence of the board. Recognizing that the open space law was a test, the legislature had provided separately for the financing for the open space program by appropriating for the metropolitan area a share of the State cigarette tax. The flow of money went directly to the Metropolitan Council and the former board became an advisory body to the Council. A budget for $2 million of State money, matched fifty-fifty with other funds, was approved in August 1971, and guidelines for the acquisition of land were approved in January 1971.

With the decision to establish the zoo as a State facility, the Council's role was limited to approval of the site. A location in the southern suburb of Apple Valley was conditionally approved in June 1970, and a concept plan for development in February 1971.

Health. The advisory committee designing a comprehensive health planning arrangement recommended in April 1970, that the Council itself become the 314(b) agency. A Metropolitan Health Board was consequently established by the Council in June. Members were appointed in July, and in September the Health Board absorbed the pre-existing Metropolitan Hospital Planning Agency, a voluntary planning arrangement among major hospitals for the review of capital expansion programs. The Health Board was drawn early into a major decision in Hennepin County because of a new hospital proposed for development two blocks away from a major private hospital complex, which was itself in the process of reconstruction. The Health Board decided not simply to review the two plans separately when submitted, but to move in the early stages of planning with guidelines covering the relationship desired between the two institutions. A special study committee appointed early in 1971, concluded that the two institutions should be co-located and physically contiguous. These guidelines were affirmed by the Health Board, and a $70-million joint development, with substantial sharing of facilities between the public and private institutions, proceeded into final planning and development.

Emergence of Major Controversies

During this period the Council also began addressing itself to unresolved issues from 1968-69.

The Metropolitan Airports Commission had chosen not to appeal to the 1969 legislature, the Council's suspension of its Ham Lake site proposal. The question of a new major airport therefore went into a period of joint study by the staffs of the two agencies in the summer of 1969. No basic agreement was reached, however, and in November 1970, the Metropolitan Airports Commission resubmitted the Ham Lake proposal. It was again suspended by the Council. The Council then applied to the Federal government for a grant to begin the preparation of a metropolitan airport plan.

Transportation Planning. By early 1969, a decision had been reached on the reconstruction of the transportation planning program. Its essence was a contract between the Council and the Minnesota Highway Department under which the highway commissioner would delegate to the Council his responsibilities under the 1962 Federal act for the development of a continuous, comprehensive, and coordinated transportation program. The original proposal for a management committee composed of the highway commissioner, the Metropolitan Council chairman, and the Transit Commission chairman was broadened, at the insistence of local government, to include one member each from the counties and municipalities. The city engineer of St. Paul was hired to direct the program, and a new travel behavior inventory was begun. The first corridor study in this joint framework was initiated in September 1970. The Council's transportation section of the development guide was brought to hearings in January 1971, and approved the next month. Through this period, too, the Council was involved in specific disputes over the design of various highway interchanges, generally resisting the over-provision of access desired by local units and developers.

First steps were also taken to begin development of the public transit system. The Council had been required by 1969 legislation to approve the Metropolitan Transit Commission's acquisition of the area's private bus company. Studies began in 1969 and acquisition of the major operator was approved in August 1970. Studies were also initiated toward the development of a new transit system.

Sewers. Difficulties began to occur with the sewer program as the Sewer Board moved aggressively to get major interceptors out to fringe area communities. The need of these smaller communities for sewage outlets was difficult to deny, but the Council was concerned about opening up large areas to development as the interceptors reached across open country toward the problem areas. A serious struggle with the Sewer Board occurred in the preparation of the 1971 construction program. It was finally approved by the Council with certain exceptions and conditions, including the requirement that the Sewer Board prepare a five-year advance program, and a reaffirmation by the Council that *it* was to retain the paramount role in the planning of the system.

Housing. The housing section of the development guide was completed in late 1970 and moved to public hearing in February 1971. The hearing was distinguished by the lobbying of the Greater Metropolitan Federation, organized in 1970 as an extension of the social action programs of churches in suburban Hennepin County. The federation brought several busloads of its members to the hearing to insist on the retention, in the guide, of the so-called "policy 13" under which the Council would assign a lower priority, in the review of all grant applications, to municipalities felt not to be meeting their obligations in the provision of low- and moderate-income housing.

Open Space and Parks. The Council was also encountering difficulty in securing agreement on a bill for the reconstitution of the Park Reserve District. The board itself, which had been retained as an advisory body, proposed that it be given legal status, with broadened membership and incorporating the Hennepin County Park Reserve District. However, the idea of an operating metropolitan district was resisted by the revived Metropolitan Inter-County Council, which had set as its goal a major park program to be operated through the county government, and by the Hennepin County Park Reserve District, which had acquired and paid for a substantial park reserve program in the preceding decade.

All these controversies, combined with a somewhat relaxed attitude on the part of Council members following the 1969 success, were producing visible strains in the relationship with local government as the 1971 legislative session approached. This stress was reinforced by the decision, particularly in the creation of the open space board, not to name local officials to the subordinate boards. The Council attempted during this period to improve its contacts with local government by reorganizing and strengthening its community services staff, under the direction of a former suburban mayor. The Council also proposed a work program for 1971 focused on the relationship between regional programs and local actions in the implementation of a total metropolitan development program. An areawide conference on the topic of planned unit development was held in February 1971. But, far from reassuring local officials, this tended in some ways to agitate municipal government about the preservation of what local officials regard as their central function: the control of land use and zoning.

The 1971 Legislative Session

With the preceding 18 months so largely absorbed by implementation of the 1969 program, the Council had less time to prepare for the 1971 legislature. It did not, as before, appoint advisory committees. The Council marked out fiscal problems as its own top priority as sewerage had been in 1969. Since members never really mastered the complexities of the issue, it proceeded essentially as staff work. As a result, more effort was expended on negotiations for repassage of the park program and for a new metropolitan housing program.

In the fall of 1970, metropolitan issues were overshadowed by a major dispute in the gubernatorial campaign over State assumption of responsibility for the financing of public education. Some of the strongest legislative supporters of the Council's programs did not stand for re-election. Also, in November, Rosenmeier was defeated and a DFL governor was elected. The Council thus began the 1971 session with a drastically altered legislative setting, and with the prospect of a turnover of five board members plus its chairman, whose terms expired in January.

Newspapermen covering the 1971 session reported that a subtle but real change in the climate of opinion meant the Council's legislative program was in trouble.

Heavy opposition developed to the open space bill. The Inter-County Council vigorously resisted the recreation of an areawide operating district. Its concerns were shared by landowners in the northern suburbs, who were opposed to the acquisition of the Lino Lakes area as a major metropolitan park area as proposed by the Council's guide. Despite this, after intense hearings and close votes, the bill moved ahead through subcommittee and full committee in both houses. The legislators recognized that rapidly disappearing land along streams and lakes was not likely to be preserved without the financial resources and condemnation power of an agency operating in the interests of the entire area. However, in the House the bill was successfully delayed in the Government Operations Committee by its opponents until the session expired.

Financing was provided for the Metropolitan Transit Commission, with the Council able to get a separate law requiring the Metropolitan Transit Commission, in developing its program, to follow the transportation section of the Council's guide. Watershed districts were made subject to the Council's planning controls. Also, county plans were made subject to the same review as municipal plans. Council efforts were indispensable in adoption of the plan for pooling and sharing a portion of the growth of the area's commercial-industrial tax base.

The Council's bill for a metropolitan housing assistance agency failed. Also, the legislative session did not pass a bill making the Metropolitan Airports Commission a subordinate board under the Council. Both houses failed to move on the basic question of electing the Council.

The Transfer of Leadership

The new governor, Wendell Anderson, a former state senator, did replace the five members whose terms expired. The new appointees, who took their seats in March, reflected his political thinking. All were DFL people. The black representation from the central district in St. Paul was continued.

In a statement in late April, Governor Anderson gave strong support to the Council's legislative program, including support to make the Council elective in 1974. A special session of the legislature dragged on until November. But in June, the House leadership declined to consider metropolitan issues further, and the Council therefore turned its attention to repairing the weakness made evident during the previous two years.

A long-simmering controversy between Executive Director Jorvig and his director of planning over staff organization and the relative emphasis to be given to comprehensive versus functional planning, came to a head in June: The staff was reorganized in such a way as to strengthen its capability to deal with the functional agencies. As a result, the planning director resigned.

Gradually, in a series of individual changes, more and more people with relatively stronger backgrounds in politics and government began moving into key positions. The Council strengthened its position on the Sewer Board by filling one vacancy with one of its own former members, and a second with a 20-year veteran of the Minneapolis City Council who has been, in recent years, the director of the city's capital budgeting agency. Steps were taken to rebuild relationships with local government. The community services department went through yet another reshuffling and was expanded. Chairman Hofstede also established a special committee to review the key issues in the Metropolitan Council program and structure. In the summer, offices were moved into downtown St. Paul, and the Council began a regular program of meeting occasionally in suburban village halls. The Council's willingness to talk about the relationship with local government was matched by a growing willingness by local officials to state their complaints frankly. Chairman Hofstede proved to be an understanding but forceful bargainer in these private sessions. In June 1972, in an effort to get this issue fully discussed prior to the fall legislative campaign, the Council opened a set of four weekly hearings to which it invited both local officials and citizen groups for a discussion of basic questions about the Council such as role, structure, and election. The feeling was that these issues would again complicate the legislative program in 1973 if they were not resolved.

In early 1972, the Council also tried to clear the air with legislators by inviting the chairmen of the Senate and House metropolitan affairs committees to express their feelings, and appearing itself before the joint meeting of the two legislative committees for a progress report on the status of its program. The chairman of the development guide committee frankly expressed to the legislators his disappointment with the guide as it stood. The Council members and MTC chairman also met with members of the Minnesota congressional delegation in an effort to keep them informed.

The Drive for Decisions

Establishing the relationship of the Metropolitan Council to functional agencies was the major thrust of its work at the end of 1971. Sensitive and complex issues remained in the areas of airport planning, open space, the dispersal of low- and moderate-income housing, transportation, and the Council's promised "total development framework."

Sewage. The sewer program seemed full of troubles. The Sewer Board was constructing too many interceptors too fast, thereby opening many areas to premature development. The difficult question of "metropolitan benefit" had to be settled: Which areas were so significant that the costs of effluent removal should be spread across the entire region? And there were growing doubts about the wisdom of the "reserve capacity" policy, which authorized the financing of oversized construction to handle future need. By the end of the summer, the Council had resolved matters. A trimmed-down five-year capital program asserting the Council's primary role in sewerage planning was adopted; the metropolitan benefit issue was handled in the course of a shift to a new system of charges for the financing of reserve capacity, according to which all municipalities would pay debt service in proportion to the amount of new construction each year. Eight developing municipalities, led by Mayor Cohen, challenged the new system in court.

Transportation. It was the transportation program, however, that was presenting the largest and most urgent issues. Even the settled routes in the Highway Department's program were coming into growing controversy. A proposal for a new freeway through the east side of St. Paul had been voted down by the city's council. An extension of the interstate system directly west from downtown Minneapolis, through a heavily traveled corridor, was encountering mounting citizen protest against both the design and the idea of any route. Within Minneapolis and St. Paul, vigorous opposition rekindled against the completion of interstate segments for which some land had already been acquired and cleared. Encouraged by these highway difficulties, the Metropolitan Transit Commission was moving aggressively toward its proposal for a new transit system which it would present to the 1973 legislature. Real concern existed in the Council that it would find itself forced to react to an undesirable specific plan proposed by an aggressive regional body, but for which it would have no alternative.

This concern about transportation guidelines promoted the judgment that these issues could not be resolved in inter-agency staff discussion, but only by the increased involvement of policy officials. Conviction grew that what was required were not "plans," but policy decisions.

In December, Chairman Hofstede realigned the Council's committees and made Graven, chairman of the Development Guide Committee, responsible for policy proposals for the major regional systems. The guide committee's meetings were doubled, and focused on the transportation issue almost exclusively. The staff and its consultants were put under great pressure to shape issues for decisions.

The first consequence was to force a reappraisal of the drift of discussion about transit, which had been emerging as a debate between rapid rail and personalized rapid transit. Convinced that the option of reserved-right-of-way bus must at least be discussed, the Council, early in 1972, directed the MTC to add busways to the four new systems it had under study. By summer the Council had reached its own conclusion that busways represented the most prudent solution in the near future.

By late 1972, the need to resolve the transportation issue had become critical. Convinced the MTC was too committed to an essentially rail system to give the busway a fair examination, the Council conducted a study of its own. By fall a strong preference for a reserved-right-of-way bus was emerging. In November, the MTC voted 7-2 for a transit system with a 37-mile "backbone" of automated 40-passenger cars, fed by buses. In December, increasingly attracted by the dual-mode potential of the bus, the Council's Development Guide Committee voted unanimously for the busway. This was confirmed by the full Council the following week. Some MTC members, supported by the City of Minneapolis, indicated they would pursue their argument in the 1973 legislature.

In January, on the basis of discussions with the Metropolitan Airports Commission, the Council concluded that any new airport, wherever located and whenever built, would be a replacement for, rather than an addition to, the region's major air carrier field. In July, it proposed a system plan itself. For the new site, it went north, instructing the Metropolitan Airports Commission to look within a 60-square-mile "search area" in west central Anoka County. It also recommended a long-deferred start on eight additional satellite fields.

Open Space. Early in 1972, the advisory Park Reserve Board, whose members were strongly identified with the effort to get a statutory regional park agency, resigned *en masse,* giving the Council an opportunity for a fresh start on the open space question. The Council appointed a new Open Space Advisory Committee, with a larger membership which included representatives of county government, and named as chairman a lawyer who had been executive secretary to Governor LeVander from 1967 to 1971. The task force reported in October, after deciding to compromise with the counties on a State-financed, regionally-planned, and county-operated parks program. No regional board was recommended.

In the spring, the Council reached a decision on its stated policy of distributing Federally subsidized housing more widely around the region, particularly into the first-tier suburbs. After some hesitation it vetoed an application for open-space funds from a first-tier suburb found not to have made an effort on low- and moderate-income housing. The new policy, combined with the work of the Housing Advisory Committee and the help of Mayor Philip Cohen of Brooklyn Center, produced a broad if not overly enthusiastic support for the allocation plan and the creation of a regional housing authority. By the time of the public hearing in December, it was evident that municipalities might prefer to contract with the Council instead of creating their own authority.

Council Structure. Pressed by these controversies with the special districts, Council members also reached a decision at the end of the year on their preference for metropolitan structure. They voted to seek authority to name the members and chairmen of the subordinate boards, and for the first time publicly favored a directly elected Metropolitan Council.

By the eve of the 1973 legislative session, the Council had established itself as the center of attention in governmental affairs in the Twin Cities area. There was a feeling of a political decision-making process underway by the Metropolitan Council. Affected agencies' representatives were careful to be present, listening, as the Development Guide Committee and the Council debated its alternatives. The debates became front-page news and received prime time on television. The basic question of the future of the Council and its legislative program became the most salient issue in the fall legislative campaign in the metropolitan area.

The November election provided no clear view of the Council's prospects. Some supporters and some opponents would not be returning; turnover was unusually heavy. Probably the most important fact was that for the first time in history the DFL took control of both House and Senate, providing dependable majorities for Governor Anderson, who, with the five additional appointments due in January, would become primarily responsible for the success of the Metropolitan Council and its programs.

THE STRUCTURE
OF REGIONAL GOVERNANCE

The regional level of government has not evolved in the Twin Cities area in the form of a multiple-purpose service district or as a kind of council/manager form writ large. Nor does it resemble the executive/legislative arrangement traditional in state government. It has been described as an "umbrella," with a number of special-purpose agencies drawn under the overall policy responsibility of a politically representative council.

Its distinguishing feature is the separation between the regional policy council and the operating agencies, whether other regional bodies, local units, or private organizations. Clearly evident from the Twin Cities experience is a willingness by the public and political officials to move much more rapidly toward regional arrangements in the area of policy making than in the area of program operations. There is a real reluctance to build a new administrative apparatus at the regional level. As a result, it is possible to see the overall structure in the form of contracts between the Metropolitan Council and the various private and public agencies managing development and providing services as determined by the policy body.

The Policy Institutions

The decision-making structure of the Metropolitan Council consists of the council and staff, and a set of policy boards and advisory committees through which the Council extends itself into program areas for which it is responsible.

The council itself consists of 14 members appointed by the Governor for overlapping six-year terms from districts created by combining the reapportioned state senate districts by twos, with each member representing about 100,000 people. A chairman serves at large at the pleasure of the Governor. Members are divided between two major committees: the Development Guide Committee, which receives plan proposals from the staff and advisory boards and committees and translates them into Council policy guidelines; and the Referral Committee, which reviews all applications from local units and private parties for Federal assistance. A few members overlap onto a Personnel and Work Program Committee, which also deals with questions of staff and Council structure. The chairman is designated the principal executive officer. With Council approval, he appoints an executive director, who supervises the 125-man staff.

The policy boards or committees are both permanent and temporary. Their membership typically mixes citizens and representatives of the interests under study. Some of them are further subdivided into task forces which reach for their membership still further out into the community. As of 1972, three committees could be considered permanent:

1. A 19-member Metropolitan Health Board, which prepares the initial plan and reviews projects in the health care system, with sub-groups for mental health, hospital construction, long-term care, emergency care, and community health, and with *ad hoc* study committees on specific project applications as required.
2. A 35-member Criminal Justice Advisory Committee, with representation balanced as required by Federal guidelines among professionals, local officials, and citizens.
3. A five-member Management Committee, with no citizen representation, to supervise transportation planning, along with related committees on local public officials and transportation professionals.

Three 25-member temporary committees exist:

1. An Open Space Advisory Board with task forces on recreation, open-space protection, fiscal resources, and implementation.
2. A Housing Advisory Committee with subcommittees on municipal relations, communications, legislation, and national legislative review.
3. A Cable TV Advisory Committee.

The Operating Structure

As noted, other levels of government and private organizations are part of the implementing or operating structure. At the regional level, the basic arrangement for implementing regional policy is best thought of as a set of variations on what has come to be known as the "Sewer Board model." This involves a regional agency legally separate from, but subordinate to, the Metropolitan Council, vested with the ownership of facilities and charged to carry out the program. In practice, some variation continues to exist in Council/board relationships in different functional areas.

The prototype, the *Metropolitan Sewer Board,* was created by the legislature in 1967. Its chairman and seven members are appointed by the Metropolitan Council. Each member represents a precinct created by combining the Metropolitan Council districts by twos. It exists to implement the sewer section of the Council's Development Guide. Operating and capital budgets are approved by the Council, and the Council sells the bonds to finance its work. It shares offices with the Council.

The *Metropolitan Transit Commission* was created in 1967 by law with nine members appointed by local government officials. It is charged with carrying out the Transportation Guide as developed by the Council. The MTC capital budget is subject to approval by the Council, but it issues its own bonds after consultation with the Council. It also shares offices with the Council.

The *Metropolitan Airports Commission* was created by law in 1943 and consists of four representatives from each central city and one non-resident of the area appointed by the Governor. The legislature has left its relationship to the Council unclear by authorizing the Council to suspend MAC plans, but failing to direct that MAC shall follow the Council's guidelines. The Council has no role in its financing. The MAC has offices at the airport.

The *Minnesota Highway Department* builds regional facilities in the Twin Cities Area. With the exception of the planning contract referred to earlier, the Minnesota Highway Department has no formal relationship to the Metropolitan Council. However, the Highway commissioner has indicated that he wants to rely on Council plans.

The counties joined together in 1959 in a regionwide agency to operate the mosquito abatement program. This district is governed by a board of two commissioners from each county. A similar arrangement has been proposed by the counties for the regional enforcement of State air pollution control regulations.

At the present time, there is no regionwide structure for the solid waste disposal program or the acquisition of parks and open space. The individual county governments establish landfill sites in line with the Council's guide. Counties and municipalities acquire major open-space property at metropolitan sites designated by the Council.

Inter-local Cooperation

One hundred thirty-two cities and villages, representing about 90 percent of the region's population, are organized in a voluntary Metropolitan Section of the League of Minnesota Municipalities. Separate, somewhat competitive, leagues of municipal elected officials exist on a countywide basis in Hennepin, Ramsey, and Anoka Counties. Municipal professional employees such as police chiefs and finance officers meet informally on a regional or sub-regional basis.

The seven county boards (plus Wright County to the northwest) are organized in a *Metropolitan Inter-County Council (MICC)*, whose board is composed of two commissioners from each member county. The MICC has committees for county professional persons in the areas of administration, personnel, transportation, finance, criminal justice, health and welfare, housing, environment, and parks. Sheriffs, attorneys, auditors, and treasurers also have regional associations.

Forty-two of the 49 school districts in the region are members of the *Educational Research and Development Council,* which provides in-service training for administrators, curriculum development, legislative analysis, and program evaluation service. The ERDC is governed by a board of eight superintendents elected by representatives of the member districts. Informally, the metropolitan superintendents also meet regularly on a regional basis, particularly for the consideration of legislative proposals.

The *Metropolitan Library Service Agency (MELSA)* was established in 1969 under the Joint Powers Act. Membership is open to cities of the first class and the seven counties within the metropolitan area. Carver County, which does not have a library system, is the only county which has not yet joined. MELSA is governed by a Board of Trustees, consisting of one appointee from each of the member library jurisdictions. It has three major goals: to improve library service in the metropolitan area; to coordinate total library service; and to work with other systems in statewide interlibrary cooperation. Financing is from State and Federal aids which totaled $400,000 in 1972.

REGIONAL FUNCTIONS

Broadly, the regional agencies perform three functions: policy making, the operation of facilities and programs, and the provision of research and advisory services to the public and local units of government. The general principle is that functions are not assigned exclusively to the regional level but are shared, with the State above and with the local units below. There are three separate sources which authorize the undertaking of regional functions: the Minnesota legislature, the Congress and the Federal agencies which issue regulations, and the joint powers authority of local governments within the region.

Making General Community Policy

By State law, and by its designation as the "regional clearinghouse," the Metropolitan Council is established as the body to resolve conflicts and to speak for the region. Council policy statements sometimes represent final action. On decisions, where authority rests at higher levels, the Council's policy represents significant local consensus which permits the other body to act without a full-scale review of the issues on its own. This policy-making function appears in several forms: consensus for the legislature, the Development Guide, review of local comprehensive plans, and project review.

Consensus for the Legislature. The 1967 law specifically charges the Council to make recommendations on the control and prevention of air pollution; a program of major parks and open spaces; the control and prevention of water pollution; the development of long-range planning *in* the area (by other than metropolitan bodies); a program for solid waste disposal; the tax structure and ways to equalize tax resources; assessment practices; surface water drainage; the need for the consolidation of services of local units; and the advance acquisition of land for development purposes. Recommendations are to cover also the organizational and financial aspects of the solutions proposed.

The Development Guide. The same law directs the Council to say, specifically and with respect to a broad range of physical and social problem areas, what should be done in order to promote the orderly and economic growth of the region. In exercising this function, the Council creates policy guidelines for all relevant public and private agencies. They are contained in sections of the Development Guide, which to date have been completed on sewers, solid waste, parks and open space, transportation, total development (the pattern of major activity centers), and housing. Sections on airports, water resources, health care, and the criminal justice system are in preparation. Revisions in the direction of increased concreteness are continuous. The MTC is directed by law to follow the Council's Development Guide, as is the Sewer Board, and the counties with respect to refuse disposal. Under the 1971 State "certificate of need" law, the Council's determination is also generally relied on by the State Health Department with respect to proposals for health care facilities in excess of $50,000. The Council's role is more than advisory also with respect to multi-jurisdictional special districts: It may suspend the plans or projects of these agencies. The agency may appeal to the legislature. The guide is also the basis for the advisory A-95 reviews.

Review of Local Comprehensive Plans. The Council is authorized to review the plans and projects of municipalities and counties in relation to regional policy and each other. On occasion, a municipality will bring to the Council a request for it to study an action by an adjoining municipality which it feels has some adverse spillover effect. Where the Council believes, either raises an issue of metropolitan significance, it can "hold" for 60 days and attempt to mediate the differences. One area in which a stronger review exists is that of municipal sewer plans: these are required under the 1969 Act, and in approving them the Council can make suggestions and set conditions.

Review of Projects. As the designated A-95 clearinghouse, the Council reviews applications for Federal assistance. It screens projects proposed for funding under the Safe Streets Act, and makes recommendations to the Governor's Crime Commission. It reviews applications from private as well as public parties for aid for hospitals and health facilities construction. Partly by law and partly by contract with the Highway Department, it reviews proposed highway construction projects. It reviews applications from developers for Federally assisted housing. It also advises the Minnesota Municipal Commission with respect to proposed incorporations and annexations.

Operating Programs

Under the framework of Metropolitan Council plans and policies, region-wide operating programs have come to be organized in three different ways: First, as a program of State government, perhaps decentralized to the seven-county region; second, as a new and separate agency created directly by the legislature on a seven-county basis; and third, as a regionwide joint effort of local units, particularly the counties.

Current operating programs include highways, a State-county undertaking; transit, controlled by MTC; airports, operated by the two central cities through MAC; sewerage, handled by the Metropolitan Sewer Board; mosquito control, run by the counties under a joint agreement; and open-space site designation, over-seen by the Metropolitan Council, which recommends funding to individual counties.

Research and Service

The Metropolitan Council coordinates the census in the Twin Cities area.

It publishes and distributes population, housing, fiscal, and other data. It advises and assists local units on their own planning and on applications for Federal aid. And it is currently undertaking jointly with the State and local units the development of a regionwide system for the coordination of management and planning data.

Research and advisory services, and mechanisms for the joint study of regional problems, are also made available to municipalities, counties, and school districts by the three associations of local governments.

REGIONAL FINANCING

No explicit or coherent policy on the financing of regional programs has been worked out by the legislature. Like the structure, the financing is evolving on an *ad hoc* basis. Nevertheless, some patterns are discernible.

Generally, the capital and operating costs of the major regional systems are being financed by a combination of user charges and, where a general revenue subsidy is required, *ad valorem* property taxes. General non-property taxes are not in use at the regional or the local levels. Local costs are, wherever possible, supplemented by Federal grants-in-aid. In recent years, the State has begun to provide a small stream of grants-in-aid toward the regional programs. But with the exception of Federal aid most revenues for regional programs are raised at the regional level by the regional agencies where they are so authorized by the legislature. The exception is the sewer program, in which the Metropolitan Sewer Board and the Metropolitan Council simply apportion costs and bill the municipalities, which are then responsible for actually raising the revenue from whatever combination of *ad valorem* taxes and sewer use charges they individually see fit. Bonding authority has been provided in most cases in order to make a fast start on the construction of the infrastructure such as sewers. Both State highways and major county roads are on a pay-as-you-go basis.

The decision to use the property tax must be seen in the context of overall State policy toward the financing of local government. In addition to increasing State aid for education, the legislature has acted to drive down the level of property taxes in the total fiscal "mix," with a 4 percent sales tax and a 22 percent increase in income taxes in 1971. In 1972, mill rates were about 10 percent below the previous year's level, even though State-local expenditures have increased. Property tax rates are more uniform across the region and the State, with State-collected non-property revenues used increasingly to offset the interlocal differences in valuations and in needs. Within this larger State-local system, the legislature has felt it appropriate for the regional agencies to return, in a limited way, to the property tax, with usually uniform areawide tax rates.

Finances of Individual Agencies and Programs

The Metropolitan Council operates on an annual budget (for 1973 just over $3 million), about half provided by Federal grants and half by a region-wide property tax levy. It assumed upon its creation the .5 mill levy of the Metropolitan Planning Commission (the MPC having been almost the first such agency in the country to get this kind of assured public funding). The levy was increased to .7 mill by the legislature in 1969. The grants have come from a variety of Federal agencies: HUD, though its proportion has been declining, EPA, FAA, LEAA, DOT, HEW. Stability was a problem. In 1972, the Council was able to enter into an arrangement with the Federal agencies through the Federal Regional Council for an integrated annual grant for planning for 1973. The Council hopes that if this can produce a multi-agency plan and program the Council will not need to be so concerned about whether the capital grant money actually passes through its hands: The important thing is that the Council will have been able to determine the use of these capital dollars. At present, it can only influence this flow of funds, which move to the program agencies directly from the Federal government or from legislative authorizations. The Council has no general fund for capital or program. It makes no grants to local units for capital or operations, though an aid program for local planning is included in its 1973 budget.

The Council receives no cut of Federal revenue sharing, though hopes remain this can be achieved. It gets no private contributions. And it depends in no way on voluntary contributions from local government units. Its transportation planning program relies heavily on monies contributed by the State Highway Department.

With respect to the operating programs, the Council has its largest role in the financing of the Metropolitan Sewer Board. It both approves that agency's budget and sells the sewer bonds. For this program the Council assumed about $208 million of debt issued by the sewer districts acquired in the formation of the metropolitan system, and through the summer of 1972 had borrowed an additional $104 million for construction. In early fall, it approved a 1972-76 program calling for the expenditure of an additional $211 million. The current annual operating budget is $26 million. Interceptor costs originally apportioned within six sewer areas will, under the 1972 revision, now be spread areawide, as are costs for treatment plants.

The Council approves the budget of the Metropolitan Transit Commission, but the MTC sells its own bonds. Over $9 million was received in Federal grants and $6 million borrowed locally for the acquisition of the private bus company and for new buses. The annual operating budget of the MTC is about $20 million—about three-fifths of which is provided by farebox collections and charter service. The debt service and the operating subsidy are funded from a property-tax levy within a defined "transit taxing district" covering areas served. The legislative policy here is significant. In 1971, it was noted that in the seven-county area almost three-fourths of the county and municipal road system was still financed in one way or another by charges to property—almost $50 million a year. The legislature began an effort to shift more of this cost to road users, by mandating a reduction in county road and bridge property levies, authorizing the counties to impose a $5-per-vehicle wheelage tax to replace the lost property tax revenue, and authorizing a new property tax for the MTC—all in recognition that the road system can now support both capital and operations from users, and that this general-revenue subsidy ought to be used for the start-up of the transit system. Depending on the vehicle system selected, it is estimated this will cost between $300 million and $1 billion.

The Council really plays no role in the financing of the Metropolitan Airports Commission, except, as noted, to approve the projects on which money can be spent. Currently, MAC has a $42-million development program under way at its existing airport, in which it now has $104 million invested. The new major airport, and the eight proposed new satellite fields, have recently been estimated to cost in excess $1 billion. MAC bonds are secured against the tax base of the two central cities, and for a time tax levies were made to pay debt service and operating deficits. In recent years, revenues from users have been sufficient to support both operating and capital costs.

The solid waste program is financed by charges of from 40 to 90 cents per cubic yard for trucks using the landfills. In most cases, the sites are acquired privately, in line with the Council's plan, and operated under license by the counties.

The major open-space program has moved slowly. Relatively little of the $3.5 million of cigarette-tax money made available by the legislature since 1969 has been spent—partly due to the complex approvals required among the localities, the Council, the Federal government, and the legislative Minnesota Resources Commission.

The seven-county Metropolitan Mosquito Control District is financed by a per-capita assessment on each of the counties, collected by them through a property tax levy on their valuations.

The Council plays a key role indirectly in the financing of the area's hospital system since under the State's 1971 certificate-of-need legislation the Minnesota Health department, which parcels out the Hill-Burton aids, normally abides by the decisions on capital expansion made by the regional agencies—in the Twin Cities area, the Metropolitan Health Board.

Financing Local Government

Dramatic changes were made in 1971 in the financing of the State's counties, municipalities, and school districts. Substantial increases in State revenue were provided, mainly for schools, with formulas increasingly moving away from "place of collections" or "per capita" toward new measures of need and "tax effort."

School finance was essentially taken over by the State. Each district will continue to make a local property levy, amounting to about 30 mills in 1972. But this can just as well be regarded as a State-mandated, or statewide, levy. Whatever this produces in dollars, the State will then supplement for 1972, up to $750 per pupil unit. The implications of this far-reaching change are only now being absorbed. It means that for school operating purposes and up to $750 per pupil unit the valuation of a district or the valuation of any individual house is basically irrelevant, since the State guarantees the financing no matter how many children reside there. It was recognized even before the legislative debate ended that this alone would be disadvantageous to the central cities whose relatively high valuations per pupil meant they would receive little in non-property State aids. The legislature offset this with special credits for children in AFDC families and with an expanded program of revenue-sharing for municipalities.

No comparable amount of new money was provided for general local government. But a number of existing aid programs were abolished and a new State revenue-sharing system was established. In general, it tends to provide larger shares for municipalities than for counties and to recognize the special problems of the larger developed cities. In the Twin Cities area it takes an essentially metropolitan approach. The seven-county area is treated as a unit in the statewide per capita "first cut." This "pot" is then divided between municipalities and counties. Of the municipal share, the central cities receive a "cut" proportionate to their levies as a proportion of total regional municipal levies. The remainder is then divided among the suburbs on a per capita basis. In an effort to protect the tax sources necessary to fund this revenue-sharing program, the legislature also enacted a prohibition against any local unit's increasing a present, or levying a new tax on sales or income.

Local finances will eventually be affected also by the Metropolitan Development Act of 1971, which provides for a limited sharing of the growth of the non-residential property tax base in the seven-county area. Beginning in 1972, 40 percent of the net growth of non-residential valuations will be excluded from entering directly into the tax base of the jurisdictions where the buildings are located, pooled at the seven-county level, and shared among all jurisdictions. This will be done essentially on a population basis, but weighed so that a part of the region where valuations per capita are above the regional average will receive a slightly smaller share, and vice versa.

This program is intended to diminish somewhat the fiscal factors in such development decisions by municipalities as zoning, the location of freeway interchanges, the acceptance of open space, etc. The immediate tax-base advantages to be gained from such fiscal zoning will be somewhat reduced and municipalities will begin to experience some growth of tax base from the assured growth of the area as a whole, no matter where commercial or industrial buildings may be located. A delicate balance had to be struck here. The legislature did not want to change incentives so far as to encourage municipalities to resist all non-residential development.

It is too early to tell what the consequences will be, in terms of the way the tax base distributes, or in terms of municipal council reaction. It may be of particular help to the central cities, where losses of valuation due to relocation of commercial activity and the demolition of properties will tend to reduce the contribution to the pool from their new development. (In one instance, following passage of the new Act, the State commission which rules on the extension of municipal boundaries revised its stand on incorporation, adopted originally for "tax base" reasons.

The law is being contested by an aggressive Dakota County municipality seeking growth. But the timing of the decision will not prevent the base-sharing from going into effect for the first year. If it continues in effect, it should reinforce the tendency in the legislature's revenue-sharing program toward a greater sense of regional unity. The Council was not the author of the plan but its legislative analysis and explanation were critical to its passage. Nor is the Council involved in the operation of the base-sharing. The legislature enacted it partly as an alternative to the creation of both a metropolitan taxing district and a metropolitan government, since it redistributes resources among local units to be taxed locally within the existing fiscal system.

AN EVALUATION OF PERFORMANCE

No systematic evaluation of the Metropolitan Council has been done. However, some judgments are possible.

Making Regional Decisions

Regional decision making has remained the central objective of the Council. Effectiveness has been defined not primarily in terms of functional achievements, but in terms of the ability to assert a regionwide policy interest in the programs of operating agencies.

The first major accomplishment was the decision to organize the sewerage system on a fully regional basis, plus the related decision to finance the cost of treatment plants regionwide and to introduce the metropolitan benefit concept. The Council's decision here resolved an eight-year deadlock within the legislature, and in less than two years the regional system was fully established with a major expansion program underway. Discharges of effluent into lakes are being rapidly eliminated; in October 1972, it was reported there had been a 60 percent reduction in algae in Lake Minnetonka, the region's largest recreational water body. In 1972, in approving the five-year capital improvement program for sewers, the Council was able to reduce the rate of new interceptor construction by requiring the Sewer Board to proceed only as Federal aid became available.

The second major decision was veto of the MAC proposal for a new major airport, first in early 1969 and again in late 1970. The vetoes represented an assertion of essentially environmental considerations felt not to have been adequately considered in MAC planning. This decision, too, has been effective. On neither occasion did MAC choose to appeal the Council's action to the subsequent legislative session as it was authorized to do by law. In the summer of 1972, after months of work by a joint Council-MAC committee, agreement was reached on a general plan for the expansion of the airport system. The technical merits of the alternative north and south locations were approximately equal; the Council's decision was felt to be based essentially on a desire to balance development, which had been drifting to the south and southwest.

A third major decision was the Council's adopted revision of its Development Guide, which favors a transportation system consisting essentially of no new freeways within the central urban area, a grid of freeways on new alignments in the developing fringe, and a transit system consisting of buses.

In its effort to distribute low- and moderate-income housing more broadly throughout the region, the Council decided in December 1971, to move toward the first- and second-tier suburbs, except those in which the market had concentrated low-income tract developments. It also insisted that projects be well located with respect to commercial facilities and transit. The HUD area director encouraged potential developers to contact the Council early. Thus, the Council's staff has been able to advise early on where such housing should be proposed. Through 1971 and 1972 more Federally subsidized housing was approved in the suburbs than in all the years of the program up to that date. Looking toward the 1973 legislative session, the Council is proposing that it be designated a Metropolitan Housing Authority so that it could be contracted with by suburban municipalities for the development of public or publicly assisted housing.

Improving Service Inadequacies

Major improvements in airports and transit await action by the 1973 legislature. But the bus system has already been vastly upgraded with the acquisition of the private operator, the purchase of 325 new buses, the extension of the system from 500 to 700 route miles, and the upgrading of service on existing routes. A trend of declining ridership has been reversed, and patronage rebuilt from about 50 million to about 54 million riders per year.

The closing of small treatment plants has reversed the deterioration of important recreational lakes, and central sewer service has come to areas which had depended on septic tanks. Most of the approximately 60 open burning dumps have been closed, and about a dozen sanitary landfills substituted. Little has been done in the acquisition of open space, largely as a result of a court decision which invalidated the Park Reserve District. State funding problems and county opposition prevented the legislature from acting on a new board in 1971. In health care, the Council has directed Hennepin County to plan neighborhood primary care centers along with the new general-hospital/private-hospital complex.

Costs and Economies

The argument for creating a regional structure never rested on the expectation that it would reduce service costs. Rather it was advanced with the recognition that the regional agencies would undertake activities not being performed, and that costs previously absorbed by the environment or appearing as sub-optimal development would, in the future, be expressed in public budgets. And these budgets have in fact increased substantially. As a result, pressures are appearing for the Council to begin setting cross-functional priorities among the major regional programs and to develop an overall capital budget.

Sewer Board administrators assert that their large treatment plants provide economies of scale as compared with the smaller sub-regional plants that would otherwise have developed. Hospital officials have testified that the joint development of Hennepin General and the private complex will save $4 million in construction costs and $1 million a year in operating costs. A reduction in bed supply, also involved, may improve hospital utilization, producing savings in insurance rates.

The Reduction of Disparities

The extremes in wealth and service levels are to be found among suburbs, not between the central cities and the suburbs. These disparities have been significantly reduced since the creation of the Metropolitan Council in 1967. The important actions were, necessarily, taken by the State legislature, but the work of the regional agencies played an important part both in establishing the problem and in implementing the solutions.

Some equilization of sewer service costs has resulted from the decisions to spread treatment costs areawide and to base operating costs on volume of flow, rather than on distance from the plant, within sub-regional service areas. The principles of uniformity and ability to pay will be considerably extended by the new financing system, under which the annual debt service for major sewer construction will be collected annually from charges based on the amount of new development occurring in a municipality.

The 1971 school aid changes have also had a dramatic effect. In the large Anoka-Hennepin school district in the northern suburbs, for example, (which in 1970 had a per pupil valuation of $3,700, compared with $14,000 in Golden Valley and $17,700 in Minneapolis) property-tax levies dropped from $10.3 million in 1971 to $4.3 million in 1972—a decrease of 57 percent.

Impact on Local Planning

There has been little impact on local planning, partially because the Council has not established its exact role in providing guidelines for municipal development. Localities feel its advice wavers between the overly general and the overly specific. As the Council sees it, its job is to set regional plans within which the localities can make their own planning and development decisions.

One exception is local sewer planning. Since comprehensive sewer plans must be reviewed by the Council, it has an opportunity to specify where sewers should be extended and recently when as well. One major limitation is that although the law provides for Council review of plans when prepared, no law mandates their actual preparation.

Intergovernmental Cooperation

The Metropolitan Council has mediated some interlocal disputes. It has also at times pointedly refused to be drawn into disputes it did not consider of metropolitan significance.

The regional governance mechanism is supplemented by the separate areawide associations of municipalities, counties, and school districts. Intergovernmental cooperation, therefore, is largely a function of these associations, which are cooperating extensively on such matters as labor relations.

Overall, the conclusion must be that the existence of the Metropolitan Council has increased the tension of intergovernmental relations. Municipalities, given their numbers and their diversity in size and interests, have not been affected greatly. However, the metropolitan counties are large enough and strong enough to believe they should and can move affirmatively to substitute themselves, singly or in groups, for the State-created regional operating agencies the Council would like to bring into existence.

The Metropolitan Council is a political body. Many of its members, appointed by the Governor, have public affairs backgrounds. Also, it has replaced the major city councils as the logical focus of attention from the news media. Policy decisions have been made with an eye toward their effects on relationships with local officials and the legislature, although these effects do not always override other factors. The Council's political character has been set largely by its members' willingness to involve themselves deeply in both internal deliberations and public debate.

Within the Council, its political character has been reflected in important votes which have rejected recommendations from its staff, policy boards, and advisory committees. Votes are frequently close. Yet no permanent factions have appeared; no continuing central city versus suburban or Republican versus DFL division has been evident. In 1972, for example, Mayor Cohen was a leading supporter of the metropolitan housing development program while he was preparing to take the new sewer availability charge to court.

Increasingly, the Metropolitan Council is being lobbied by private organizations. It was pressure from the Greater Metropolitan Federation, which bussed 400 people to its hearing, that originally persuaded the Council to adopt its "policy 13" regarding low- and moderate-income housing. When considering approval for the new Hennepin County General Hospital, the Council was pressed by inner-city organizations to establish a priority instead on neighborhood primary care. Pressure groups representing both developers and residents have been active in the Council's decision on the location for the new major airport. And more than 40 representatives, mostly from private groups, appeared at a hearing on the proposed new transportation guide.

Minorities

An estimated 32,000 blacks represent about 2.8 percent of the region's population. About 17,000 persons are of Spanish extraction, and approximately 10,000 are Indians. There is no electoral district at any level where a non-white majority exists. Three blacks are in elective office. (The two black suburban elected officials ran successfully for the State legislature in November 1972. Both are from Hennepin County.)

This political situation has fundamentally shaped the attitude of the minority community toward regional affairs. With no prospect of controlling any unit of government, they see clearly that their efforts must be to push the majority-dominated institutions into policies favorable to them and to their interests. On the whole, regional government has not been very close to the top in the priorities of the leaders in the black and minority community. This may be because the Council's work to date has concentrated largely on the physical development of regional systems. As the Council and its agencies begin to raise issues about housing, health care, man-power development, and tax burdens—which could not be raised effectively among a collection of independent local units—leaders in the minority community may tend to be supportive.

The Council has had a black member since its inception. About 10 percent of the staff is non-white, though few occupy professional positions. Representatives of the black and Indian communities serve on the Council's advisory committees and subcommittees dealing with criminal justice, open space, and health care, in numbers beyond their proportion in the total population.

The significance of the role played by the State of Minnesota can scarcely be overemphasized. Although not originally proposed by the State, the Council and the operating agencies were created by it through general State law. And the State provides the metropolitan agencies with their revenue or the authority to raise revenue.

The Role of the State

The Governor's role has been an important one. He is involved, of course, in the policy process as the State makes its decisions on changes in the system of regional governance, and he is the appointing authority for the chairman and members of the Metropolitan Council. When campaigning for governor in 1966, Harold LeVander supported establishment of a metropolitan council. Once elected, he made it a part of his legislative program. His principal effort came during 1969 in efforts to help pass the metropolitan sewerage legislation. His successor, Governor Wendell Anderson (who as a senator in 1967 had moved the narrowly defeated amendment to make the Council elected) sent a special message to the legislature in the spring of 1971, reaffirming his support for the Council's program at a time when it was in legislative difficulty.

The State's role is exercised principally, however, by the legislature, which determines structure, establishes functions, and authorizes financing for the Metropolitan Council and the other regional agencies. The law required the governor to consult with legislators within each Council district prior to making his appointments. Senate consent is required on the appointment of the members and chairman. Perhaps most important, it is the legislators, as representatives of their districts, who are contacted first by citizens and local officials displeased by some action (or inaction) of the Metropolitan Council. In the fall of 1972, the debate over the future of the metropolitan arrangement was occurring largely in the legislative campaign materials and meetings.

Overall, the Twin Cities experience underscores strongly what Larry Margolis of the Citizens Council on State Legislatures means when he says: "The urban crisis is in the State legislatures."

By contrast with its intimate involvement in regional policy making, the State's role in regional administration is slight. The Attorney General's opinion permitted the Metropolitan Council to evolve basically as a separate, regional level of government. Consequently, it does not use the State Treasurer for its fiscal services, the Attorney General's office for its legal services, the State Civil Service for its personnel services, or the State Department of Administration for its purchasing services. The State Planning Director told the Council at its structure hearings in July 1972, that the administration regards the regional agencies statewide as entities of local government.

Legislators are ambivalent about the Metropolitan Council. Like many local officials, they tend to support a regional approach when an issue arises within a particular functional area. Also, like local officials, they become hesitant when it is suggested that the variety of functions appearing at the regional level be drawn together into an overall general government. They are responsive to the complaints of local officials, particularly about appearances of unresponsiveness or bureaucracy in the Council. They appear to enjoy criticizing the Council, and pushing it to perform. Yet they rely on it for advice and decisions with which they can resolve disputes which would otherwise fall with full force on the legislature itself. Overall, and considering even the Council's record in the 1971 session, it is fair to say that the legislature since 1967 has not weakened the Council or the metropolitan structure, but cautiously and critically has continued to expand its scope and authority.

In 1969, two years after the creation of the Council, the legislature moved into a statewide program of regional districts. This will likely be supportive of the Metropolitan Council in the long run. In the short run, however, it has been disruptive. Before 1969, the question of how best to govern the State's major metropolitan area was perceived by non-metropolitan legislators as a matter of statewide policy which affected them scarcely at all in their own districts. After 1969, with the passage of the new law, regionalization became a major issue in many of their districts. Efforts to begin organizing the outstate regional commissions were not always skillful and provoked in many areas a boiling controversy among the several county seat towns in each region, each either hoping to become the "regional capital" or fearing that its competitor might win this designation. This statewide bill came totally without the kind of education on the need for regional cooperation which had preceded creation of the Metropolitan Council. In 1971, therefore, outstate legislators, acutely conscious that whatever they did with the Twin Cities area might become a precedent for proposals later in their own regions, were extremely cautious about expansion of the Council's authority. All this is now, however, quieting. Regional commissions have been successfully established in three areas outside the Twin Cities area. (The Metropolitan Council's structure is not serving as a model for these outstate commissions which are made up as a combination of citizen members and elected local officials.)

The State government seems to be moving away from direct provision of services and operation of facilities. The adopted long-range plan for the Department of Public Welfare, for example, calls for a termination of State operation of major hospitals and other institutions and a devolution of these responsibilities to regional organizations or to individual communities. The whole field of social services lies open for regional organizations in a way that is only beginning to be realized.

Volunteerism

The arrangements for regional governance in Minnesota are not a formalization of earlier voluntary arrangements. Each piece of the structure, almost without exception, was either created by law or established pursuant to a legal requirement.

When established in 1957, the Metropolitan Planning Commission was created in law. For five metropolitan counties provision was made for additional contiguous counties to join at the request of their county boards. Two later did. The original Minneapolis-St. Paul Sanitary District was established by the legislature in 1933; the Metropolitan Airports Commission in 1943.

The Metropolitan Transit Commission is an exception. It was formed as a voluntary agency by several municipalities in the Twin Cities area in 1966, after the failure of a bill for a statutory agency in 1965. It was then made statutory in 1967. In retrospect, it might have been better to wait for the 1967 legislation since the joint powers board, selected by local officials, was carried forward into the new Transit Commission, and has operated with considerable difficulty.

The voluntary approach has existed and continues to exist in the Twin Cities area separate from and parallel to the statutory regional governance structure. Voluntary associations of municipalities, counties, and school districts at the regional and sub-regional levels, and in specialized functional and geographic groupings, are strong and productive.

Centralization and Decentralization

The Twin Cities area has not been explicitly implementing a two-tier concept of regional governance. The new metropolitan level is coming in without a clear policy decision to take any existing level out. There are people, particularly in the business community, concerned about this addition of a level of government to an already complicated pattern, but the issue has not really been sharpened. In fact, pressure from municipal and county officials to keep the metropolitan level within bounds tends to preserve the rationale for a three-level local system.

Nevertheless, the relationships will not remain static. There is some structural change, notably the increasing size of municipalities as a result of the Minnesota Municipal Commission's policy on incorporations, and as a consequence of occasional mergers. A movement for neighborhood organizations is beginning. And there is the continuing reorganization of governmental structure, most noticably, since 1963, the dramatic upgrading of the competence of the county governments. Whether major change will occur, or in what direction, is hard to see clearly. From time to time municipal officials privately express their feeling that the county level could just as well be divided, with some functions being transferred up to the metropolitan level and others downward to the municipalities. County officials, on the other hand, have been heard to express belief that they could handle the first tier functions more effectively and economically than the municipalities, perhaps in conjunction with some essentially advisory councils organized at the neighborhood level.

The really significant movement has been not in structure but in functions. Interestingly, this does not heavily involve the metropolitan agencies, which developed primarily to undertake activities never performed by any local units. Functions are being transferred most actively between municipal and county governments, particularly in Hennepin County. In the last decade, the City of Minneapolis has transferred to Hennepin County most of its major specialized facilities and programs, so that the city, even though larger in territory and population, is now, functionally, virtually the equivalent of a suburban village.

A 1970 study by the Citizens League (a nonprofit public affairs research organization in the metropolitan area) proposed that Minneapolis establish a citywide framework of "community councils." This was urged partly as a way of better representing minorities (not only racial) in city decision making, and partly as a way of getting participation in decisions on major city projects from the neighborhoods. Essentially, it argued that citizen participation exists, if only in the form of people lying down in front of bulldozers. The prudent course, therefore, would be to structure participation so that it could be rewarding, rather than disruptive; constructive rather than negative; and productive of decisions rather than frustration.

In the fall of 1970, the league was asked by the Minneapolis Model City project to advise on the application of the small-unit-election system it had proposed for community councils in the Model City area, which was then governed by a large (105-member) and unwieldy board. Ultimately, a new board with about 60 members elected from regular city precincts (other members were added from caucuses and interest groups) was negotiated with the City Council. Elections were held in September 1971, and this board is now in operation.

The issue of community participation also became a factor in the campaigns for St. Paul City Council and mayor in the spring of 1972, the first election under the new "strong mayor" form of government. Partly because no element of district representation exists in St. Paul's governmental structure, the question of a new form of citizen participation came on with some strength. The DFL-endorsed candidate, Lawrence Cohen, endorsed the idea of community councils. He was elected, and in the fall of 1972 a committee was attempting to transform his campaign pledge into program specifics.

FUTURE DIRECTIONS

In 1973, the regional arrangement in the Twin Cities area is on trial both as to concept and as to performance. The Council is engaged in a major test of strength with the three major areawide operating agencies as it seeks to assert comprehensive planning and development considerations and overall budgetary considerations into their program proposals. Local government is seeking a definition of metropolitan and local roles. The relationship with the legislature is uncertain, after one session of considerable success and one of some disappointment. And it remains to be seen, as the Council's relations with other units of government fall into the normal competitive pattern of intergovernmental relations, how broad a range of private and citizen interests will identify their values with the general-purpose regional policy-making structure.

Who Is the Constituency
for the Regional Government?

One constituent of the regional government is the State, particularly in Minnesota, where its prosperity depends so largely on the continued strength and health of the dominant Twin Cities region. How far the local units of government feel themselves served by the Council and its agencies remains an open question. The Council is trying to expand its service to local units, not only with plans and proposals, but also with assistance in grant applications and with information and data services. The attitude of the citizenry also remains unknown. The Council itself continues to emphasize that it represents people. Without the debate that comes with election campaigns, however, the Council has only begun to be visible as it begins to achieve real decisions about the location of airports, freeways, transit lines, and sewers—which affect particular individuals, neighborhoods, and economic groups.

Few patterns are yet clear. An airport site, north and south, will please some landholders and displease many homeowners. The Council's inclination toward a bus, rather than a rail, transit system, tends to please suburban areas, and to displease the central cities. Just the opposite had resulted from its tendency to insist on the distribution of low- and moderate-income housing in the suburbs. This has aroused the opposition of municipal officials. It has also activated for the first time the interest of social action and minority groups. Environmentalists worry about the impact of the airport, yet they know that environmental factors would scarcely have been considered at all, without the Council and its veto of the MAC's Ham Lake proposal.

The problem of the Metropolitan Council is the problem of every general government, which must make choices among conflicting values. On any given issue its opponents will be specific and vociferous; its supporters probably distant and perhaps unaware they have benefited. A great deal will depend on the Council's ability to arouse the interests of those served by its decisions in order to balance the displeasure of those offended.

Will the Metropolitan Council
Become Elective?

Intricate issues surround the question of electing Council members, which has been central since the Metropolitan Council was first proposed in 1966. Election was vigorously advocated then by legislators, local officials, and citizens in the metropolitan area, partly as a counter to the system of gubernatorial appointment which seemed to establish the Council as a State agency. Their original fervor has cooled somewhat, as they have watched the Council work as a local agency, and move with some genuine competence, determination, and courage on major areawide issues. Also, the cry for election has increasingly been taken up by Council opponents who see elections as the way to temper its aggressiveness.

There is confusion as to what should be the test of the need for the Council's election. The idea remains from the 1967 debate that it should become elective when it becomes an operator of programs and facilities. Others argue, however, that election depends not on whether the Council lets contracts or hires laborers, but on whether it is in fact making major policy decisions. This is, increasingly, the Council's own view.

Some see election clearing the way for an expansion of the Council's powers. Others argue that the Council should be made elective before it is given additional responsibilities, hoping perhaps that the thrust against election will thereby prevent the Council from expanding its authority.

There are also political implications. Both parties, and most major officeholders, are on record in favor of an elected Council. The political character of the Council now depends largely on the Governor. Under election, it would depend on the regional distribution of political power, particularly on the nature of political control of the suburbs.

In November 1972, the Council for the first time took a position in favor of election—for six-year, staggered terms, with no member permitted to serve two consecutive terms. Council members said they would not push this as legislation; it represents a *position,* in the event some legislator attaches an election amendment to the redistricting bill likely in the 1973 legislative session.

Council members themselves are ambivalent, and not solely because of their individual uncertainty about standing for election. Election would, they recognize, give them a political credibility to match that of other levels of government. Yet there is a special status conferred on them, even if intangibly, by the tie to the legislature and to the governor, a status above other local governments, co-equal with the major state departments.

How Many Issues Can Be Handled?

A remarkably broad charge has been given to the Metropolitan Council from its three major sources of authority. The 1957 MPC law (incorporated into the Council's authority) charges it to "make plans" for the physical, social, and economic development of the region. The 1967 law specifically directs it to carry on a continuous program of study, with recommendations, in ten major problem areas. Federal regulations direct it to review applications for Federal aid on a broad range of program categories. All these present a major problem of priorities. No functions are wholly local or wholly regional. There are regional aspects to almost all problems. Yet, clearly, the Council cannot allow itself to be drawn into everything at one time.

It had tried to move first on the major problems of physical development. Yet responsibilities in social program areas have been thrust upon it, particularly by Federal law, as in criminal justice, health care, and housing patterns. There are specific charges in its 1967 legislation to which the Council has not yet begun to respond, for example the recommendation of a program for the advance acquisition of land for public facilities. Yet it has chosen on occasion, as with cable television, to move into areas not specified as a part of its responsibility. With some reluctance, it has played no role in planning the rapidly expanding system of junior colleges and area vocational schools.

Even within the range of issues in which it has become involved, difficult choices are forced simply by the amount of time required for Council members to master planning, policy, and political implications, to the point where they can assert the Council's point of view effectively. In 1972, for example, the urgent need to concentrate at one time on vital decisions about the airport system, the transit system, and the sewer program made it impossible to work out the basic policies needed for the exercise of Council responsibilities in reviewing projects for the expansion of the health care system. To the considerable frustration of its health board, the Council handled individual applications for nursing home and hospital expansion on an *ad hoc* and essentially political basis. The Council has little enthusiasm for the effort it saw developing by the counties, in early 1972, to create in effect a metropolitan special district for air pollution control, but it simply had no capacity to move adequately on this issue, given its other commitments.

The Council has been able to enter as many fields as it has basically by spreading itself broadly, creating extensions of itself in the form of permanent and temporary advisory committees, each of which has been able to move into a particular area in some real depth, and to shape for the Council a proposal which it could consider in a reasonably limited period of time.

How Should Operations Be Structured?

There is an intimate relationship between the Metropolitan Council's capacity to consider policy issues and its capacity to supervise the administration of program operations. This relationship has proved difficult for the Council as it moves toward the 1973 legislative session.

Some decision must be made about the structuring of new programs as they are added to the regional governance system. Some governmental unit must be responsible for the construction, operation, and maintenance of the facilities. In the Council's hearings during the summer of 1972 on regional organization, three general models were identified: (1) The function might be directly assigned to the Council, so that the Council itself would begin to develop an executive/administrative staff in addition to the staff serving, planning, and policy functions. (2) The legislature might create a regional operating entity, separate from, but subordinate to, the Council on the "Sewer Board model," or might assign the new program to one of the existing subordinate boards. The Sewer Board, in the hearings, did propose that it be given operating responsibility for the forthcoming air pollution control program and for the solid waste disposal program. (3) The function might be assigned to some existing local government units, most likely the counties, or to some agency created voluntarily by them.

The Council's own attitude appeared to be ambivalent. Members did not uniformly relish the thought of more intense, difficult struggles of the sort they were then having with the Sewer Board, the MTC, or MAC, but neither did they eagerly seek the load of detailed decisions that would come with full responsibility for program operations. From the public point of view the issue was perhaps clearer. The deliberate structuring of a divided responsibility, between the general policy council and the specialized program agency, has in all cases produced an increasingly well-informed and open debate on major regional issues.

Program operations were contracted out to individual local units in 1969 when the legislature provided for the individual counties to implement the Council's plan for landfill sites. The same arrangement has now been recommended by the Council's Open Space Advisory Committee in its consensus for the 1973 session on a metropolitan park program.

In general, a distinction seems to be developing between programs in which the facilities truly need to be operated as a system, and programs in which the facilities need simply to be planned as a system. Day by day and hour by hour, for example, what happens at one airport must be related to what happens at another airport, and what happens at one sewage treatment plant must be related to what happens at another treatment plant on the same river. This is not the case with park sites.

What Does the Federal Government Want?

It seems clear that the National government is disinclined to try, through its own agencies, to become the delivery system for programs within urban areas. Rather, it appears committed to local planning, decisions, and implementation. The National government appears also to feel, however, that the existing local structure is inadequate, particularly in its inability to plan and to arrive at policy decisions on a regional or metropolitan basis. This is, at any rate, strongly suggested by the stream of laws and regulations since the mid-1960s, which increasingly mandate an "areawide" definition of "local."

As the 1971 annual report of the Advisory Commission on Intergovernmental Relations notes, the government continues to be essentially ambivalent both about the nature of these metropolitan arrangements and about the process by which they should be brought into existence. This ambivalence is clearly reflected in the six years' experience with the Metropolitan Council in the Twin Cities area.

In a sense, the Metropolitan Council record poses a dilemma for the Federal government. This regional policy council is clearly not structured in the manner presently specified, or preferred, by Federal law and regulations. It is not a council of local governments. Its structure represents rather a determination by the legislature that a different—an equal-population district—pattern of representation and voting would be more desirable and/or workable for this region. Yet the Metropolitan Council's performance may surpass that of other regional bodies in the Nation.

What, then, does the Federal government want? If it moves toward regionalism, should it specify the organizational arrangements for the regional bodies? Or should it simply set a performance requirement, probably in terms of an ability to produce decisions, and let the States or metropolitan regions themselves design whatever structure seems to them workable in achieving the result required? The question is, by whom should regional bodies be created? By federal regulations, local governmental units, or the State legislature?

Congress and the executive departments recognize the importance of the orderly physical and social development of the great metropolitan areas. The government is deeply involved in assisting this development financially. Its vital interest would seem to be, therefore, in the emergency of effective regional institutions, which can make the political decisions required.

Regional institutions of this kind, with authority to act in the interests of the region, can be created only by the state legislatures, in which reside constitutionally the power to make and to remake the basic institutional rules by which urban development proceeds. However, concerning regional governance, the Federal government relates scarcely at all to the legislatures. Rather, it has tried to relate mainly to local units. It has tended to specify, in its laws and regulations, the organization of regional bodies which it requires for the review of applications for its aid, and for the preparation of areawide plans against which these applications can be evaluated.

These arrangements are, in most cases, inconsistent with the bases on which the Metropolitan Council was created and has become effective. This has meant that the regional arrangements in Minnesota are in jeopardy on almost every occasion when a new law extending these planning and review requirements to a new Federal aid program is adopted, or when regulations implementing such a law are written.

The Metropolitan Council tends to be strengthened, on the other hand, when the Federal government requires simply the existence of a regional institution competent to make the decisions required, and leaves to the State legislature the decisions about its structure and system of representation.

The future of the regional arrangement in Minnesota depends, to a significant degree, on a choice by the Federal government between emphasis on the organizational specifics, or on the performance, of regional institutions.

SUMMARY

The question of replicability requires, first, a decision on what are the central features of the Twin Cities area regional arrangement.

These conclusions emerge:

- The definition of regional functions or activities varies enormously among regions, and even within a particular urban region such as the Twin Cities area through time. This is probably both inevitable and desirable.
- The arrangements for the implementation of programs, the operations of facilities, the delivery of services, and the process of development are almost infinitely complex, even just within the Twin Cities area. They consist of a network of private and public, state, regional, and local agencies influenced by the Metropolitan Council's policy guidelines. These, too, are changing through time.
- The essential element of the urban governance system is the general regional policy council, which will at the direction of, or with the concurrence of, the State legislature, write the definition of regional functions and design the arrangements for program operations.
- The principal distinguishing feature of the general regional policy council—in the Twin Cities area, the Metropolitan Council—is not its particular structure, but rather the process by which it was created, by the legislature, under its authority over the system of local government. The Council's grant of authority from the State gives many of its policy decisions the force of law.
- The general regional policy council has been established not as a replacement for, but parallel with, school, county, and municipal governmental units.

With respect to replicability, then:

- The definition of state, regional, and local functions will and should vary from state to state. The particular definition arrived at in Minnesota for the Twin Cities area is not replicable.

- The arrangements for the implementation and operation of programs and facilities will vary from one urban area to another. The peculiar combination of State, regional, and local agencies used in the Twin Cities area to implement the policy guidelines of the Metropolitan Council is not replicable.

- The decision to establish a general regional policy council, separate from the associations of local government units, is replicable. The policy council does not replace, but exists with, the organizations created to voice the legitimate interests of the local units in matters of regional policy.

- The complete, particular structure of the Metropolitan Council as to size, districts, method of selection of members, system of voting, selection of chairman, relationship with staff and other regional agencies, probably is not replicable. It works in and for the Twin Cities area. But certain aspects of the structure, such as the selection of members, can be transferred to other areas.

- The statutory character of the regional policy council in the Twin Cities area is replicable.

- The situation which impelled the legislature to create a regional policy council for this metropolitan area is replicable. The particular citizen and local official pressure which led to legislative action for the creation of the Metropolitan Council in Minnesota is not likely to be duplicated elsewhere. But it is possible to substitute for this the pressure of the Federal government, given a decision by it that regional institutions do in fact need to be created, and that they must be statutory in order to be effective.

The central message of the Minnesota experience is the importance of moving toward the State legislature for the creation of a regional policy body competent both to do regional planning and to make regional decisions. If held accountable for the effectiveness of this regional body, the legislature will then face the critical issues about equity of representation, systems of voting, and authority for implementation, all the questions which have so far been dodged in the formation of most regional bodies.

It should be of no importance to the Federal government that the particular organizational forms created by the legislatures might vary from region to region. Its central objective—the creation of competent decision-making bodies at the regional level in the major metropolitan areas—would have been achieved, and without the Federal government's having itself to enter the thicket of issues surrounding the question of regional governmental structure.

NOTES

1. Beginning in 1973, the legislature will be able to use its 120 days within the first six months of either year.
2. The relevant laws are to be found in Minnesota Statutes Chapter 473 (A) (B) (C) (D) (E).

Standard Metropolitan Statistical Areas

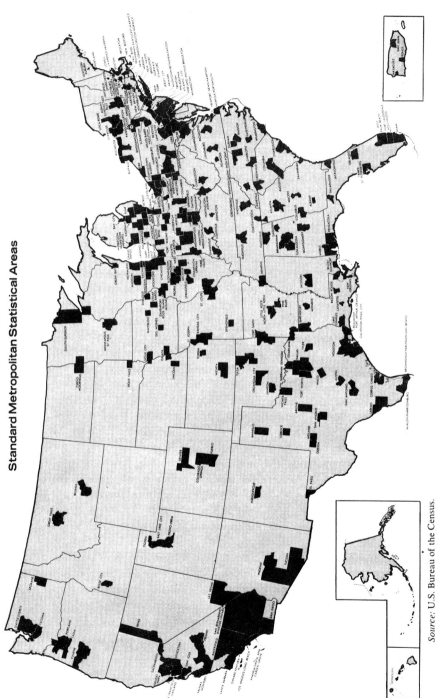

Source: U.S. Bureau of the Census.

Index